George Whitefield Powers

Important Events

George Whitefield Powers

Important Events

ISBN/EAN: 9783337417796

Printed in Europe, USA, Canada, Australia, Japan

Cover: Foto ©Suzi / pixelio.de

More available books at **www.hansebooks.com**

A Book of Dates

HISTORICAL, BIOGRAPHICAL, POLITICAL, RELIGIOUS, LITERARY, SCIENTIFIC, AND INDUSTRIAL

COMPILED BY

GEORGE W. POWERS

———

NEW YORK: 46 EAST 14TH STREET

THOMAS Y. CROWELL & COMPANY

BOSTON: 100 PURCHASE STREET

PREFACE.

THIS book is a compilation intended for the use of the general reader. In condensing the recorded history of 6,000 years within the limits deemed desirable, many events are necessarily omitted which might be considered of equal importance with those selected. This is unavoidable. No attempt has been made to compete with the many-volumed encyclopedias and works of historical reference from which the materials for this work have been derived. It has been the aim of the compiler rather to present a thread of history running through the careers of the nations which have played a more or less important part in human affairs, that may assist the reader of current news and literature in better understanding the present by a glance at the past. More than one-half of the space has been devoted to the continent of America, the larger portion to affairs in the United States. The minor States of America, North and South, have received comparatively more attention than their relative importance in the world's history would suggest; but the rapidly growing political, commercial, and social intercourse of our own country with these peoples, and our

recent war with Spain and the resultant close connection with Spanish Americaus, give an especial
interest to their previous history. It has been
impossible to reconcile the conflicting dates in
what are considered "standard" authorities.
This would have involved an amount of research
entirely outside the scope of this work. The dif-
ficulty encountered by every one who has given
the least attention to chronological matters is so
clearly expressed by Mr. Louis Heilprin, the able
editor of the historical and biographical data in
the Appletou publications and author of "Historical Reference Book," that a few words from the
preface of the latter work will clearly illustrate
this feature of chronology. "It is little under-
stood to what extent encyclopedic publications
contradict each other in the matter of dates. A
vast amount of confusion prevails, even with
regard to the events of ordinary history. Uniform accuracy is seldom achieved, owing to the
amount of labor involved. . . . Even able and
conscientious historians will often slip into chronological errors. The utmost confusion prevails in
books respecting dates in the seventeenth century
and the first half of the eighteenth century. . . .
[This resulted from the changes brought about
by the Gregorian Calendar, adopted by the European nations at different times. In England the
change took place in 1752. when the day following Sept. 3 was reckoned as the 14th.] The same

writer will not unfrequently use the old style in one place, and the new in another," etc. Many other causes for the discrepancies of dates in historical matters exist, which it would require a treatise rather than a preface to explain. Therefore, if any reader of this book should find that the dates do not always correspond with his favorite " authority," he will readily see the reason. The principal authorities consulted, and to which the compiler is very much indebted, are the " Encyclopædia Britannica," Appleton's publications, Heilprin's " Historical Reference Book," Haydn's " Book of Dates," Harper's " Manual of Facts," Drake's " American Biography," " Canadian Biography," " Chambers's Encyclopædia," " Review of Reviews," " Current History," Duruy's and Fiske's Histories, " Century Dictionary of Names," Webster's " International Dictionary," and New York *World Almanac*. Special histories of the different countries have also been consulted.

G. W. P.

Boston, *May*, 1899.

IMPORTANT EVENTS.

A BOOK OF DATES.

NORTH AMERICA.

Semi-Mythical, Traditional, and Conjectural History,
500–1400.

A.D.

500 Pre-Toltec Period.

503 Mexican history begins.

600 Toltecs established throughout Mexico.

861 The Norseman, Nadodd discovers Iceland.

982 Eric the Red discovers and names Greenland.

985 Bjarni sights land at Cape Cod or Nantucket.

1000 Leif Ericsson sails for Western land.

1002 Thorwald, Leif's brother, visits Vinland.

1004 Thorwald killed in a skirmish with the
natives.

1005 Thornfinn Karlsefne lands in Rhode Island,
and stays in Vinland three years.

1050 End of the Toltec power in Mexico.

1090 Aztecs begin their journey towards Mexico.

1325 Aztecs found the city of Mexico.

1

1349 Esquimaux appear in Greenland.

1400 Communication with Greenland ceases.

Period of Authentic Discovery, Exploration, and Conquest, 1492–1616.

1492 Columbus sails from Palos. Aug. 3; lands on Guanahani, Oct. 12; discovers Cuba, Oct. 28.

1493 Columbus sails on his second expedition, Sept. 25.

Cattle first brought to Amer. by Columbus.

1494 Columbus discovers Jamaica, May 3.

1497 John Cabot dis. N. Amer. continent, June 24.

1498 Columbus sails on his third voyage, May 30.

1499 First voyage of Amerigo Vespucci.

1500 Gaspar Cortereal discovers Labrador.

1501 Negro slaves imported into Hispaniola.

1502 Columbus sails on his fourth voyage, May 9.

1504 Columbus finally leaves the New World for Spain.

Cape Breton discovered by French fishermen.

1506 Columbus d. at Valladolid, May 20; b. 1436?

1511 Velasquez subjugates Cuba.

1512 Florida discovered by Juan Ponce de Leon.

1513 Vasco de Balboa discovers Pacific Ocean.

1517 Mexico discovered by Fernando de Cordova.

1519 Hernando Cortez lands in Mexico.

1524 Verazzano enters bay of New York, April.

1534 Jacques Cartier enters Gulf of St. Lawrence.

1535 Grijalva's expedition discovers California.
1540 De Soto conquers Louisiana.
1562 Jean Ribault explores coast of Florida.
1565 St. Augustine, Fla., founded by Menendez.
1583 Sir Humphrey Gilbert takes possession of Newfoundland.
1584 Raleigh's first exp. lands in Virginia, July 13.
1585 John Davis discovers Davis Straits. [10.
1586 Sir Francis Drake visits Roanoke Inlet, June
1587 Virginia Dare, first English child born in America, Aug. 18.
1602 Bart. Gosnold discovers Cape Cod, May 14.
1605 De Monts takes possession of Maine, May.
1609 Henry Hudson explores Hudson River, Sept. 11–22.
1614 Capt. John Smith explores New Eng. coast.
1616 Great mortality among Indians in New Eng.

Colonial Period - British America.

1603 Simon Bradstreet, col. gov. of Mass., born; d. March 27, 1697.
1604 John Eliot, Apostle to the Indians, born; d. May 20, 1690.
1607 John Harvard, founder of Harvard College, b.; d. Sept. 11, 1638.
Jamestown, Va., set. by the Eng., May 13.
Capt. John Smith saved by Pocahontas, Dec.
1611 Stephen Daye, first printer in N.E., born; d. Dec. 22, 1668.

1614 Manhattan (New York) settled by the Dutch.
New Jersey settled by the Dutch.

1616 Slaves first brought to Va. by the Dutch.

1618 Powhatan, Indian sachem in Va., dies. [17.

1620 *Mayflower* sails from Plymouth, Eng., Sept.
Peregrine White, first white child born in
New England, Nov.; d. July 22, 1704.
Mayflower reaches Plymouth, Mass., Dec. 16;
Pilgrims land, Dec. 21.

1621 John Carver, first gov. of Plym. col., dies.
Miles Standish captain of Plymouth colony,
Feb. 17.
Samoset, first Indian who vis. the Pilgrims.
Treaty between Plymouth colony and Mas-
sasoit, Mar. 22.
William Bradford governor of Plymouth.
First Thanksgiving in Plymouth, Sept.
Fortune arrives at Plymouth, Nov. 11.
Cotton-seed planted in Virginia.

1623 New Hampshire settled.
Lord Baltimore founds a colony at **Ferry-
land**, Newfoundland.
Ship *Anne* arrives at Plymouth, Aug.

[The *Mayflower*, *Fortune*, and *Anne*, are usually
spoken of as the " Pilgrim " ships.]

1628 John Endicott governor of Mass., May 30.

1629 John Winthrop governor of Mass., Aug. 20.
Transfer of Mass. govt. to New England.

1630 First church of Boston gathered at Charlestown, July.

1630 Boston (Indian Shawmut) settled, Sept. 17.
Famine in Massachusetts Bay Colony.

1632 Edward Winslow governor of Plymouth.

1633 Wouter Van Twiller gov. of New York.
Connecticut settled by the English.

1634 Maryland settled by Lord Baltimore.

1636 Rhode Island set. by Roger Williams, June.
John Mason, capt., founder of N. H., d. Dec.
Pequot war begins in Mass. ; ends, 1637.

1637 John Winthrop gov. of Mass., dies Mar. 26,
1649.

1638 William Kieft governor of New York.
Delaware settled by the Swedes.
John Harvard bequeaths his library to found
a college, Sept. 14.
New Haven settled.

1639 Printing-press estab. at Cambridge, Mass.
Cambridge, Mass., selected as site of Harvard
College, March 13.
First Baptist church in America, at Provi-
dence, R.I.
First Constitution of Conn. adopted, April.
Increase Mather, pres. of Harvard College,
born June 21 ; dies Aug. 23, 1723.

1640 Reformed Dutch Church estab. in New York.
Manufacture of cloths began in Mass.
Thomas Gorges dep. gov. of Maine, Mar. 10.

1642 First Commencement at Harvard College.
Sir William Berkeley gov. of Virginia.

1643 Anne Hutchinson, religious enthusiast, dies.

1643 Brewster dies at Plymouth, Mass., April 18.
Swedes settle in Pennsylvania.

1644 Anabaptists banished from Massachusetts.

1645 Free schools established at Roxbury, Mass.

1646 John Eliot preaches first sermon to Indians,
Oct. 28.

1647 Peter Stuyvesant gov. of New York, May 11.
Law passed in Mass. estab. grammar schools.

1648 Margaret Jones, first witch executed in Mass.
Elihu Yale, patron of Yale College, born;
dies July 22, 1721.

1650 Baptists arrested and fined in Mass.

1652 John Cotton, Puritan minister, d.: b. 1585.
Mint established in Boston, John Hull mint-
master.
Samuel Sewall, jurist, born; dies 1730.
Pres. Dunster of Harvard indicted for reli-
gious opinions, and forced to resign.

1653 North Carolina settled, July.

1654 Charles Chauncy, pres. of Harvard; d. 1672.
Col. Wood explores Kentucky.

1655 Edward Winslow, gov. of Plymouth colony,
dies; born 1595.
Delaware brought under Dutch rule, Sept.

1656 Anne Hibbins executed as a witch in Boston.
Quakers arrive in Boston, July.

1657 Wm. Bradford, 2d gov. of Plymouth colony,
dies; born 1589.

1658 Sir Richard Saltonstall dies; born 1586.

1659 Quakers hung in Boston.

1660 Whalley and Goffe, regicides, ar. in Boston.
1661 Eliot translates New Testament into Indian.
1663 Cotton Mather, b. Feb. 12 ; d. Feb. 13, 1728.
1664 First Baptist church in Massachusetts.
Surrender of Fort Amsterdam to English,
Sept. 8.
Richard Nicolls gov. of New York.
1665 John Endicott, gov. of Mass., d. ; born 1588 ?
John Winthrop, Jr., gov. of Connecticut.
Philip Carteret, first Eng. gov. of N. Jersey.
Prov. government estab. in Maine, June 23.
1668 Francis Lovelace gov. of New York, Aug. 28.
1670 John Davenport, Puritan divine, d. ; b. 1597.
South Carolina settled ; W. Sayle first gov.
1671 French settle in Michigan.
First slaves come to South Carolina.
1672 George Fox, founder of Quakers, visits R.I.
1673 New York and New Jersey surrendered to
the Dutch.
1674 New Netherlands and New Jersey restored
to England.
Edmund Andros gov. of New York, July 1.
1675 King Philip's Indian war in Mass.
1676 Nathaniel Bacon rebellion in Virginia.
Philip (*King Philip*) Pometacom, Indian
chief, shot.
1680 Government of Maine organized by Mass.
John Buckner brings a printing-press to Va.
1681 William Penn receives charter of Pennsylvania, March 4.

1682   Penn lands at Newcastle, Penn., Oct. 27.

1683   First assembly in New York under Eng. rule.

1684   Charter of Mass. revoked by England.

1685   First printing-press in Philadelphia.
First Episcopal church in New Jersey.

1686   First Episcopal church in Boston.
City of Albany incorporated, July 22.

1687   Thomas Prince, divine and hist., b. ; d. 1758.

1689   Gov. Andros arrested by people of Boston.

1690   Sir William Phipps (or Phips) captures Port Royal, N.S., April–May.
Colonial Congress called at New York, Apr. 2.
First paper-mill in America, built by Rittenhouse, in Pennsylvania.
Huguenots of France come to Virginia.

1691   Maine united with Massachusetts, Oct. 7.
Second charter granted Mass. by Eng., Oct. 7.

1692   Witchcraft delusion begins at Salem, Mass., March.
William and Mary Coll. chartered, Va., Feb.

1695   First Episcopal church in Philadelphia.

1696   Sir Wm. Pepperell, general, b. June 29 ; d. July 6, 1759.

1697   Remarkable escape of Mrs. Hannah Dustin from Indians, March.

1699   Capt. Kidd, pirate, arrested in Boston ; hung in London, May 24, 1701.

1700   First quarantine act passed in Penn.
Williamstown made capital of Virginia.

1701   Charter for Yale College granted, Oct. 9.

1701 Philadelphia incorporated as a city, Oct. 28.

1702 First issue of paper money in America, in South Carolina.

1703 Jonathan Edwards, met., born ; dies 1758.

1704 *Boston News Letter*, first paper in Boston, April 24.

1705 First Baptist church in Connecticut.
First church in North Carolina built.

1706 Benjamin Franklin born in Boston, Jan. 17 ; dies April 17, 1790.

1707 Stephen Hopkins, signer of Declaration of Independence. b. Mar. 7 ; d. July 19, 1785.

1709 Slave-market estab. in Wall Street, N. York.
Thomas Short, first printer in Connecticut.

1710 3,000 German Lutherans arrive in New York, June 14.

1714 Schooners first built, at Cape Ann, Mass.

1716 First iron-works established in Pennsylvania.
Philip Livingston, signer Dec. of Ind., born Jan. 15 ; d. June 12, 1778.

1718 Israel Putnam, Rev. gen., b. Jan. 7 ; d. May 29, 1790.
Esek Hopkins, first com. of Am. navy, born ; d. Feb. 26, 1802.
David Brainerd, missionary to the Indians, b. April 20 ; d. Oct. 9, 1747.   [1644.
Wm. Penn dies in Eng., July 30 ; b. Oct. 14,

1719 Scotch-Irish settle in New Hampshire.

1721 Inoculation against small-pox practised in Boston.

1721 Roger Sherman, signer of Dec. of Ind., b. April 19; d. July 23, 1793.

Peyton Randolph, pres. of first Am. Congress, born; d. Oct. 22, 1775.

1722 Samuel Adams, Rev. patriot, b. Sept. 27; d. Oct. 2, 1803.

1723 Franklin arrives in Philadelphia, Oct.

1724 Father Sebastian Rasle, French priest, killed at Norridgewock, Me., Aug. 12.

1725 James Otis, orator and patriot, b. Feb. 5; d. May 23, 1783.

New York Gazette, first paper in N. Y., Oct.

1726 Wm. Prescott, Rev. col., b. Feb. 20; d. Oct. 13, 1795.

1727 Artemas Ward, Rev. gen., b. Nov. 27; d. Oct. 27, 1800.　　　　[d. May 12, 1795.

Ezra Stiles, pres. of Yale College, b. Dec. 15;

Wm. Ellery, signer of Dec. of Ind., b. Dec. 22; d. Feb. 15, 1820.

First newspaper printed in Maryland.

1728 Horatio Gates, gen., b.; d. April 10, 1806.

John Stark, gen., b. Aug. 28; d. May 8, 1822.

1729 Brit. government formally recognizes Newfoundland as a colony.

1730 Baltimore laid out.

1731 Robert Treat Paine, signer of Dec. of Ind., b. March 11; d. May 11, 1814.

Samuel Huntington, signer of Dec. of Ind., b. July 3; d. Jan. 5, 1796.

Wm. Moultrie, Rev. gen., b.; d. Sept. 27, 1805.

1731 Franklin founds library of Phil., Nov. 8.

1732 Richard Henry Lee born Jan. 20 ; d. June 19,
  1794.   [1795.
  Francis Marion, Rev. gen., born ; d. Feb. 27,
  George Washington born Feb. 22 ; d. Dec.
  14, 1799.
  First stage runs between Boston and N. Y.
  Poor Richard's Almanac issued.

1733 Gen. Oglethorpe settles Georgia.
  Savannah, Georgia, founded.   [7, 1806.
  Robert Morris, financier, b. Jan. 20 ; d. May
  Trustees prohibit rum in Ga., Aug. 11 ; re-
   pealed by order of House of Commons,
   July 14, 1742.
  First Freemasons' lodge in Amer., in Boston.

1734 Francis L. Lee, signer of Dec. of Ind., b.
  Oct. 14 ; d. April, 1797.   [1818.

1735 Paul Revere, patriot, b. Jan. 1 ; d. May 10,
  John Adams (2d pres.) born Oct. 19 ; dies
  July 4, 1826.

1736 Ann Lee, founder of the Shakers in Amer-
  ica, b. Feb. 29 ; d. Sept. 8, 1784.
  John Wesley preaches at Savannah, March 7.
  Patrick Henry born May 29 ; d. June 6, 1799.
  Virginia Gazette, first newspaper in Va., Aug.

1737 John Hancock b. Jan. 12 ; d. Oct. 8, 1793.
  John S. Copley, historical painter, b. July 3 ;
  d. Sept. 9, 1813.
  Charles Carroll, last surviving signer of Dec.
  of Ind., b. Sept. 20 ; dies Nov. 14, 1832.

1738 Francis Hopkinson, signer of Dec. of Ind., born; d. May 9, 1791.

Rufus Putnam, gen., and pioneer settler of Ohio, b. April 9; d. May 4, 1824.

Benjamin West, painter, b. Oct. 10; d. Mar. 10, 1820.

1739 Richmond, Va., settled by Wm. Byrd.

Geo. Clinton, vice-pres. U. S., b. July 26; d. April 20, 1812.

1740 George Whitefield arrives in Amer. July 23.

Negro insurrection in South Carolina.

Jonathan Trumbull, statesman, b. Aug. 7; d. 1809.

Arthur Lee, diplomatist, b. Dec. 20; d. Dec. 14, 1792.   [b. June 11.

1741 Joseph Warren, gen., killed at Bunker Hill,

John Murray, founder of Universalism in Amer., b. Dec. 10; d. Sept. 3, 1815.

1742 Faneuil Hall built in Bos., by Peter Faneuil.

Joseph Brant, Mohawk chief, born; d. 1807.

Nathaniel Greene, Rev. gen., b. May 27; d. June 19, 1786.

1743 John Fitch, inventor (steamboat), b. Jan. 21; d. July 2, 1798.

Amer. Philos. Soc. estab. in Phil. by Franklin.

Thomas Jefferson (3d pres.) b. April 2; d. July 4, 1826.

James Rumsey, inventor (steamboat), born; d. Dec. 23, 1792.

1744 Hostilities with Six Nations (Indians).

1744 Josiah Quincy, Jr., Rev. patriot, b. Feb. 23;
d. April 26, 1775.

Elbridge Gerry, signer of Dec. of Ind., born
July 17; d. Nov. 23, 1814.

1745 Louisburg captured by N. E. troops, June 17.

Francis Asbury, first Meth. bishop in Amer.,
b. Aug. 20; d. March 31, 1816.

John Jay, first chief-justice of U. S., b. Dec.
12; d. May 17, 1829. [16, 1826.

Lindley Murray, grammarian, born; d. Feb.

1746 College of New Jersey (Princeton) incor.

1747 John Paul Jones, com., b. July 6; d. July
18, 1792.

Robert R. Livingston, statesman, b. Nov. 27;
d. Feb. 26, 1813.

Scotch Highlanders settle in N. Carolina.

1748 Harper's Ferry named after Robert Harper.

1749 *North Carolina Gazette*, first paper in N. C.

1750 Christopher Gist explores the Ohio country.

Stephen Girard, banker, founder of Girard
College, b. May 21; d. Dec. 26, 1831.

Henry Knox, gen., b. July 25; d. Oct. 25, 1806.

Nicholas Biddle, naval com., b. Sept. 10; d.
March 7, 1778.

1751 James Madison (4th pres.) born Mar. 16; d.
June 28, 1836. [1816.

1752 Gouverneur Morris b. Jan. 31; d. Nov. 6,

Timothy Dwight, pres. of Yale College, born
May 11; d. Jan. 11, 1817.

Franklin experiments on electricity, June 5.

1752 First theatre in the Colonies opened at Williamsburg, Va., Sept. 5.

1753 Benj. T. Rumford, count, b. March 26; d. Aug. 21. 1814.

Wm. Hull, gen., b. June 24; d. Nov. 29, 1825.

First regular theatre in New York City opened in Nassau St., Sept. 17.

Phillis Wheatley, negro poetess, b. in Africa; d. Dec. 5, 1784.

1754 Kentucky settled by Daniel Boone.

King's College (now Columbia) founded.

Convention at New York to consider Colonial Confederacy, June 19.   [5, 1822.

1755 Thomas Truxtun, com., b. Feb. 17; d. May

Rufus King, vice-pres., born March 24; dies April 29, 1827.   [June 17.

French Acadians removed from Grand Pré.

Gen. Braddock defeated at Fort Duquesne, July 9.

Battle of Lake George, Sept. 8.   [1835.

John Marshall, jurist, b. Sept. 24; d. July 6,

1756 Henry Lee ("Light-Horse Harry") b. Jan. 29; d. March 25, 1818.

Aaron Burr, third vice-pres. U. S., b. Feb. 6; d. Sept. 14, 1836.

New Hampshire Gazette established, Aug.

Fort Oswego sur. to Montcalm, Aug. 14.

Richard Dale, com., b. Nov. 6; dies Feb. 24, 1826.

First general hospital opened at Phil., Dec.

1757 Alex. Hamilton b. Jan. 11; d. July 12, 1804.
Fort William Henry sur. to French, Aug. 9.

1758 Fisher Ames b. April 9; d. July 4, 1808.
James Monroe (5th pres.) b. April 28; dies
July 4, 1831.
Charles Pinckney born; d. Oct. 29, 1824.
Fort Frontenac sur. to English, Aug. 27.
Noah Webster, lexicographer, b. Oct. 16; d.
May 28, 1843.
Newport Mercury established. [1818.

1759 Joshua Barney, com., b. July 6; dies Dec. 1,
Fort Niagara captured by British, July 25.
Battle of Quebec (Plains of Abraham),
Wolfe and Montcalm killed, Sept. 13.

1760 Montreal sur. to the British, Sept. 8.
Mason and Dixon line surveyed.

1761 Albert Gallatin b. Jan. 29; d. Aug. 12, 1849.
Edward Preble, com., b. Aug. 15; d. Aug.
25, 1807. [June 9, 1826.
Jedidiah Morse, geographer, b. Aug. 23; d.
Bennington, Vt., settled.

1762 English settle in New Brunswick. [17.

1763 First newspaper in Ga., *Georgia Gazette*, Apr.
Pontiac war on frontiers. [1848.
John Jacob Astor b. July 17; d. March 29,
Massacre of Wyoming, Oct. 15.
Wm. Franklin last royal gov. of New Jersey.

1764 *Hartford Courant* established.
Brown University chartered as College of
Rhode Island.

1764 Stephen Van Rensselaer (The Patroon) born Nov. 1; d. Jan. 26, 1839.

1765 Robert Fulton, engineer and inventor, b.; d. Feb. 24. 1815.   [May 30.

Speech of Patrick Henry on Stamp Act. Delegates from Anglo-American colonies meet in New York, Oct. 7.

Stamp Act passed by British Parliament, March, goes into effect Nov. 1.

Eli Whitney (cotton-gin) b. Dec. 8; d. Jan. 8, 1825.

1766 Robert B. Thomas, founder of *Old Farmer's Almanack*, b.; d. May 19. 1846.   [1813.

Alex. Wilson, ornithol., b. July 6; d. Aug. 23.

First Methodist Society in Amer. organized in New York.

First Medical Society in American colonies, New Jersey, org. July 23.

1767 John Quincy Adams (6th pres.) b. July 11; d. Feb. 23, 1848.

Andrew Jackson (7th pres.) b. March 15; d. June 8, 1845.

1768 Pittsburg (Penn.) *Gazette* established.

Tecumseh. Indian chief, b.; d. Oct. 5, 1813.

James Barron. com., born; d. April 21, 1851.

1769 De Witt Clinton b. March 2; d. Feb. 11, 1828.

Term "doctor" first applied to medical practitioners in America.

Jonathan Trumbull gov. of Connecticut ("Brother Jonathan").

1769 Daniel Boone explores Kentucky.

Dartmouth College (Hanover, N.H.) chartered, Dec. 30.

1770 Boston Massacre, March 5.

Joseph Hopkinson, author ("Hail Columbia"), b. Nov. 12; d. Jan. 15, 1842.

Rutgers College, New Jersey, chartered.

1771 Hosea Ballou, eminent Universalist, b. Apr. 30; d. June 7, 1852.

Isaac T. Hopper, Quaker philanthropist, b. Dec. 3; d. May 7, 1852.

John Rodgers, com., born; d. Aug. 1, 1838.

North American, Philadelphia, established.

Wm. Tryon, last royal gov. of New York.

"Green Mountain Boys" organized.

1772 Josiah Quincy, mayor of Boston, b. Feb. 4; d. July 1, 1864.

William Wirt, b. Nov. 8; d. Feb. 18, 1834.

1773 Wm. H. Harrison (9th pres.) b. Feb. 9; dies April 4, 1841.   [16, 1838.

Nathaniel Bowditch b. March 26; d. March

John Randolph of Roanoke, b. June 2; dies May 24, 1833.

Tea thrown overboard in Boston Harbor, Dec. 16.   [first issued.

Maryland Journal and Baltimore Advertiser

1774 Passage of Boston Port Bill by British Parliament, March 7.   [1833.

Wm. Bainbridge, com., b. May 7; d. July 28,

First Cont. Cong. meets at Phil., Sept. 5.

1774 Congress adopts a declaration of Colonial rights, Oct. 14.   [Feb. 1.

1775 Prov. Cong. of Mass. meets at Cambridge, Isaac Hull, com., b. March 9 ; d. Feb. 13, 1843.

First Antislavery society formed in Phil., April 14.

Battles of Lexington and Concord, April 19.

Second Cont. Cong. meets in Phil., May 10.

Ethan Allen capt. Ft. Ticonderoga, May 10.

Crown Point surrenders, May 12.

Benedict Arnold captures St. Johns, Can., May 16.   [May 20.

Articles of Union and Confederation adopted,

Washington appointed commander-in-chief of American forces, June 15.

Battle of Bunker Hill, June 17.

Washington takes command of army at Cambridge, July 3.

Lyman Beecher, preacher, born Oct. 12; dies Jan. 10, 1863.

Gen. Montgomery capt. Montreal, Nov. 13.

Montgomery attacks Quebec, and is killed, Dec. 31.

1776 First Union flag unfurled at Cambridge, Mass., Jan. 1.

" Common Sense " published by Thomas Paine, Jan. 8.

British evacuate Boston, March 17.

Congress authorizes privateering, March 23.

Declaration of Independence, July 4.

Events in British American Colonies after formation of the United States.

1788 King's College, Windsor, N.S., founded.

1791 Canada divided into Upper and Lower.

1796 Thomas C. Haliburton, judge and humorist ("Sam Slick"), b. Dec.; d. Aug. 27, 1865.

1798 Sir Wm. E. Logan, geologist, born April 20; dies June 22, 1875. [May 8, 1887.

1799 Sir Wm. Young, chief justice N. S., b.; dies

1800 The Sault Ste. Marie, the first canal in Can.

1807 Sir Francis Hincks, statesman, born Dec. 11; dies, Aug. 18, 1885.

1809 R. D. Wilmot, statesman, born Oct. 16.

1814 Sir A. G. Archibald, statesman, born May 18. Sir George E. Cartier b. Sept. 6; d. May 20, 1873.

1815 Thomas Galt, judge, born Aug. 12.

1817 Sir Alex. Galt, statesman, b. Sept. 6; d. Sept. 19, 1893. [June 25, 1896.

1818 Sir Leonard Tilley, statesman, b. May 8; d.

1820 Sir J. W. Dawson, geologist, born. Elzear A. Taschereau, cardinal, b. Feb. 17; dies April 12, 1898.

1827 Sir Charles Tupper, statesman, b. July 2.

1832 Newfoundland obtains a colonial legislature.

1833 *Advertiser*, the first daily newspaper in Montreal.

1836 First railway in Canada opened.

1837 Papineau and Mackenzie rebellion in Canada.

1838 Canadian rebellion suppressed.

1840 Upper and Lower Canada reunited.

1841 Sir Wilfred Laurier, statesman, b. Nov. 24.

1844 John Rose. jurist. born Oct. 11.

1847 George E. Foster, statesman. born Sept. 3.

1850 Riots in Montreal, Parliament House burned.
Canadian clergy reserves abolished.

1854 First oil-wells dug.   [8.

1855 Niagara Falls suspension bridge opened, Mar.

1856 Grand Trunk railroad opened.

1858 Ottawa made capital of Canada.
Decimal system of coinage adopted.

1860 Prince of Wales visits Canada.
Victoria railroad bridge over St. Lawrence at Montreal opened, Aug. 25.

1861 Gold found in Nova Scotia.

1862 J. S. Macdonald premier of Canada.

1864 Southern U. S. Confederates in Canada plan raids.   [Mar. 7.

1865 Confederation rejected by New Brunswick,

1866 Invasion of Canada threatened by Fenians.
Canadian Parliament first meets at Ottawa.

1867 Dominion of Canada formed Mar. 29. by union of Upper and Lower Canada, Nova Scotia, and New Brunswick.
Lord Monck sworn as viceroy of Can., July 2.
New parliament meets at Ottawa, Nov. 6.

1868 Agitation against confederation in N.S., Jan.

1868 Murder of Thomas D'Arcy McGee, cabinet minister, April 7.

Fenian raid into Canada repelled, May.

Sir John Young governor-general, Nov. 27.

1869 Newfoundland refuses to join the Dom., Mar.

Hudson Bay Ter. purchased by Dominion of Canada, Nov.   [completed.

Clifton suspension bridge at Niagara Falls

1870 Rupert's Land made the Province of Manitoba, Aug.

1871 British Columbia united to the Dominion.

Departure of last bat. of royal troops, Nov.

Uniformity of currency established through the Dominion.

1872 Lord Dufferin governor-gen., inaug., June 25.

1873 Sir Joseph Howe, lieut.-gov. of N.S., d. June; born Dec. 1804.   [81.

J. W. Johnston, statesman, d. Nov. 21, aged

Prince Edward Island joins the Dominion.

1875 Icelanders settle in Northwest Territories.

1876 Intercolonial railroad opened from Quebec to Halifax.

1877 Great fire at St. John, N.B., June 20–22.

Canada and U. S. Fishery Com. at Halifax, June–Nov.   [Canada, Oct. 14.

1878 Marquis of Lorne appointed governor-gen. of

Halifax fishery award paid by U. S., Nov. 21.

1879 Dominion Industrial Exhibition at Ottawa opened, Sept. 24.

1880 Royal Canadian Academy of Arts founded.

1881 Contract for new Pacific railway ratified, Feb. 1; opened, May 18, 1885.

Victoria, steamer, sunk on the Thames, great loss of life, May 24.

1882 Northwest Ter. beyond Manitoba divided into four new ter., — Assiniboia, Saskatchewan, Alberta, Athabraska, July.

Sir Hugh Allan, founder of Allan line of steamers, d. Dec. 7; b. Sept. 20, 1810.

First colony of Russians settle in N. W. Ter.

1883 Conflicts between Orangemen and Catholics in Newfoundland.   [20.

Niagara Falls cantilever bridge opened, Dec.

Standard time adopted in Canada.

1884 Marquis of Lansdowne, governor-general of Canada, Oct. 22.

1885 Insurrection in Northwest Ter., led by Louis David Riel, about March 20.

Riel surrenders May 15; hanged, Nov. 16.

1886 Fisheries dispute with the United States.

Vancouver City founded.

1887 Great railway bridge over St. Lawrence at Lachine completed, July 30.

Joint committee on fisheries dispute appointed, about Aug. 30.

Anthracite coal first mined in Canada.

1888 Lord Stanley app. gov.-gen. of Can., June 11.

1890 Dominion Commons unanimously resolve on adhesion to Great Britain, Jan. 29.

Great storms in Newfoundland.

1891 Indians of Ontario and Quebec petition for leave to elect their own chiefs, Feb. 4.

Canadian Pacific Railway completed, Mar. 28.

First mail steamer of the Pacific mail service arrives at Vancouver from Yokohama, April 28.

Sir John Macdonald, statesman, d. June 6; born 1814.

Hon. Joseph C. Abbott becomes premier, June 14.

Fishery disputes among English, American, and French fishermen in Newfoundland.

Motion in favor of unrestricted reciprocity with U. S. rejected, July 29.

Sir Hector Louis Langevin and other officials charged with corruption ; Langevin exonerated, July–Sept.

St. Clair Tunnel, connecting Canadian and U. S. Railways, opened Sept. 19.

1892 Dominion discriminates against U. S. in use of Welland canal, April 4.

Alexander Mackenzie, former premier, dies April 17, aged 70.

Great fire in St. John's, Newfoundland, July 8–11.   [25.

Sir Wm. Ritchie, chief-justice, d. about Sept.

Sir John S. D. Thompson, premier, Nov.

1893 Canal tolls arranged with the U. S., Jan. 14.

Treaty for reciprocal trade between France and Canada, Feb. 9.

1893 Destructive fire and hurricane at Halifax, N.S., Aug. 12.

Earl of Aberdeen, gov.-gen., arrives at Ottawa, Sept 25. [72.

Sir John Abbott, statesman, d. Oct. 30, aged

1894 Intercolonial Cong. op. at Ottawa, June 28.

Prominent members of Newfoundland Assembly unseated for bribery.

1895 First exhibition at Regina, N. W. Canada, July 30.

1896 Prof. Cox of McGill University locates a ball by Röntgen rays, Feb. 7.

W. C. McDonald gives $500,000 to McGill Univ., bringing his gifts up to $2,000,000, March 25.

Sir Charles Tupper, premier, May 1.

T. W. Anglin, ex-speaker H. C., d. May 3.

A new rail route between Quebec, St. John, and Halifax opened, June 22.

Wm. D. Balfour, statesman, d. Aug. 19.

Central Canada Exhibition opened at Ottawa, Sept. 21.

Lieut.-gov. Fraser of N. Brun. d. Nov. 24.

Behring Sea Claims Commission in session at Victoria, B.C., Nov. 25.

Newfoundland government purchases railway system, Dec. 2.

1897 School question settled in Manitoba, Mar. 25.

Commission for Yukon gold region appointed, Aug. 9.

1897 British Science Association in session at
Toronto, Aug. 18.

Meeting of the World's W. C. T. U. in Toronto, Oct. 23.

Joint commission to settle difficulties with
U. S., Nov. 19.

1898 Sir F. D. Middleton, gen., d. Jan. 24, aged 72.

Influx of miners to Yukon gold region.

Colonial Period. — French America.

1607 Poutrincourt estab. first permanent French
settlement in America at Port Royal.

1608 Champlain settles Quebec, July 3.

1611 French Jesuits reach Port Royal.

1613 Port Royal burned by Gov. Argall of Va.

1620 Champlain governor of Canada.

1628 Port Royal taken by English.

1629 Sir David Kirke captures Quebec.

1632 Richelieu obtains restoration of territory,
March 29.

1634 Jesuits send missionaries to Indians.

1639 Ursuline Convent established at Quebec.

1640 French at Green Bay, Wisconsin.

1641 Montreal founded.

1659 Laval, first bishop of Quebec.

French fur traders explore Lake Superior.

1668 Marquette establishes mission at Sault Ste.
Marie, April.

1669 La Salle sails down the Ohio to the Miss.

1670 Maine, east of the Penobscot, occupied by the French.

1671 The French occupy about Lakes Huron and Superior.

1672 Count de Frontenac governor of Canada.

1673 Fort Frontenac (Kingston, Ont.) built.
Marquette and Joliet in Iowa.

1679 French at Niagara Falls.

1682 La Salle descends the Mississippi to the Arkansas, and names the valley Louisiana.

1685 French in Texas under La Salle.

1689 French occupy Hudson Bay Territory.
Iroquois capt. Montreal and Lachine, Aug. 25.

1690 Settlements at Salmon Falls, N.H., and Falmouth, Me.

1691 Acadia retaken by the French.   [Jan.

1692 York, Me., attacked by French and Indians,

1696 Frontenac invades New York.

1698 Frontenac dies Nov. 28 ; born 1620.

1699 D'Iberville enters the Mississippi from the Gulf.   [troit, July.

1701 La Motte Cadillac establishes a post at De-Bienville in command in Louisiana.

1702 French settle in Alabama, on bank of Mobile River.

1703 Philippe de Rigaud, Marquis de Vaudreuil. governor of Canada.

1710 Port Royal, Acadia, captured by Eng. fleet.

1713 Treaty of Utrecht gives Acadia to the Eng.
French establish a trading-post at Natchez.

1716 French in the Ohio valley.

1717 Illinois joined to Louisiana.

1718 New Orleans founded.

1719 Negroes brought from Africa to Louisiana.

1720 French fortify Louisburg.

1722 New Orleans made capital of Louisiana.

1725 Vaudreuil governor of Canada.

1729 Massacre of French at Natchez by Indians.

1731 French established at Lake Champlain.

1733 Baton Rouge, Louisiana, settled.

1736 Verendrye builds Fort Rouge, near present Winnipeg.

1745 Marquis Gallissonière governor of Canada.
Louisburg captured by British provincials.

1749 Fort Rouille (Toronto) built by the French.

1751 Sugar-cane introduced into Louisiana.

1752 English trading-posts destroyed by French.
De Menneville, Marquis Duquesne, governor of Canada.

1753 French build forts in the Ohio country.

1754 Geo. Washington captured by the French.

1755 Acadians transported from Grand Pré.
French defeat Braddock at Fort Duquesne.

1756 Montcalm in Quebec.
Acadians arrive at New Orleans.

1757 Fort William Henry captured by French.

1758 Louisburg captured by Gen. Amherst, July.
Fort Frontenac surrenders to Col. Bradstreet.
French abandon Fort Duquesne.

1759 Quebec surrenders to English, Sept. 18.

1760 Pierre François, Marquis de Vaudreuil, last French governor of Canada.

Canada surrendered to the British.

1762 Louisiana ceded to Spain.

1763 Acadia permanently ceded to the British.

1800 Spain cedes Louisiana to France.

1803 Pres. Jefferson purchases La. from France Apr. 30; end of French power in Amer.

Colonial Period. — Spanish America.

1511 Havana founded by Velasquez.

1519 Panama settled by Pedrarias.

Cortez lands in Mexico.

1521 Captures the city of Mexico.

1522 Mexico constituted a kingdom.

1528 Spaniards land in Florida.

1535 Mendoza establishes mint in New Spain.

1567 Menendez builds fort at St. Augustine.

1586 Sir Francis Drake destroys fort at St. Augustine.

1665 St. Augustine pillaged by Eng. buccaneers.

1719 French capture Pensacola.

1722 Pensacola restored to Spain.

1740 Oglethorpe, gov. of Georgia. attacks Florida.

1762 Louisiana acquired from France, Nov. 3.

1763 Florida ceded to Great Britain, Feb. 10.

1764 English troops occupy Baton Rouge, Feb.

1766 Large colony of Acadians arrive in La.

Antonio d'Ulloa takes possession of La.

1768 Revolt of French against Spanish rule in La.

1779 Baton Rouge captured from the British.

1789 Settlers from No. Carolina arr. in Louisiana.

1795 Sugar first produced from cane in Louisiana.
United States allowed to deposit merchandise in New Orleans, Oct. 27.

1800 Louisiana transferred to France by Spain.

1817 Unsuccessful insurrections in Mexico.

1821 Mexico becomes independent of Spain.

1850 Cuba invaded by American filibusters under Lopez.

1851 Second invasion by filibusters; Lopez shot.

1868 Insurrection of Creoles in Cuba, under Cespedes, Sept.

1869 Filibusters again attack Cuba.

1870 Continual insurrections in Cuba.

1873 Slavery abolished in Porto Rico, March 23.
American steamer *Virginius* captured by Spanish gunboat, Oct. 31.

1878 Surrender of insurgent gov. in Cuba, Feb. 21.

1880 Gradual emancipation of slaves promulgated, Feb. 18.

1886 Slavery absolutely abolished in Cuba.

1888 Destructive cyclone in Cuba, 1,000 lives lost, Sept. 4.

1895 Insurrections break out afresh in Cuba.
Marshal Campos arrives in Cuba, April.
Yellow fever epidemic, great mortality, July.
Cuba demands autonomy under Spain, July.
Guerrilla warfare continues, August, *et cet.*

1895 Spanish warship, *Christopher Colon*, wrecked off the coast of Cuba, about 200 lives lost, Sept. 29.

1896 Weyler issues his famous reconcentrado order, Oct. 21.

Gen. Maceo, Cuban leader, killed, Dec. 7.

1897 Weyler recalled, and Blanco appointed captain-general, Oct. 2.

1898 Hostile demonstrations at Havana against Americans, Jan. 15–20.   [15.

Battleship *Maine* blown up at Havana, Feb.

Court of Inquiry begins its sessions at Havana, Feb. 20.

Armistice offered by Spain to the Cuban insurgents, March 12.   [March 19.

Maine Court of Inquiry completes its labors,

Consul-general Lee leaves Havana, Apr. 9.

The blockade of Cuban ports begun, Apr. 22.

Nashville captures *Buena Ventura*, first prize, April 22.

Batteries at Matanzas bombarded, April 27.

Attack on Cienfuegos by torpedo-boat *Winslow*, Ensign Bagley killed, May 11.

Sampson bombards San Juan, Porto Rico, May 12.

Cervera in Santiago harbor, May 19.

Forts at harbor of Santiago bomb., May 31.

Sampson joins Schley at Santiago, June 1.

Lieut. Hobson sinks the *Merrimac* in Santiago harbor, June 3.

1898   Marines win vict. at Guantanamo, June 12.

Fight at El Caney by Gen. Shafter, July 1, 2.

Cervera's fleet totally destroyed, July 3.

Santiago surrenders, July 17.

Gen. Miles lands in Porto Rico, July 25.

Blockade of Cuba raised, Aug. 12.

American army and navy take possession of
    Porto Rico, Oct. 18.

Gen. Garcia, Cuban leader, dies in Washing-
    ton, Dec. 11.

Columbus's bones removed to Spain, Dec. 12.

Fitzhugh Lee back in Havana, Dec. 14.

1899   Spanish power ceases in America, Jan. 1.

UNITED STATES.

1776 United States declares its indepen. July 4.
British Gen. Howe lands in N. Y., Aug. 22.
Americans evacuate New York, Sept. 14.
Battle on Lake Champlain, Oct. 11–13.
Fort Washington capt. by British, Nov. 16.
Washington crosses the Delaware, Dec. 8.
Third Continental Congress meets at Balti-
    more, Dec. 20.
Battle of Trenton, N.J., Dec. 26.

1777 Battle of Princeton, Jan. 3.   [Mar. 4.
' Fourth Continental Congress meets at Phil.,
Roger B. Taney b. Mar. 17 ; d. Oct. 12, 1864.
Henry Clay, statesman, born April 12 ; dies
    June 29, 1852.
Union flag adopted by Congress, June 14.
British evacuate New Jersey, June 30.
Lafayette commis. major-general, July 31.
Battle of Bennington, Vt., Aug. 16.
Battle of Brandywine. Sept. 11.
Count Pulaski com. brigadier-gen., Sept. 15.
British army occupy Philadelphia. Sept. 27.
Fifth Cont. Cong. meets at Lancaster, Penn.,
    Sept. 27.   [Sept. 30.
Sixth Cont. Cong. meets at York, Penn.,
Battle of Germantown, Oct. 4.
Battle of Saratoga, Oct. 7.
Surrender of Burgoyne, Oct. 17.

1777 Articles of Confederation adopted, Nov. 15.
American army at Valley Forge, Dec. 18.

1778 Treaty of alliance with France, Feb. 6.
Baron Steuben joins American army, Feb.
Rembrandt Peale, painter, b. Feb. 22; dies
Oct. 3, 1860.
Treaty with France ratified by Cong., May 4.
British evacuate Philadelphia, June 18.
Battle of Monmouth, N.J., June 28.
Seventh Cont. Cong. meets at Phil., July 2.
Massacre of Wyoming by Indians and Tories,
July 4.   [Nov. 7, 1869.
Charles Stewart, admiral, b. July 18; dies
French fleet ent. Narragansett Bay, July 29.
Battle of Rhode Island, Aug. 29.
Franklin app. minister to France, Sept. 14.
Massacre at Cherry Valley, Nov. 10.
John Jay chosen pres. of Congress, Dec. 10.
British capture Savannah, Ga., Dec. 29.

1779 First Soc. of Universalists in U.S., org. Jan. 1.
Stephen Decatur, Jr., com., b. Jan. 5; dies
March 22, 1820.
British driven from Port Royal, S. C., by
Moultrie, Feb. 3.
Battle of Kettle Creek, Ga., Feb. 14.
Fort Stony Point capt. by Wayne, July 16.
Francis S. Key, poet ("Star-spangled Banner"), b. Aug. 1; d. Jan. 11, 1843.
Benj. Silliman, physicist, b. Aug. 8; dies
Nov. 24, 1864.

1779 James K. Paulding, author, b. Aug. 22 ; dies
April 5, 1860.

Joseph Story, jurist, born Sept. 18; dies
Sept. 10, 1845. [Sept. 23.

Paul Jones capt. British war-ship *Serapis,*

Samuel Huntington of Conn., pres. of Congress, Sept. 28.

Pulaski killed at siege of Savannah, Oct. 9.

British evacuate Rhode Island, Oct. 11–25.

Washington Allston, painter, born Nov. 5 ;
dies July 9, 1843.

Amer. army in winter quarters at Morris-
town, Dec. [Jan. 10.

1780 Gen. Chas. Lee dismissed from Amer. army,

David Porter, com., b. Feb. 1 ; d. Mar. 3, 1843.

Bank of Penn. (first in U. S.) chart., Mar. 1.

Wm. Ellery Channing, b. April 7 ; dies Oct.
2, 1842. [10.

Gen. Clinton besieges Charleston, S.C., April

John J. Audubon, ornithologist, born May 4 ;
dies Jan. 27, 1851.

" Dark Day " in New England, May 19.

Battle of Ramsour's Mills, N.C., June 20.

First Free-will Baptist church in America,
organized in Durham, N.H., June 30.

French army under Rochambeau reaches
Newport, R.I., July 10. [16.

Battle of Camden, S.C., Amer. defeated, Aug.

Richard Rush b. Aug. 29 ; d. July 30, 1859.

Benedict Arnold turns traitor, Sept.

1780 Major André capt., Sept. 23 ; hanged, Oct. 2.
Battle of Charlotte, N.C., Sept. 26.
Battle of King's Mountain, S.C., Oct. 7.
Gen. Nathaniel Greene supersedes Gates,
Oct. 14.

1781 Phillips Academy, Exeter, N.H., founded.
Lemuel Shaw, jurist, b. Jan. 9 ; d. Mar. 30,
1861. [17.
Battle of Cowpens, S.C., Amer. vict., Jan.
Robert Morris app. supt. of finances, Feb. 20.
Bat. of Guilford Court House, N.C., Mar. 15.
Augusta, Ga., captured by Amer., June 5.
Thomas McKean of Del., pres. of Conti-
nental Congress, July 10.
Cornwallis retires to Yorktown, Aug. 4.
French fleet arr. in the Chesapeake, Aug. 30.
Benedict Arnold burns New London, Conn.,
Sept. 6.
Battle of Eutaw Springs, S.C., Sept. 8.
James Lawrence (com. of *Chesapeake*) born
Oct. 1 ; dies June 5, 1813.
Wm. Miller, prophet of the Millerites, born ;
dies Dec. 20, 1849.
Richard M. Johnson, 9th vice-pres. of U. S.,
born Oct. 17 : dies Nov. 19, 1850.
Cornwallis surr. at Yorktown, Oct. 19.
John Hanson of Maryland pres. of Continen-
tal Congress, Nov. 5.
Bank of N. America estab. at Phil., Dec. 31.

1782 First Eng. Bible printed in U. S., at Phil.

1782 Nicholas Longworth b. Jan. 16 ; d. Feb. 10, 1863.

Daniel Webster b. Jan. 18 ; d. Oct. 24, 1852.

John C. Calhoun b. Mar. 18 ; d. Mar. 31, 1850.

Holland recognizes indep. of U. S., April 19.

Congress adopts Great Seal of U. S., June 20.

Savannah, Ga.. evac. by British, July 11.

Jesse D. Elliott, com., born July 14 ; dies Dec. 10, 1845.

Last blood of Revolution shed, in Georgia ; Col. John Laurens killed in a skirmish, Aug. 27.   [at Phil.

First manuf. of fustians and jeans in U. S.,

Lewis Cass b. Oct. 9 ; d. June 17, 1866.

Elias Boudinot of N. J., pres. of Continental Congress, Nov. 4.   [Nov. 30.

Preliminary articles of peace signed at Paris,

Martin Van Buren (8th pres.) born Dec. 5 ; dies Oct. 13, 1862.

British evacuate Charleston, S.C., Dec. 14.

French army embarks from Boston, Dec. 24.

1783 Washington College. Chestertown, Md., org.

Sweden recognizes indep. of U. S., Feb. 5.

Denmark recognizes indep. of U. S., Feb. 25.

Spain recognizes indep. of U. S., Mar. 24.

Washington Irving, author, b. April 3 ; dies Nov. 28, 1859.   [11.

Cong. proclaims cessation of hostilities, Apr.

Cong. ratifies preliminary treaty with Great Britain, April 15.

1783 Order of Cincinnati formed, May 13.

Eighth Cont. Cong. meets at Princeton, N.J., June 30.   [July.

Independence of U.S. recognized by Russia,

Samuel C. Reid, designer of the U.S. flag, b. Aug. 25; d. Jan 28, 1861.

Treaty of peace with Gt. Brit. signed, Sept. 3.

Washington's Farewell Address to the army, Nov. 2.   [gress, Nov. 3.

Thomas Mifflin of Penn. pres. of Cont. Con-

American army disbanded, Nov. 3.

British evacuate Long Island, Dec. 4.

Thos. McDonough, com., b. Dec. 23; d. Nov. 16, 1825.

Washington resigns commission as commander-in-chief, Dec. 23.

1784 St. John's College, Annapolis, Md., organized.

First cotton sent to England.

Congress adopts decimal currency.

University of State of New York established.

American Daily Advertiser, first daily newspaper in America, issued at Phil.

Congress ratifies treaty of peace, Jan. 14.

Charles Morris, com., b. July 26; d. Jan. 27, 1856.

Joseph E. Worcester, lexicographer, b. Aug. 24; d. Oct. 27, 1865.

Zachary Taylor (12th pres.) b. Sept. 24; dies July 9, 1850.   [Nov. 1.

Tenth Cont. Cong. meets at Trenton, N.J.,

1784 Methodist Episc. Ch. organized at Baltimore, Dec. 24.

1785 City Directory of Phil., first pub. in U. S.

Eleventh Cont. Cong. meets at N.Y., Jan. 11.

Samuel Woodworth, poet ("Old Oaken Bucket"), b. Jan. 13; d. Dec. 9, 1842.

John Adams appointed minister to Great Britain, Feb. 24.

Thomas Jefferson appointed minister to Fr., March 10.   [1866.

John Pierpont, poet, b. April 6; d. Aug. 27,

First Episcopal ordination in U. S. at Middletown, Conn., Aug. 3.

Treaty between Prussia and U. S., Aug. 5.

Oliver H. Perry, com., b. Aug. 23; d. Aug. 23, 1819.

Twelfth Cont. Cong. meets at N. Y., Nov. 7.

John Hancock of Mass., pres. of Cont. Cong., Nov. 23.   [March 11, 1848.

Henry Wheaton, publicist, b. Nov. 27; dies

1786 James Rumsey propels boat by steam on Potomac, March.

Wm. R. King, vice-pres. of U. S., b. April 7; dies April 18, 1853.

Amos Lawrence b. Apr. 20; d. Dec. 31, 1852.

Thomas Nuttall, naturalist, b.; d. Sept. 10, 1859.

First spinning-jenny in U. S., at Prov., R. I.

Nathaniel Gorham pres. of Cont. Cong., June 6.

1786   Winfield Scott b. June 13 ; d. May 29, 1866.
Ordinance establishing coinage passed, Aug.
Daniel Shays' rebellion in Western Mass.
David Crockett, backwoodsman, b. Aug. 17 ;
     d. March 6, 1836.   [passed, Oct. 16.
Ordinance to establish United States Mint
Thirteenth Cont. Cong. meets at N.Y., Nov. 6.
Wm. L. Marcy b. Dec. 12 ; d. July 4, 1857.

1787   Arthur St. Clair of Penn. pres. of Congress,
     Feb. 2.
Geo. W. Rodgers, com., b. ; d. May 21, 1832.
Convention to form constitution for U. S.
     meets at Phil., May 25.
Congress enacts ordinance for Northwest
     Territory, July 13.
Treaty between U. S. and Morocco, July 18.
First manuf. of cotton in U. S., at Beverly,
     Mass.
Manufacture of salt at Syracuse, N.Y., begun.
First newspaper published in Kentucky, at
     Lexington, Aug.
John J. Crittenden, b. Sept. 10 ; d. July 26,
     1863.   [5.
Fourteenth Cont. Cong. meets at N.Y., Nov.
Richard H. Dana, b. Nov. 15 ; d. Feb. 2, 1879.
Thom. H. Gallaudet, founder of first inst. in
     America for instruction of the deaf and
     dumb, b. Dec. 10 ; d. Sept. 9, 1851.

1788   Cyrus Griffin of Virginia pres. of Cont. Con-
     gress, Jan. 22.

1788 First lead-mining in America, near Dubuque, Ia.

Joshua Bates born ; dies Sept. 24, 1864.

James Gadsden (*Gadsden Purchase*) b. May 15 ; d. Dec. 26, 1858.

Adoniram Judson, b. Aug. 9 ; d. Apr. 12, 1850.

Alexander Campbell, founder of the Campbellites. b. Sept. 12 ; d. March 14, 1866.

Last Cont. Congress adjourns, Oct. 21.

1789 Tammany Society formed.

Electors vote for first pres. of U. S., Feb.

First U. S. Congress meets at N. Y.; George Washington chosen pres. of U. S. and John Adams vice-pres., April 6.

Washington takes oath of office, April 30.

Jared Sparks b. May 10 ; d. Mar. 14, 1866.

First U. S. tariff bill passed, July 4.

Dep't of Foreign Affairs organized, July 27.

War and Navy Dep'ts organized, Aug. 7.

Treasury Department organized, Sept. 2.

Supreme Court of U. S. estab., Sept.

James Fenimore Cooper b. Sept. 15 ; dies Sept. 14, 1851.

Washington visits Northern States, Oct. 15.

Levi Woodbury b. Dec. 22 ; d. Sept., 1851.

Catherine M. Sedgwick b. Dec. 28 ; d. July 31, 1867.   [4.

1790 Second session of Cong. meets in N. Y., Jan.

Sec. Hamilton reports on public debt, Jan. 14.

First copyright law passed.

1790 Act passed ordering census, March 1.

John Tyler (10th pres.) b. March 29 ; d. Jan. 18, 1862.

Franklin dies at Phil., April 17, aged 84.

Fitz-Greene Halleck b. July 8; d. Nov. 19, 1867. [July 10.

Act passed for acquisition of Dist. of Col.,

First mechanical patent issued, July 31.

Columbia, Capt. Robert Gray, first American ship to make voyage round the world, returns to Boston, Aug. 10.

Wm. B. Shubrick, adm., b. Oct. 31 ; d. May 27, 1874.

Third session of Cong. opens in Phil., Dec. 6.

1791 Anthracite coal discovered in Pennsylvania.

Vermont (14th State) admitted, Jan. 18.

United States bank incorporated, Feb. 8.

Peter Cooper, founder of Cooper Institute, b. Feb. 12 ; d. April 4, 1883.

First Congress adjourns, March 3.

James Buchanan (15th pres.) b. April 23 ; d. June 1, 1868.

Samuel F. B. Morse, inventor (telegraph), b. April 27 ; d. April 2, 1872.

George Ticknor, author, b. Aug. 1 ; d. Jan. 26, 1871. [Aug. 7.

Great Britain appoints first minister to U. S.,

Lydia H. H. Sigourney b. Sept. 1 ; d. June 10, 1865.

Second Congress opens at Phil., Oct. 24.

1791   Charles Sprague, poet, b. Oct. 26 ; d. Jan.
1875.

Amend. to Const., I.–X., ratified, Dec. 15.

1792   Corner-stone of White House, Wash., laid.

Lowell Mason b. Jan. 8; d. Aug. 11, 1872.

Congress grants bounty for fishing-vessels,
Feb. 16.

United States Mint established, April 2.

Matthew Vassar (*Vassar Coll.*) b. April 29 ;
d. June 23, 1868.

Laws passed organizing militia, May 8.

Capt. Robert Gray discovers mouth of river
Columbia, May 11.

Kentucky (15th State) admitted, June 1.

John Howard Payne b. June 9; d. April 10,
1852.

Chester Harding, portrait painter, b. Sept. 1 ;
d. April 1, 1866.

Second presidential election, Nov. 6.

Abbott Lawrence, founder of Scien. School
at Harvard, b. Dec. 16 ; d. Aug. 18, 1855.

1793   Thaddeus Stevens b. April 4; d. Aug. 11,
1868.

First Synod of German Reformed Church,
at Lancaster, Pa.

Sentinel, first newspaper of the Northwest,
appears at Cincinnati, O.

U. S. Mint at Phil. begins to coin money.

Washington receives all the electoral votes ;
John Adams, vice-pres., Feb. 13.

1793 Sam. Houston b. March 2; d. July 25, 1863.

Henry R. Schoolcraft, ethnologist, b. March 28; d. Dec. 10, 1864.

Eli Whitney invents cotton-gin.

Pres. issues proc. of neutrality, April 22.

Edward Hitchcock, geologist, b. May 24; dies Feb. 27, 1864.

Great Britain and France seize neutral ships with war supplies, May–June.

S. G. Goodrich ("Peter Parley"), b. Aug. 19; d. May 9, 1860. [ington, Sept. 18.

Corner-stone of U. S. Capitol laid by Wash-

Political parties assume names of Republican and Federalist.

Third Congress opens at Phil., Dec. 2.

1794 New York *Commercial Advertiser* appears.

Le Moniteur, first newspaper in Louisiana.

First regular theatre in Boston opens in Federal St., Feb. 4.

Amend. XI. to Constitution adopted, Mar. 5.

Act authorizing formation of U. S. N., March 11.

American vessels forbidden to supply slaves to another nation, March 22. [26.

Embargo laid on shipping for 60 days, March

Matthew C. Perry, com., b. April 10; dies March 4, 1858.

Edward Everett b. Apr. 11; d. Jan. 15, 1865.

Cornelius Vanderbilt b. May 27; dies Jan. 4, 1877.

1794 Neutrality act passed, June 5.

Post-office department permanently estab.

Whiskey insurrection in Pa., July–Nov.

Sylvester Graham, vegetarian advocate, b. ; d. Sept. 11, 1851.

Wm. Cullen Bryant b. Nov. 3; d. June 12, 1878.

Ed. T. Taylor ("Father Taylor"), preacher, Boston, b. Dec. 25 ; d. April 5, 1871.

1795 Anti-Rent troubles begin in N. Y., Jan. 7.

Stringent naturalization law passed, Jan. 29.

Hamilton, secretary of treasury, resigns, Jan.

Act passed for redemption of public debt.

University of Tenn. at Knoxville opened.

University of N. Carolina opened, Feb. 13.

Geo. Peabody b. Feb. 18; d. Nov. 4, 1869.

James Harper, founder of Harper & Bros., publishers, b. April 13; d. Mar. 27, 1869.

Silas Wright b. May 24 ; d. Aug. 27, 1847.

Josh. R. Giddings b. Aug. 6 ; d. May 27, 1864.

J. Rodman Drake b. Aug. 7 ; d. Sept. 21, 1820.

Washington signs treaty with Eng., Aug. 14.

James Gordon Bennett, founder *New York Herald*, b. Sept. 1 ; d. June 1, 1872.

Treaty with Algiers, Sept. 5.

James G. Percival b. Sept. 15; d. May 2, 1856.

Robert F. Stockton, com., b. ; d. Oct. 7, 1866.

Treaty with Spain opening Miss., Oct. 20.

John P. Kennedy, secretary of navy, b. Oct. 25; d. Aug. 18, 1870.

1795 James K. Polk (11th pres.) b. Nov. 2; dies
June 15, 1849. [7.

Fourth Congress opens at Philadelphia, Dec.

1796 Congress sustains Jay's treaty with England,
April 30.

Junius Brutus Booth, English tragedian, b.
May 1; d. Nov. 30, 1852.

John G. Palfrey, historian, b. May 2; dies
April 26, 1881. [1859.

Horace Mann, educator, b. May 4; d. Aug. 2,

William Prescott, historian, b. May 4; d.
Jan. 28, 1859. [1876.

Reverdy Johnson born May 21; d. Feb. 10,

Tennessee (16th State) admitted, June 1.

John M. Clayton b. July 24; d. Nov. 9, 1856.

First gaslight in America at Phil., Aug.

Washington issues his " Farewell Address,"
Sept. 19.

Third presidential election, Nov. 8. [6.

Second session of Cong. opened at Phil., Dec.

1797 Electoral votes declare John Adams pres. ;
Thomas Jefferson vice-pres., Feb. 8.

Mary Logan, founder of Mt. Holyoke Sem.,
b. Feb. 28; d. Mar. 5, 1849.

Gerrit Smith b. Mar. 6; d. Dec. 29, 1874.

Special session of Cong. to consider relations
with France, Mar. 25.

Theophilus Parsons, jurist and writer, born
May 17; d. Jan. 26, 1882. [appears.

Medical Repository, first med. journal in Am.,

1797 Cong. prohibits privateering against friendly
nations, June 14.

Cong. authorizes raising 80,000 militia for
three months, June 24.   [Oct. 4.

Commissioners app. to treat with France,

Thurlow Weed, journalist, b. Nov. 15; dies
Nov. 22, 1882.   [1878.

Hiram Paulding, adm., b. Dec. 11; d. Oct. 20,

1798 R. Dunglison ("Dunglison's Med. Dict."),
b. Jan. 4; d. April 1, 1869.

Charles Wilkes, adm., b.; d. Feb. 8, 1877.

Mississippi Territory organized, April 3.

"Hail Columbia" written, April 29; first
sung, May.   [May 4.

Harper's Ferry selected as site for armory,

Congress auth. provisional army, May 28.

Congress auth. seizing of hostile French vessels, May 28.

Imprisonment for debt abolished, June 6.

Commercial intercourse with France suspended, June 12.

Washington com.-in chief of army, June 17.

Uniform rule of naturalization adopted,
June 18.   [July 14.

Alien and sedition laws passed, June 25,

Marine corps organized, July 11.

John A. Dix b. July 24; d. April 21, 1879.

Samuel G. Drake b. Oct. 11; d. June 14, 1875.

Silas H. Stringham, adm., b. Nov. 7; d. Feb.
7, 1876.

1799 General post-office estab., March 2.

John Lowell, founder of Lowell Institute, Boston, b. May 11 ; d. March 4, 1836.

Baltimore American begins pub., May 14.

Rufus Choate b. Oct. 1 ; d. July 13, 1859.

A. Bronson Alcott b. Nov. 29 ; d. Mar. 4, 1888.

Sixth Cong. assembles at Phil., Dec. 2.

1800 University of Vermont opened.

Millard Fillmore (13th pres.) b. Jan. 7 ; dies Mar. 8, 1874.   [*geance*, Feb. 1.

Constellation defeats French frigate *La Ven-*

Ter. of Indiana organized, May 7.

John Brown "of Ossawattomie " b. May 9 ; executed Dec. 2, 1859.

Law passed against slave-trade, May 10.

U. S. gov. removes to Washington, July.

First vaccination in U. S. performed at Harvard College, July.

Treaty with France, spoliation claims adjus.

Daniel S. Dickinson b. Sept. 11 ; d. April 12, 1866.

Henry S. Foote b. Sept. 20 ; d. May, 1880.

Spain cedes Louisiana to France, Oct. 1.

[See *Spanish Colonies.*]

George Bancroft b. Oct. 3 ; d. Jan. 17, 1891.

Benj. F. Wade b. Oct. 27 ; d. Mar. 2, 1878.

Fourth presidential election, Nov. 11.

Chas. Goodyear, inventor (vulcanized rubber), b. Dec. 29 ; d. July 21, 1860.

1801 *New York Post* established.

Merino sheep imported from Spain.

Thos. Jefferson chosen president by electors, Feb. 11; inaugurated, March 4.

Congress assumes jurisdiction over District of Columbia, Feb. 27.   [July 24, 1882.

Geo. P. Marsh, philologist, b. March 17; d.

Wm. H. Seward b. May 16; d. Oct. 10, 1872.

Brigham Young b. June 1; d. Aug. 29, 1877.

Tripoli declares war against U. S., June 10.

David G. Farragut b. July 5; d. Aug. 14, 1870.   [1869.

Robert J. Walker b. July 23; d. Nov. 11,

Theodore D. Woolsey, pres. of Yale College, b. Oct. 31; d. July 1, 1889.

Sam. G. Howe, philanthropist, b. Nov. 10; d. Jan. 9, 1876.

1802 Mark Hopkins, pres. of Williams College, born Feb. 4; dies June 17, 1887.

Congress recognizes war with Tripoli, Feb. 6.

Lydia M. Child b. Feb. 11; d. Oct. 20, 1880.

Naturalization laws of 1795 restored, Apr. 14.

Washington incorporated as a city, May 3.

Gideon Welles, sec. of U. S. N., b. July 1; dies Feb. 11, 1878.

John Wilson, Scottish-American printer and author, born; dies Aug. 3, 1868.

Geo. Ripley, journ., b. Oct. 3; d. July 4, 1880.

Geo. P. Morris, poet and journ., b. Oct. 10; dies July 6, 1864.

1803 *News and Courier*, Charleston, S.C., estab.

Albert S. Johnston, Confederate gen., born Feb. 3; killed at Shiloh, April 6, 1862.

Ohio (17th State) admitted, Feb. 19.

Louisiana purchased for $15,000,000, Apr. 30.

Ralph Waldo Emerson b. May 25; d. April 27, 1882.

John Ericsson, builder of *Monitor*, born July 31; dies March 8, 1889.

Samuel F. Dupont, admiral, b. Sept. 27; d. June 23, 1865.

Eighth Congress opens, Oct. 17.

Frigate *Philadelphia* wrecked and captured in Tripoli, Oct. 31.

New Orleans delivered to the U. S., Dec. 20.

1804 First experiments in artificial propagation of fish in U. S., in South Carolina.

Com. Decatur destroys *Philadelphia* in Tripoli harbor, Feb. 16.

Neal Dow, temperance reformer, b. Mar. 20; dies Oct. 2, 1897.

Severe hurricane in South Carolina.

Nathaniel Hawthorne b. July 1; dies May 19, 1864.

Vice-president Burr kills Alex. Hamilton in a duel, July 11.

Twelfth Amendment to the Constitution adopted, Sept. 25.

Franklin Pierce (11th pres.) b. Nov. 23; d. Oct. 8, 1869.

1805   Territory of Michigan formed from Indiana,
          Jan. 11.

          David D. Field, jurist, b. Feb. 13 ; dies Apr.
          13, 1894.

          Electors choose Jefferson president, Clinton
          vice-pres., Feb. 13.

          Louis M. Goldsborough, adm., b. Feb. 18 ;
          dies Feb. 20, 1877.

          Jefferson and Clinton inaugurated, March 4.

          Theodorus Bailey, adm., b. April 12 ; d. Feb.
          10, 1877.

          Treaty of peace with Tripoli, June 3.

          Robert Anderson, gen., defender of Ft. Sum-
          ter, b. June 14 ; dies Oct. 27, 1871.

          Chas. T. Jackson, discoverer of etherization,
          b. June 21 ; dies Aug. 29, 1880.

          Hiram Powers, sculptor, b. July 29 ; d. 1873.

          Horatio Greenough, sculptor, b. Sept. 6 ; dies
          Dec. 18, 1852.

          Ninth Congress opens, Dec. 2.   [1879.

          Wm. Lloyd Garrison, b. Dec. 12 ; d. May 24,

          Joseph Smith, founder of the sect of Mor-
          mons, b. Dec. 23 ; killed at Carthage, Mo.,
          June 27, 1844.

          University of S. C. opens at Columbia. ·

          Dorothea L. Dix born ; dies July 19, 1887.

1806   Matt. F. Maury, b. Jan. 14 ; d. Feb. 1, 1873.

          Nath'l P. Willis b. Jan. 20 ; d. Jan. 20, 1867.

          Edwin Forrest, actor, b. March 9 ; d. Dec.
          12, 1872.

1806   Pennsylvania Academy of Fine Arts incor.,
        March 26.   [d. Nov. 19, 1869.
        Wm. P. Fessenden, statesman, b. March 31 ;
        John P. Hale b. March 31 ; d. Nov. 19, 1873.
        Wm. G. Simms b. April 17 ; d. June 11, 1870.
        Andrew H. Foote, admiral, b. Sept. 12 ; dies
        June 26, 1863.
        Treaty with Gr. Brit. signed by com., Dec. 3.
1807   Robert E. Lee b. Jan. 19 ; d. Oct. 12, 1870.
        Joseph E. Johnston, Conf. gen., b. Feb. 3 ;
        d. March 21, 1891.   [Feb. 7.
      · Act to prohibit importation of slaves passed,
        Aaron Burr arrested for treason, Feb. 19 ;
        acquitted, Sept. 15.
        Henry W. Longfellow b. Feb. 27 ; dies Mar.
        24, 1882.
        Act passed prohib. import. of slaves, Mar. 2.
        Louis J. R. Agassiz b. May 28; d. Dec. 11,
        1873.
        British frigate *Leopard* fires into U. S. frigate
        Chesapeake, June 22.
        Richard Hildreth, historian, b. June 28 ; d.
        July 11, 1865.
        American ports closed to British ships, July.
        Chas. Francis Adams b. Aug. 18 ; d. Nov.
        21, 1886.
        First steamboat (Fulton's *Clermont*) sails
        from N. Y. to Albany, Sept. 14.
        Tenth Congress opens, Oct. 26.   [1862.
        Cornelius C. Felton, b. Nov. 6 ; d. Feb. 26,

1807 John G. Whittier b. Dec. 17 ; d. Sept. 7, 1892.

Embargo Act, prohib. for. commerce, Dec. 22.

1808 Salmon P. Chase b. Jan. 13 ; d. May 7. 1873.

Alvan Clark b. March 4 ; d. Aug. 19, 1887.

Embargo act modified, March 12.

Jefferson Davis b. June 3 ; d. Dec. 6, 1889.

Hamilton Fish b. Aug. 3 ; d. Sept. 7. 1893.

Samuel F. Smith, author of "America," b. Oct. 21 ; d. Nov. 16, 1895.

Sixth presidential election, Nov. 8.

Stephen C. Rowan, adm., b. Dec. 25 ; d. March 31, 1890.   [1875.

Andrew Johnson (17th pres.) b. Dec. 29 ; d.

Andover (Mass.) Theological Semin. opened.

1809 Mammoth Cave, Kentucky, discovered.

Territory of Illinois established, Feb. 3.

Electors choose Jas. Madison pres., Feb. 8.

Abraham Lincoln (16th pres.) b. Feb. 12 ; d. April 15, 1865.

Embargo Act repealed, March 1.

Non-intercourse Act with Great Britain and France, March 1 ; terminated, April 19.

Benj. Peirce, math., b. Apr. 4 ; d. Oct. 6, 1880.

Robert C. Winthrop b. May 12 ; d. Nov. 16, 1894.

Eleventh Congress opens, May 22.

Hannibal Hamlin, vice-pres. U. S., b. Aug. 27 ; d. July 4, 1891.

Oliver Wendell Holmes b. Aug. 29 ; d. Oct. 7, 1894.

1809 John A. Dahlgren, admiral, b. Nov. 13; d.
July 12, 1870.

1810 General post-office estab. at Wash., Apr. 30.
First Agricultural exhibition in U. S. at
Georgetown, D.C., May 10.
Theodore Parker, theol., b. Aug. 24; d. May
10, 1860.   [29, 1873.
John A. Winslow, adm., b. Nov. 19; d. Sept.
P. T. Barnum, showman, b.; d. Apr. 7, 1891.

1811 Charles Sumner, statesman, b. Jan. 6; d.
March 11, 1874.
Edgar Allan Poe b. Jan. 26; d. Oct. 7, 1849.
Horace Greeley, founder of *N. Y. Tribune*,
b. Feb. 3; d. Nov. 29, 1872.
Trading-posts first established among Indi-
ans, March 2.
Engagement between U. S. frigate *President*
and Brit. sloop-of-war *Little Bell*, May 16.
First number of *Niles' Register* issued in
Baltimore, Sept. 7.
Twelfth Congress convenes, Nov. 4.
General W. H. Harrison defeats Indians at
Tippecanoe, Nov. 7.
Wendell Phillips b. Nov. 29; d. Feb. 2, 1884.
First steamboat on the Ohio, the *New Orleans*.
Elihu Burritt ("The Learned Blacksmith")
b. Dec. 8; d. March 7, 1879.   [4, 1892.
Noah Porter, pres. of Yale Coll., b.; d. Mar.
Theatre at Richmond, Va., burned, gov. and
many others perish, Dec. 26.

1812 First steam vessel on the Mississippi, Jan.
Alex. H. Stephens b. Feb. 11 ; d. Mar. 4, 1883.
Embargo on all vessels in U. S. for 90 days,
    April 4.   [20.
Vice-pres. Clinton dies at Washington, Apr.
Louisiana (18th State) admitted, April 30.
Territory of Missouri established, June 4.
Harriet Beecher Stowe b. June 15 ; d. July
    1, 1896.
War declared against Gt. Britain, June 18.
Am. *Constitution* cap. Brit. *Guerrière*, Aug. 19.
Richard M. Hoe (*Hoe's Lightning Press*) b.
    Sept. 12 ; d. June 7, 1886.
Am. Antiquarian Soc. incorporated at Wor-
    cester, Mass., Oct. 12.
Battle of Queenstown, Canada, Oct. 13.
Am. *Wasp* capt. British *Frolic*, Oct. 18.
Henry Wilson, vice-pres., b.; d. Nov. 22, 1875.
Fight at St. Regis, N.Y., Oct. 23.
Frigate *United States* capt. Brit. *Macedonian*,
    Oct. 25.
Presidential election, Nov. 10.
Wm. Warren, Jr., comedian, b. Nov. 17 ; d.
    Sept. 21, 1888.
U. S. *Constitution* capt. British *Java*, Dec. 29.
Term "gerrymander" originates in Mass.
National Academy of Art estab. by Act of
    Cong. in Dist. of Columbia.   [Jan.

1813 Brit. adm. Cockburn blockades Amer. coast,
John C. Frémont b. Jan. 21 ; d. July 13, 1890.

1813 Electors choose James Madison pres.; Elbridge Gerry vice-pres., Feb. 10.

Am. *Hornet* capt. British *Peacock*, Feb. 24.

Christopher P. Cranch, artist and poet, born March 8; d. Jan. 20, 1892.   [1861.

Stephen A. Douglas b. April 23; d. June 3, York (Toronto) captured, April 27.

Thirteenth Congress convenes, May 24.

Brit. *Shannon* capt. Am. *Chesapeake*, June 1.

David D. Porter, adm., b. June; d. Feb. 12, 1891.   [1887.

Henry Ward Beecher b. June 24; d. Mar. 8.

Boston Daily Advertiser established.

Am. *Enterprise* capt. Brit. *Boxer*, Sept. 5.

Victory of Com. Perry on Lake Erie, Sept. 10.

John Sedgwick, gen., b. Sept. 13; d. May 9. 1864.   [d. Mar. 16, 1868.

1814 David Wilmot (*Wilmot Proviso*) b. Jan. 20;

Samuel J. Tilden b. Feb. 9; d. Aug. 4, 1886.

Thomas Crawford, sculptor, b. Mar. 22; dies Oct. 10, 1857.   [Mar. 28.

Brit. *Phœbe* and *Cherub* capt. Amer. *Essex*,

John L. Motley b. Apr. 15; d. May 29, 1877.

Am. *Peacock* capt. Brit. *Epervier*, April 29.

Am. *Wasp* capt. British *Reindeer*, June 28.

Fort Erie surr. to Gens. Scott and Ripley, July 3.

Battle of Chippewa, July 5.

Samuel Colt, inventor (revolver), b. July 19; d. Jan 10, 1862.

1814 Battle of Lundy's Lane, July 25.   [9–12.
Stonington, Conn., bomb. by Brit. fleet, Aug.
Capitol at Washington burned, Aug. 24.
Amer. *Wasp* defeats British *Avon*, Sept. 1.
Vict. of Com. McDonough on Lake Champlain, Sept. 11.
"Star-spangled Banner" written by Francis
    Scott Key, Sept. 13.   [*genet*, Sept. 26.
Sea-fight of *Gen. Armstrong* and Brit. *Planta*-
Elbridge Gerry, vice-pres., dies at Washington, Nov. 23.   [Dec. 15.
Hartford Convention to oppose war meets,
Edwin M. Stanton, sec. of war, b. Dec. 19;
    d. Dec. 24, 1869.   [Jan. 8.

1815 Gen. Jackson's vict. at bat. of New Orleans,
Amer. *President* capt. by British *Endymion*,
    Jan. 15.   [Feb. 17.
Treaty of peace with Great Britain ratified,
Constitution captures *Cyane* and *Levant*, Feb.
U. S. declares war against Algiers, Mar. 3.
Amer. *Hornet* capt. Brit. *Penguin*, Mar. 23.
Handel and Haydn Society organized in
    Boston, April 20.
Treaty of peace with Morocco, June 30.
Richard H. Dana, Jr., b. Aug. 1; d. Jan. 7,
    1882.   [1879.
Joseph Hooker, gen., b. Nov. 13; d. Oct. 31,
Clark Mills, sculptor, b. Dec. 1; d. Jan. 12,
    1883.
Fourteenth Congress convenes, Dec. 4.

1816 First savings bank in the U. S., at Phil.

Henry W. Halleck, gen., b. Jan. 16 ; d. Jan. 9, 1872. [1894.

Nathaniel P. Banks b. Jan. 30 ; d. Sept. 1, *Boston Recorder*, first religious newspaper in U. S., appears. [31, 1895.

Ebenezer R. Hoar, jurist, b. Feb. 21. d. Jan.

U. S. Bank chartered by Congress, April 10.

Amer. Bible Society organized, May 8–13.

John G. Saxe, poet, b. June 2 ; dies Mar. 31, 1887. [d. Feb. 8, 1876.

Charlotte S. Cushman, actress, born July 23 ;

Geo. H. Thomas, gen., b. July 31 ; d. Mar. 28, 1870.

First steamboat on the Gt. Lakes, the *Ontario*.

George G. Meade, gen., b. ; d. Nov. 6, 1872.

Presidential election, Nov. 12.

Elizabeth Cady Stanton, reformer, b. Nov. 12.

Benj. Silliman, Jr., physicist, b. Dec. 4 ; dies June 14, 1885.

Indiana (19th State) admitted, Dec. 11.

American Colonization Society formed, Dec.

1817 Presidential electors choose James Monroe pres. ; Dan'l Tompkins vice-pres., Feb. 12.

Mississippi territory divided, March 1.

Seth Green, fish culturist, born Mar. 19 ; dies Aug. 20, 1888. [Savannah.

Frederic Tudor of Boston first ships ice to

Pierre G. T. Beauregard b. May 23 ; d. Feb. 20, 1893.

1817 John B. Gough b. Aug. 22; d. Feb. 18, 1886.
First coast-survey work.
Frederick Douglass, orator, formerly a slave,
b.; d. Feb. 20, 1895.
Fifteenth Congress convenes, Dec. 1.
Mississippi (20th State) admitted, Dec. 10.
First instruction of deaf mutes in Amer., by
T. H. Gallaudet.
James T. Fields b. Dec. 31; d. Apr. 26, 1881.

1818 Geo. S. Boutwell, statesman, b. Jan. 28.
Wm. M. Evarts born Feb. 6.
American Farmer, first agricul. paper in U. S.
Pensions granted to Rev. soldiers in need,
Mar. 18.   [19, 1898.
Don Carlos Buell, gen., b. Mar. 23; d. Nov.
Act establishing flag of U. S., April 4.
Gen. Jackson takes Pensacola, May 24.
John A. Andrew, war gov. of Mass., b. May
31; d. Oct. 30, 1867.
Maria Mitchell, astron., b. Aug. 1; d. June
28, 1889.
Irvin McDowell, gen., b. Oct. 15; d. May 5,
1885.
Treaty with England, Oct. 20.
Benj. F. Butler b. Nov. 5; d. Jan. 11, 1893.
Illinois (21st State) admitted, Dec. 3.
Lucy Stone, advocate of woman's rights, b.;
d. Oct. 18, 1893.   [1893.

1819 Philip Schaff, scholar, b. Jan. 1; d. Oct. 20,
Central Coll. at Danville, Ky., incor., Jan. 19.

1819 Wm. W. Story, sculptor, b. Feb. 19 ; d. Feb. 8, 1895.

Treaty with Spain concluded, Feb. 22.

James Russell Lowell b. Feb. 22; d. Aug. 12, 1891.

Richard S. Greenough, sculptor, b. April 27.

First transatlantic steamship, *Savannah*, sails from Savannah to Liverpool, May 24 (passage 26 days).

Julia Ward Howe born May 27.

Walt Whitman b. May 31 ; d. Mar. 26, 1892.

Thomas Ball, sculptor, born June 3.

Maine separated from Mass., June 19.

Nathaniel Lyon, gen., b. July 14; killed Aug. 10, 1861.

First American lithographic printing, July.

Chas. A. Dana, journ., b. Aug. 8; d. Oct. 17, 1897.

Wm. T. G. Morton, dis. of the use of ether as an anæsthetic, b. Aug. 9 ; d. July 15, 1868.

Thomas W. Parsons, poet, b. Aug. 18 ; dies Sept. 3, 1892.

Cyrus W. Field, organizer of Atlantic Telegraph Co., b. Nov. 30 ; d. July 12, 1892.

Wm. S. Rosecrans, gen., b. Dec. 6 ; d. Mar. 11, 1898.

Sixteenth Congress convenes, Dec. 6.

Alabama (22d State) admitted, Dec. 14.

Isaac T. Hecker, founder of the Paulists, b. Dec. 18 ; d. Dec. 22, 1889.

1819 Oddfellowship introduced from Manchester, Eng.   [d. Nov. 25, 1885.

Thos. A. Hendricks, vice-pres. of U. S., b.;

1820 Waterville College (afterward Colby Univ.) established.   •

Henry J. Raymond, founder of *N. Y. Times*, b. Jan. 24 ; d. June 18, 1869.

Wm. T. Sherman, general, b. Feb. 8 ; d. Feb. 14, 1891.

Maine (23d State) admitted, Mar. 15.

Duel between Com. Decatur and Com. Barron ; both wounded, Decatur mortally, March 22.

Chas. Devens, general, jurist, b. April 4 ; d. Jan. 7, 1891.

Alice Cary b. April 20 ; d. April 12, 1871.

First steamship line between New York and New Orleans, June.

Indiana State Univ. chartered ; opened, 1824.

John F. Reynolds, gen., b. Sept. 20 ; killed July 1, 1863.

1821 James Longstreet, Confed. gen., b. Jan. 8.

John C. Breckinridge, vice-pres., b. Jan. 21 ; d. May 17, 1875.

Missouri Compromise Bill passed, Feb. 26, 27.

Elizabeth Blackwell, first woman in U. S. who received degree of M. D., b.

Andrew Jackson appointed gov. of Fla., Apr.

Missouri (24th State) admitted, Aug. 10.

Amherst College dedicated, Sept. 18.

1821 Seventeenth Congress convenes, Dec. 3.
Mary A. Livermore b. Dec. 19.

1822 Thos. B. Read, poet, b. Mar. 12; d. May 11, 1872.

Independence of Spanish South American States recognized, March 28.

Donald G. Mitchell (*Ik Marvel*) b. April.

Edward Everett Hale b. April 3.

Ulysses S. Grant (18th pres.) b. April 27 ; d. July 23, 1885.

Rutherford B. Hayes (19th pres.) b. Oct. 4 ; d. Jan. 17, 1893.   [b. Nov. 10.

Frederick L. Olmsted, landscape gardener,

Anson Burlingame, diplomatist, b. Nov. 14 ; d. Feb. 23, 1870.

Gaslight introduced into Boston.

Richard Grant White, Shakespearean critic, b.; d. April 8, 1885.   [20, 1863.

Geo. W. Rodgers, com. U. S. N., b.; d. Aug.

1823 First American theatre in New Orleans.

John Pope, gen., b. Mar. 16 ; d. Sept. 23, 1892.

Schuyler Colfax, vice-pres. U. S., b. March 23 ; d. Jan. 13, 1885.

John Sherman b. May 10.   [d. May 1, 1895.

John Newton, military engineer, b. Aug. 24 ;

Francis Parkman, historian, b. Sept. 16 ; d. Nov. 8, 1893.

Eighteenth Congress convenes, Dec. 1.

President Monroe proclaims " Monroe Doctrine," Dec. 2.

1824   Thomas J. Jackson (" Stonewall Jackson ")
b. Jan. 21; d. May 10, 1863.

Winfield S. Hancock, gen., b. Feb. 14; d.
Feb. 9, 1886.   [1892.

Geo. Wm. Curtis b. Feb. 24; d. Aug. 31,

Ambrose E. Burnside b. May 23 ; d. Sept.
13, 1881.

Alfred Pleasanton, gen., b. June 7 ; d. Feb.
17, 1897.

Lafayette arr. in N. Y., Aug. 15; welcomed
to House of Representatives, Dec. 10.

Phœbe Cary, b. Sept. 4 ; d. July 31, 1871.

Benj. A. Gould, Jr., astronomer, b. Sept. 27 ;
d. Nov. 26, 1896.

Ambrose P. Hill, Confed. gen., b. Nov. 9 ;
killed April 2, 1865.

Thos. Starr King b. Dec. 16; d. Mar. 4, 1863.

Amer. Sunday-school Union founded at Phil.

1825   Treaty with Russia ratified, Jan. 11.

Bayard Taylor b. Jan. 11 ; d. Dec. 19, 1878.

Quincy A. Gillmore, gen., b. Feb. 28; d.
April 7, 1888.

John Quincy Adams inaug. president, Mar. 4.

University of Virginia opens March 25.

Corner-stone of Bunker-Hill Monument laid,
June 17.

Richard H. Stoddard, poet, b. July.

Illuminating-gas comes into use in N. Y.

Randolph Rogers, sculptor, b. July 6; dies
Jan. 14, 1892.

1825 Erie Canal finished, Oct. 26.

Nineteenth Congress convenes, Dec. 5.

1826 John A. Logan b. Feb. 9; d. Dec. 26, 1886.

Duel between Clay and Randolph, April 8.

George F. Hoar, senator, b. Aug. 29.

Anti-masonic excitement on account of William Morgan, Sept.

Joseph R. Hawley, gen., b. Oct. 31.

Journal of Education, first of its kind, issued in Boston.

Lucy Larcom born; dies April 17, 1893.

Geo. B. McClellan b. Dec. 3; d. Oct. 29, 1885.

1827 *Youth's Companion*, Boston (weekly) appears.

Disciples of Christ (Campbellites) founded.

Lew. Wallace, author, b. April 10.

John T. Trowbridge b. Sept. 18.

Henry W. Slocum, gen., b. Sept. 24; dies April 14, 1894.

Alfred H. Terry b. Nov. 10; d. Dec. 16, 1890.

First railroad in the U. S., in Quincy, Mass.

Twentieth Congress convenes, Dec. 3.

1828 Second railroad in the U. S., in Penn.

Ground broken for Chesapeake and Ohio canal, July 4.

James B. MacPherson, gen., b. Nov. 14; killed, July 22, 1864.

Webster's Dictionary first published.

Oswego canal finished.

1829 Albert Bierstadt, painter, b. Jan. 7.

Joseph Jefferson, actor, b. Feb. 20.

1829 Carl Schurz b. March 2.

Andrew Jackson inaug. president, March 4.

James L. M. Smithson, founder of Smithsonian Institution, dies June 27.

First locomotive run in the U. S., Aug. 8.

First pub. school in Baltimore opens Sept. 21.

Inquirer, Philadelphia, established.

John Rogers, sculptor, b. Oct. 30.

Roscoe Conkling b. Oct. 30; d. Apr. 18, 1888.

Charles G. Halpine ("Miles O'Reilly") born Nov.; dies Aug. 3, 1868.

Twenty-first Congress convenes, Dec. 7.

Laura Bridgman, blind deaf mute, born Dec. 21; dies May 24, 1889.

Patrick S. Gilmore, musician, b.; d. Sept. 24, 1892.

1830 Gouverneur K. Warren, gen., b. Jan. 8; dies Aug. 8, 1882.

Great speeches of Webster and Hayne in U. S. Senate, Jan. 25–27.

James G. Blaine b. Jan. 31; d. Jan. 27, 1893.

Jared Sparks begins "American Biography."

First 14 miles of Baltimore and Ohio railroad opens, May 24.

Chester A. Arthur (21st pres.) born Oct. 5; dies Nov. 18, 1886.

Harriet G. Hosmer, sculptor, born Oct. 9.

Oliver O. Howard, gen., b. Nov. 8.

Mount St. Mary's College, Emmittsburgh, Md.. incorporated.

1830 Book of Mormon first published.

Evening Transcript, Boston, Mass., estab.

First gold from Georgia mines received at U. S. Mint.

Clara Barton, org. Red Cross Society, born.

1831 First locomotive built in the United States.

Copyright law radically amended.

Paul H. Hayne, b. Jan. 1; d. July 9, 1886.

William Lloyd Garrison first publishes *Liberator*, Jan. 1.

Philip H. Sheridan b. March 6; d. Aug. 5, 1888. [Aug.

Nat Turner's negro insurrection in Virginia,

Anti-Masonic party hold a National Convention, Sept. 26.

John M. Schofield, gen., born Sept. 29.

Boston Daily Post established.

University of Alabama opens.

Chloroform discovered by Samuel Guthrie of Sackett's Harbor, N.Y. [12, 1885.

Helen (Hunt) Jackson, poet, born; dies Aug.

James A. Garfield (20th pres.) b. Nov. 19; dies Sept. 19, 1881.

Twenty-second Congress convenes, Dec. 5.

1832 Red Jacket, chief of the Senecas, d. Jan. 20, a. 78.

James E. B. Stuart, Confed. gen., b.; killed, May 11, 1864. [21.

First Democratic National Convention, May

Black Hawk war, May–Aug.

1832   Cholera first appears in the U. S., June 27.

President vetoes national bank bill, July 10.

Source of Mississippi discovered by School-craft, July 13.

Jackson issues proclamation to South Carolina, against nullification, Dec. 10.

John C. Calhoun, vice-pres., resigns, Dec. 28.

John H. Vincent, founder of "Chautauqua," born Feb. 23.

1833   South Carolina railroad from Charleston to Hamburg, Ga., 135 miles, then the longest continuous line in the world, completed.

South Carolina repeals ordinance of nullification, March 16.

Benjamin Harrison (23d pres.) b. Aug. 20.

New York Sun first published, Sept. 3.

Bank deposits removed from National Bank, Oct. 1.

Edmund C. Stedman, poet, born Oct. 1.

Antislavery Society organized in N.Y., Oct. 2.

Great display of meteors, Nov. 13.

Edwin T. Booth, actor, born Nov. 13; dies June 7, 1893.   [1888.

Louisa May Alcott b. Nov. 29; dies Mar. 6,

Twenty-third Congress convenes, Dec. 2.

Am. Antislavery Society org. at Phil., Dec. 6.

Robert G. Ingersoll born Aug. 11.

Adelaide Phillips born; dies Oct. 2, 1882.

Launt Thompson b.; d. Sept. 26. 1894.

Boston Journal established.

1834 Treaty with Spain, indemnity, Feb. 17.

Charles W. Eliot, pres. of Harv. Univ., born March 20.

Chas. F. Browne ("Artemus Ward") born April 26; dies March 6, 1867.

Lafayette dies in France, May 19.

James Gibbons, cardinal, born July 23.

Whig party first so-called.

St. Ursula convent at Mount Benedict, Mass., burned by mob, Aug. 11.

McCormick reaping-machine patented.

National debt extinguished, Dec.

1835 Attempted assassination of Pres. Jackson, Jan. 30.

Seminole war begins.

New York Herald published by James Gordon Bennett, May 6.

" Loco-focos " applied to Democratic party.

Branch mint at New Orleans established.

Sam. L. Clemens ("Mark Twain") b. Nov. 30.

Phillips Brooks b. Dec. 13; d. Jan. 23, 1893.

Great fire in New York City, Dec. 16, 17.

1836 Judson Kilpatrick, gen., born Jan. 14; dies Dec. 4, 1881.

Massacre at Alamo, Texas, March 6.

Public Ledger, Philadelphia, established.

Arkansas (25th State) admitted, June 15.

Treaty with Venezuela and Peru-Bolivian confederacy.

First observatory in U. S., in Massachusetts.

1836 Sam. Houston, first pres. of **Texas,** Oct. 22.

Thomas B. Aldrich, poet, born Nov. 11.

Hugh J. Kilpatrick, gen., b.; d. Dec. 4, 1881.

Celia Thaxter born; dies Aug. 26, 1894.

Jay Gould born; dies Dec. 2, 1892.

1837 Michigan (26th State) admitted, Jan. 26.

Dwight L. Moody born Feb. 5.

William D. Howells born March 1.

Stephen Grover Cleveland (22d and 24th pres.) born March 18.

Great commercial panic, May.

Morse system of telegraphy invented.

Baltimore Sun established.

Mt. Holyoke College, South Hadley, Mass., opens.   [21.

Osceola, Seminole chief, made prisoner, Oct.

United States citizens join Canadian patriots.

Wesleyan Female College, in Georgia, oldest for women in U. S., chartered.

Rev. Elijah P. Lovejoy murdered by pro-slavery mob at Alton, Ill., Nov. 7.

Whitelaw Reid, journalist, born Oct. 27.

Wendell Phillips's first abolition speech, Dec. 8.

American steamer *Caroline* burned by Canadians, Dec. 29.

1838 Duel between Graves and Cilley, Congressmen, Feb. 24.

Great Western and *Sirius* cross the Atlantic, April.

1838 U. S. exploring expedition to the Antarctic.
John D. Long, secretary of navy, b. Oct. 27.

1839 Daguerreotypes first taken in U. S.
Vulcanized rubber patented by Goodyear.
" Aroostook war " between Me. and N. B.
First dental school in U. S. at Baltimore.
Nelson A. Miles, gen., b. Aug. 8.
Francis Bret Harte, born Aug. 25.
Henry George, political economist, born Sept.
2; dies Oct. 29, 1897. [18, 1898.
Frances E. Willard, born Sept. 28; dies Feb.
Thomas B. Reed born Oct. 18.
Liberty Party convene at Warsaw, N.Y.,
Nov. 13.
George A. Custer born Dec. 5; killed by
Indians, June 25, 1876.

1840 Steamer *Lexington* burned on Long Island
Sound, 140 lives lost, Jan. 13.
Lieut. Wilkes discovers Antarctic continent,
Jan. 19.
Washingtonian Temperance Soc. founded.
Francis A. Walker, educator, born July 2;
dies Jan. 5, 1897.
First Cunard steamer, *Britannia*, leaves Liv-
erpool for Boston, July 4; arrives July 19.
Corner-stone of State University of Missouri
laid, July 4.
Alfred T. Mahan, naval writer, born Sept. 27.

1841 Steamer *President* sails from New York for
Liverpool, and never heard from, Mar. 11.

1841   Mormon Tem. at Nauvoo, Ill., begun Apr. 6.

Horace Greeley issues *N. Y. Daily Tribune*, April 10.   [chines, May.

Pat. granted to Elias Howe for sewing-ma-

Failure of United States Bank, Oct. 11.

Brook Farm, socialistic experiment in Mass., begins.

Times, Hartford, Conn., established.

1842   Sidney Lanier b. Feb. 3 ; d. Sept. 8, 1881.

University of Mich. at Ann Arbor estab., March 18.

John Fiske, historian, born March 30.

Col. J. C. Frémont exp. Rocky Mts., May.

Dorr's Rebellion in R. I., May–June.

Order of Pocahontas introduced into U. S.

Statue of Washington placed in Capitol.

Charles Dickens visits United States.

Gold found in California.

Clara L. Kellogg born July 12.   [9.

" Ashburton treaty " with Eng. signed, Aug.

Anna E. Dickinson b. Oct. 28.

Alleged mutiny on U. S. brig *Somers*, Dec. 1.

1843   Wm. McKinley (25th pres.) b. Jan. 29.

Dr. Marcus Whitman travels from Oregon to Wash., and saves Oregon to U. S., March.

Henry James, Jr., born April 15.

Frémont's second exploring expedition, May.

Bunker Hill Monument dedicated, Daniel Webster orator, June 17.

Convention of Nat'l Liberty Party, Aug. 30.

1843 College of the Holy Cross founded at Worcester, Mass.

1844 Maryland Historical Society founded, Jan.

Louisville Courier established, Feb. 13.

Explosion of large gun on U. S. war steamer *Princeton;* Upshur, sec. of state, Gilmer, sec. of navy, and others, killed, Feb. 28.

Adolphus W. Greely, arctic exp., b. Mar. 27.

Treaty of annex. with Texas signed, Apr. 12.

Riot in Philadelphia, May 6–8.

Morse magnetic telegraph completed from Baltimore to Washington, May 20.

First telegraphic com. in U. S., May 27.

Springfield Republican (Mass.) established.

Water-cures introduced into United States.

The term " Barnburners " applied to portion of Democratic party in New York.

First screw-propeller built in United States.

Samuel Hoar, Mass. State agent, sent to protest against imprisonment of colored citizens, obliged to leave Charleston, S.C.

John Boyle O'Reilly b. June 28 ; d. Aug. 10, 1890.   [Aug. 13.

Elizabeth Stuart Phelps (Mrs. Ward) b.

1845 Florida (27th State) admitted, March 3.

James K. Polk inaug. president, March 4.

Methodist Episcopal Church South org. at Louisville, Ky., May.

United States Naval Academy established at Annapolis, Md.

1845 Petroleum obtained by boring near Pittsburg.

Texas (28th State) admitted, Dec. 29.

Will Carleton, poet, born Oct. 21.

Francis M. Crawford, novelist, b.

Martin Milmore, sculptor, b. Sept. 14; d. 1883.

1846 Hostilities between Mexico and U. S. begin,
April 25.   (See MEXICO.)   [15.

Boundary treaty with Gt. Brit. signed, June

Boston Herald established.

First application of ether by Drs. Jackson
and Morton.

U. S. National Museum org. at Washington.

Chicago Tribune established.

R. H. Hoe invents type-revolving printing-
press.

Smithsonian Institution estab. Aug. 10.

U. S. brig *Somers* sunk off Vera Cruz, Dec. 8.

Iowa (29th State) admitted, Dec. 28.

1847 Thomas A. Edison born Feb. 11.

Alexander G. Bell born Mar. 3.

Astor Place (N. Y.) Opera House opens,
Nov. 22. (Scene of the Macready riot,
evening of May 10, 1849.)

Salt Lake City, Utah, founded by Mormons.

Toledo Blade, Ohio, established.

State University of Iowa chartered ; op. 1860.

Oneida Community established.

1848 Girard College, Philadelphia, opens, Jan. 1.

Gold discovered near Colonia, Cal., by Marshal, Jan. 19.

1848 Treaty of peace, etc., with Mexico, Feb. 2.

Augustus Saint Gaudens born March 1.

John Jacob Astor d. Mar. 29; b. July 17, 1763.

Wisconsin (30th State) admitted, May 29.

University of Mississippi opens.

Spiritual rappings begin at Rochester, N.Y.

Corner-stone of Washington Monument laid,
July 4; completed, 1884.

1849 Continuous railroad connects Boston and
New York, Jan. 1.

Albert Gallatin d. Aug. 12; b. Jan. 29, 1761.

Department of Interior created, March 3.

Zachary Taylor inaug. president, March 5.

Great emigration of gold-hunters to California begins.

University of Wisconsin opens.

Collins steamship line formed.   [Apr. 19.

1850 Bulwer-Clayton treaty with Gr. Brit. signed,
Henry Cabot Lodge b. May 12.

Filibustering expedition of N. Lopez, May 21.

Eugene Field b. Sept. 2; d. Nov. 4, 1895.

California (31st State) admitted, Sept. 9.

New Mexico made a Territory, Sept. 9.

Jenny Lind gives her first concert in Castle
Garden, New York, Sept. 12.

Fugitive Slave Bill passed, Sept. 18.   [20.

Slave-trade suppressed in Dist. of Col., Sept.

Clay Compromise Bill passed, Sept. 20.

Flogging abolished in navy, Sept. 28.

Edward Bellamy b.; d. May 22, 1898.

1850 Inman steamship line organized.

Dispatch, Richmond, Va., established.

Second great fire in San Francisco.

Steam-ploughs patented. [*Era.*

" Uncle Tom's Cabin " first pub. in *National*

1851 First train on Erie Railway, April 28, 29.

Fourth great fire in San Francisco, 1,500 houses burned, May 4.

Vigilance Committee in San Francisco organized, June. [proved, June 2.

" Maine Law " to prohibit liquor-selling, ap-

Yacht *America* wins great race, Aug. 22.

Hudson River railroad opens, Oct. 8.

Grinnell arctic expedition returns, Oct.

Excitement in Boston over arrest of Shadrach and Sims, fugitive slaves.

New York Times established.

Louis Kossuth arrives at New York, Dec. 5.

Great fire in library of Congress, Dec. 24.

1852 U. S. Mint established at San Francisco, July 3.

Amer. Society of Civil Engineers organized.

Globe-Democrat, St. Louis, Mo., established.

Manufacture of galvanized iron begun in Philadelphia.

1853 Coinage of $3 gold pieces authorized, Feb. 21.

Franklin Pierce inaug. president, March 4.

Wm. R. King, vice-pres., d. April 18.

Dr. Kane sent in search of Sir J. Franklin, May 30.

1853 The Cleveland and Toledo railroad completed.

Martin Koszta affair at Smyrna, June 21.

World's Fair opens in New York, July 14.

Walker's filibustering exped. to Sonora, July.

University of Louisiana chartered.

Allan steamship line organized.

Gadsden Purchase, Dec. 20.

Steamer *San Francisco* founders; 240 U. S. soldiers perish, Dec. 23–31.

1854 Astor Library opened in New York, Jan. 9.

Chicago and Rock Island railroad, connecting Chicago with the Mississippi River, completed, Feb.

Treaty between U. S. and Japan, March 31.

U. S. branch mint opened in San Francisco, April 3.   [April 20.

Mass. Emigrant Aid Society org. in Boston,

Anthony Burns (fugitive slave) excitement in Boston, May 27, *et seq.*   [30.

Kansas-Nebraska Bill approved by Pres., May

Reciprocity treaty with Gr. Britain, June 5.

Steamer *Arctic* struck by *Vesta* off Newfoundland, over 350 lives lost, Sept. 27.

Ostend Manifesto issued, Oct. 18.

R. T. Ely, political economist, b. April 13.

Sorghum cane introduced from France.

1855 Panama railroad completed, Jan. 28.

Winfield Scott made lieut.-gen., Feb. 15.

Troubles in Kansas.

1855   *Pioneer Press*, St. Paul, Minn., established.

First agricultural college in U. S. at Cleveland, O.   [Feb. 2.

1856   Nathaniel P. Banks elected Speaker of House,

Capture of Lawrence, Kan., by pro-slavery party, May 21.

Charles Sumner assaulted in U. S. Senate Chamber, May 22.

Civil war rages in Kansas.

First Republican National Convention, June 17; John C. Frémont nominated for pres.

Steamer *Pacific* lost, with 240 persons, Sept.

1857   *Harper's Weekly* begun, Jan. 13.

Dr. Kane, Arctic explorer, d. Feb. 16; b. 1820.

Dred Scott case in U. S. Sup. Court, Mar. 6.

First attempt to lay transatlantic cable, Aug. 5–11.

Steamer *Central America* founders; 400 persons drowned, Sept. 12.

Mountain Meadow massacre by Mormons, Sept. 18.

Great financial panic in U. S., Oct.   [Oct.

Pres. Buchanan removes Brigham Young.

Cooper Union founded by Peter Cooper.

Illinois State Univ. opened at Normal, Ill.

North German Lloyd steamship line estab.

1858   Thomas H. Benton d. April 10; born March 14, 1782.

Minnesota (32d State) admitted, May 11.

Wagner's sleepers introduced; 4 in operation.

1858 Donati's comet appears, June.

Theodore Roosevelt (" Rough Riders ") b.

Second treaty with China, June 18, 1st. 1844.

First message over Atlantic cable, Aug. 16.

Crystal Palace in New York burned, Oct. 5.

1859 Oregon (33d State) admitted, Feb. 14.

Great frost throughout U. S., June 4.

Blondin crosses Niagara River on a tight-rope, June 30.

Senator Broderick of Cal. killed by Judge Terry, Sept. 16.   [16–18.

John Brown captures Harper's Ferry, Oct.

Adelina Patti makes her début in New York, Nov. 22.

Rocky Mountain News, Denver, established.

Mary Anderson, actress, born.

Railway system reaches the Missouri River by completion of the Hannibal and St. Joseph railroad.   [cars.

Patent granted Geo. W. Pullman for sleeping-John Brown hanged at Charlestown, W. Va., Dec. 2.

1860 Pemberton Mills, Lawrence, Mass., burnt; great loss of life, Jan. 10.

Morrill High Tariff Bill approved, March 2.

Steamship *Great Eastern* ar. at N. Y., June 28.

Wm. Walker, filibuster, shot, Sept. 12.

Prince of Wales visits U. S., Sept.

Football revives among University men.

Worcester's Dictionary published.

1860 San Francisco connected with New York by
     telegraph.
     New York World established.   [N. Y.
     Clara Louise Kellogg makes her début in
     South Carolina passes ordinance of secession,
        Dec. 20.
     Ralph Farnham, last survivor of Bunker
        Hill, dies Dec. 27.
     U. S. forts seized by seceders, Dec.
1861 Secession of Mississippi, Jan. 9; Florida,
        Jan. 10; Alabama, Jan. 11; Georgia, Jan.
        19; Louisiana, Jan. 26; Texas, Feb. 1;
        Virginia, April 17; North Carolina, May
        21; Arkansas, May 6; Tennessee, June 8.
     Kansas (34th State) admitted, Jan. 29.
     Jefferson Davis inaug. pres. of Confederacy,
        Feb. 18.
     Abraham Lincoln inaug. president, March 4.
     Fort Sumter bomb. April 12; sur. April 14.
     Sanitary commission organ. at Bridgeport,
        Conn., and Charlestown, Mass., April 15.
     Pres. Lincoln calls for 75,000 troops, April 15.
     Sixth Mass. Reg. attacked in Baltimore,
        April 19.
     Fight at Big Bethel, Va., June 10.
     Sanitary Commission, U. S., estab., June 13.
     Appleton's Annual Cyclopædia first pub.
     Morning Oregonian, Portland, Or., estab.
     Battle of Bull Run, July 21.   [July 22.
     McClellan appointed commander-in-chief,

1861 Battle of Springfield, Mo., Gen. Lyon killed, Aug. 10.

Gen. Butler captures Fort Hatteras, Aug. 29.

Gen. Frémont frees slaves in Mo., Aug. 31.

Siege of Lexington, Mo., Sept. 11–20.

Battle of Ball's Bluff, Va., Oct. 21.

Battle of Belmont, Mo., Nov. 7.

Mason and Slidell taken from British vessel by Capt. Wilkes, Nov. 8.

1862 Ft. Henry capt. by Grant and Foote, Feb. 6.

Battle of Roanoke Island, Feb. 8.

Grant capt. Fort Donelson, Tenn., Feb. 16.

Battle of Pea Ridge, Ark., March 6–8.

Fight between *Merrimac* and *Monitor*, Mar. 9.

Battle of Pittsburg Landing (or Shiloh), April 6–7.

Slavery abol. in Dist. of Columbia, April 16.

New Orleans captured by Admiral Farragut and Gen. Butler, April 25–May 1.

Battle of Williamsburg, Va., May 5.

Department of Agriculture estab., May 15.

Battle of Hanover Court House, May 24.

Battle of Fair Oaks, Va., May 31–June 1.

Robert E. Lee in command of Confederate armies, June 3.

Seven Days' battles before Richmond begin, June 26–July 2.

Treaty with Great Britain for suppression of African slave-trade, June 7.

Slavery prohib. in the Territories, June 19.

1862 Congress passes act to prevent polygamy in Territories, July 1.

Call for 300,000 volunteers for 3 years, July 2; for 300,000 9-months' troops, Aug. 4.

Major-gen. Halleck com.-in-chief, July 11.

Gen. Pope commands Army of Va., July 14.

Battle of Cedar Mountain, Aug. 9.

Sioux Indians attack frontiers of Minnesota, Aug. 19.

Confederates invade Kentucky, Aug. 21.

Enlistment of negroes as soldiers authorized, Aug. 25.   [Aug. 30.

Battle of Manassas (or Second Bull Run),

Battle of Chantilly, Va., Sept. 1.   [Sept. 15.

"Stonewall Jackson" capt. Harper's Ferry,

Battle of South Mountain, Md., Sept. 15.

Battle of Antietam. Md., Sept. 16, 17.

Battle of Iuka, Miss., Sept. 19, 20.

Battle of Corinth, Miss., Oct. 3, 4.

Battle of Perryville, Ky., Oct. 8.

Rosecrans com. Army of the Ohio, Oct. 30.

Burnside com. Army of the Potomac, Nov. 5.

First Gen. Council of Protestant Episcopal Church of Confederate States assembles at Augusta, Ga., Nov. 19.

Battle of Fredericksburg, Dec. 13.

Banks com. Dep't of the Gulf, Dec. 16.

Monitor founders off Cape Hatteras, Dec. 30.

Battle of Murfreesborough (or Stone River), Dec. 31.

1862 Greenbacks first issued.

University of Washington at Seattle opened.

1863 Proclamation of emancipation issued, Jan. 1.

Galveston, Tex., captured by Confed., Jan. 1.

Gold at New York, 133⅞. [Jan. 25.

General Hooker com. Army of the Potomac,

National currency provided by Congress, Feb. 25.

National Academy of Science incor., Mar. 3.

Battle of Chancellorsville, Va., May 2-1.

Battle of Champion Hills, Miss., May 16.

Battle of Big Black River, Miss., May 17.

Siege of Vicksburg begins, May 18.

Siege of Port Hudson, La., begins, May 21.

Fifty-fourth Mass. Inf., first colored regiment in Free States, leaves Boston, May 28.

Phonograph patented by Fenby, June 13.

West Virginia (35th State) admitted, June 20. [June 24–July 7.

Rosecrans finishes Tullahoma campaign,

Gen. Geo. G. Meade com. Army of the Potomac, June 27.

Battle of Gettysburg, July 1–3.

Vicksburg surrenders to Grant, July 4.

Port Hudson surrenders to Banks, July 8.

Draft riots in New York City, July 13–16.

Attack on Fort Wagner, S.C., Col. Robert G. Shaw killed, July 18.

State Agricultural Coll. in Kansas founded, July 27.

1863 Writ of *habeas corpus* suspended, Sept. 15.

Battle of Chickamauga, Sept. 19–20.

Lincoln calls for 300,000 men for 3 years, Oct. 17.

Battle of Wauhatchie, Oct. 27.

Battle of Lookout Mountain, Nov. 24.

Battle of Chattanooga, Nov. 25.

Longstreet raises siege of Knoxville, Dec. 1–4.

Activity of iron-clad fleets under Admiral Davis and Col. Ellet on Western rivers.

1864 President calls for 500,000 men for 3 years, Feb. 1.

First Fed. prisoners received at Andersonville prison, Feb. 15.

National College for Deaf Mutes established at Washington.

Theodore Thomas begins his symphony concerts in New York.

Battle of Olustee, Florida, Feb. 20.

U. S. Grant commis. lieut.-general, Mar. 10.

Draft of 200,000 men for navy ordered. March 14. [Apr. 4.

New York Sanitary Commission Fair opens,

Battles of Sabine Cross Roads, etc., Apr. 8–9.

Slaughter of garrison at Fort Pillow, Tenn.. Apr. 12.

Grant's campaign in Virginia begins, May 4.

Battle of the Wilderness, Va., May 5–6.

Battle of Spottsylvania Court House, Va., May 10.

1864 Act for postal money-order system, May 17.

Battles near Dallas, Ga., May 25-28.

Battle of Cold Harbor, Va., June 1-3.

Currency Bureau of the Treasury established, June 3.

Philadelphia Sanitary Fair opens, June 7.

Fight between *Kearsarge* and *Alabama*, June 19.

Battle of Weldon Railroad, Va., June 21, 22.

Battle of Kenesaw Mountain, Ga., June 27.

Fugitive Slave Law of 1850 repealed, June 28.

Bonds and Treasury notes issued, June 30.

Coastwise slave-trade prohibited, July 2.

Battle of Monocacy, Md., July 9.

Highest premium on gold, 285 per cent, July 16.

Pres. calls for 500,000 volunteers, July 18.

Battles in Atlanta campaign, July 20-28.

Mine explosion at Petersburg, July 30.

Capture of Mobile by Farragut and Granger, Aug. 5-22.

Battle of Winchester, Va., Sept. 19.

Battle of Fisher's Hill, Va., Sept. 22.

Price invades Missouri, Sept. 28.

Confed. cruiser *Florida* captured by *Wachusett*, Oct. 7.

Battle of Cedar Creek, Va., Oct. 19.

Confederate ram *Albemarle* blown up, Oct. 27.

Battle of Hatcher's Run, Va., Oct. 27.

Nevada (36th State) admitted, Oct. 31.

1864   Sherman begins his march to the sea, Nov. 14.

Many incendiary fires in N.Y., Nov. 25.

Battle of Franklin, Tenn., Nov. 30.

Thomas defeats Hood at Nashville, Tenn., Dec. 15, 16.

Pres. calls for 300,000 volunteers, Dec. 19.

Grade of vice-admiral established, Dec. 21.

Gen. Grierson's great raid, Dec.–Jan.

1865   Fort Fisher captured, Jan. 15.

Sherman begins march from Savannah, Feb. 1.

Peace Conference at Hampton Roads, Feb. 2–3.

Second battle of Hatcher's Run, Va.. Feb. 5.

Freedmen's Bureau established, March 3.

Abraham Lincoln inaugurated, March 4.

Confederate Congress adjourns *sine die*, March 18.

Battle of Five Forks, Va., March 31–Apr. 1.

Richmond evacuated by Confederates, Apr. 2.

Lee surrenders to Grant at Appomattox, April 9.

"Stars and Stripes" raised over Fort Sumter, April 14.

President Lincoln shot by Wilkes Booth at Ford's Theatre, Washington, D.C., April 14; dies April 15.

Vice-president Johnson sworn in as president, April 15.   [15.

Military Order of Loyal Legion formed, Apr.

J. Wilkes Booth captured, April 26.

1865 Johnson surrendered to Sherman, April 26.

Confederate Gen. Taylor surrendered, May 4.

Jefferson Davis captured, May 10.

Last fight of the war, in Texas, May 13.

Grand review of the Union armies at Washington, D.C., May 22, 23.

President proclaims general amnesty, May 29.

Society for Prevention of Cruelty to Animals organized in N.Y. by Henry Bergh.

Chronicle, San Francisco, Cal., established.

Mass. Inst. of Technology at Boston opens.

Bessemer steel first manufactured in U. S.

Execution of conspirators implicated in the assassination of President Lincoln, July 7.

Severe earthquake in California, Oct. 8.

Capt. Wirz hung for cruelty to Union prisoners, Nov. 10.   [Dec. 1.

Habeas corpus restored in Northern States,

13th Amendment ratified by 27 States, Dec.

1866 Grand Army of the Republic formed at Decatur, Ill., April 6.

Civil Rights' Bill passed over veto, April 9.

Fenian raid into Canada, May 31–June 9.

Great fire in Portland, Me., July 4.

Atlantic telegraph completed, July 27.

Railroad begun up Mt. Washington, N.H.; completed, 1869.

Steamer *Evening Star* founders at sea, 250 lives lost, Oct. 3.

Peabody Institute, Baltimore, estab., Oct. 21.

1866 National Soldiers' Home located at Togus,
Me., Nov. 10.   [by Mrs. Eddy.
Doctrine of Christian Science promulgated
Republican, Denver, Col., established.
Slaughter-houses for cattle first erec. in U.S.

1867 Evangelical Alliance of U.S. org., Jan. 30.
Nebraska (37th State) admitted, March 1.
National Bankruptcy Bill passed, March 2.
Department of Education established, Mar. 2.
Peonage in New Mexico abolished, Mar. 2.
Jefferson Davis admitted to bail, May 13.
West Virginia University, at Morgantown,
opens, June 17.   [July 19.
Supplementary Reconstruction Act passed,
Johns Hopkins University incorp., Aug. 24.
Gen'l amnesty proclaimed by pres., Sept. 7.
Mass. Agricultural College, at Amherst,
opens, Oct.
Elias Howe d. Oct. 3; b. July 9, 1819.
Organization of Grangers in Western States.
Harper's Bazar (weekly) appears.
Fisk University, at Nashville, chartered.
Alaska transferred by Russia to U. S., Oct. 9.
Cincinnati and Covington suspension bridge
completed.
Charles Dickens arrives in Boston, Nov. 19.

1868 Impeachment, trial, and acquittal of Pres.
Johnson, Feb. 25–May 26.   [May 5.
Memorial Day (30th May) ins. by G. A. R.,
Constitution, Atlanta, Ga., established.

1868 *Courier-Journal*, Louisville, Ky., established.

Southern States re-admitted to representation in Congress, June 25.

"Burlingame treaty" with China signed, July 4.

XIVth Const. Amendment adopted, July 20.

Severest earthquake yet recorded in San Francisco, Oct. 21.

1869 U. S. Grant inaugurated president, March 4.

Union Pacific railroad op. for traffic, May 10.

Great Peace Jubilee (musical) at Boston, Mass., June 15.   [July 1.

Soldiers' Monument at Gettysburg dedicated,

Franco-American cable landed at Duxbury, July 27.

University of California opens, Sept. 23.

Financial panic in N. Y. ("Black Friday"), Sept. 24.

Boston University chartered; opens, 1871.

Knights of Labor formed, at Philadelphia.

News, Indianapolis, Ind., established.

Horace Mann School for Deaf op. at Boston.

State University of Minnesota opens.

Am. Woman's Suffrage Assoc. org., Nov. 24.

Woman suffrage adop. in Wyoming, Dec. 10.

1870 Steamer *City of Boston* leaves Boston, with 177 persons on board, Jan. 28; never heard from.

Weather Bureau established, Feb. 9.

North Pacific railroad begun, Feb. 15.

1870   Hiram R. Revels, first colored U. S. senator, Feb. 25.

XVth Amendment ratified, March 30.

Am. Anti-slavery Society dissolved, April 9.

Capitol at Richmond falls, many killed and wounded. April 27.

Fenian invasion of Canada, May 25–27.

Lenox Public Library (N.Y.) incor., June 20.

U. S. Department of Justice org., June 22.

U. S. Army reduced to peace footing, July 15.

Delaware State College at Newark organized.

J. H. Rainey, 1st col. member H. R., Dec. 12.

1871   Legal Tender Act dec. constitutional, Jan. 16.

Dist. of Columbia a territorial gov., Feb. 21.

Capt. Hall sails for arctic regions, June 29; rescued, 1873.

" Tweed Ring " frauds in N. Y. exp., July 22.

Railroad accident at Revere, Mass., many killed, Aug. 26.   [2.

Brigham Young arrested for polygamy, Oct.

Great fire in Chicago, Oct. 8.   [use.

Automatic self-binding harvesters come into

Amer. Institute of Mining Engineers org.

Grand Duke Alexis of Russia in New York, Nov. 21.   [Jan. 6; d. Jan. 8.

1872   James Fisk, Jr., shot by Edward S. Stokes,

Martin J. Spalding, primate of R. C. Church in America, d. Feb. 7; b. 1810.

Yellowstone Nat'l Park, Col., estab. Mar. 1.

Imp. Japanese Embassy at Wash., Mar. 1.

1872 Arbor Day originates in Nebraska, April 22.

First narrow-gauge railroad in the U. S., the Denver and Rio Grande, opened to Pueblo, 118 miles, June.

World's Peace Jubilee (musical) begins at Boston, June 17—July 4.

Geneva Tribunal awards U. S. $15,500,000 indemnity for damages by Confederate cruisers fitted out in England, Sept. 14.

Epizoötic disease of horses in N. Y., Oct. 23.

San Juan islands awarded to U. S., Oct. 23.

Inter-Ocean, Chicago, Ill., established.

Am. Public Health Association organized.

Globe, Boston, Mass., established.

Great fire in Boston, loss $80,000,000, Nov. 9–10.

Modoc war in California, Nov. 29.   [6.

1873 Crédit Mobilier investigation in Cong., Jan.

Silver "trade dollar" ordered demonetized, Feb. 7.

U. S. Grant inaugurated president, March 4.

Gen. Canby killed by Modocs, April 11.

Polaris' arctic crew rescued, April 30.

One-cent postal cards issued, May 1.

England pays *Alabama* award, Sept.

Panic in N. Y. Stock Exchange, Sept. 20.

Hoosac Tunnel (Mass.) completed, Nov. 27.

Reformed Episcopal Church founded.

Remington type-writers constructed.

Am. Cyclopædia by Ripley and Dana begun.

1874 Chang and Eng, Siamese twins, die Jan. 17;
born April 15, 1811.

Reservoir at Mill River valley, Mass., bursts,
200 lives lost. May 16. [June 20.

Territorial gov. of Dist. of Columbia, abol.,
St. Louis bridge over Miss. completed, July 4.

Great grasshopper plague in Western States,
July–Oct.

Memnonites settle in Kansas.

State University of Nebraska opens at Elko.

Lincoln monument at Springfield, Illinois,
dedicated, Oct. 15.

King Kalakaua of Sandwich Islands visits
Washington, Dec. 18.

1875 Specie payment resumed, Jan. 14.

Centenary of battle of Lexington celebrated,
April 19.

Whiskey frauds in Western States exposed,
May 1. [17.

Centenary of battle of Bunker Hill cel., June

Smith College (for women), at Northampton,
Mass., opens, Sept. [Nov. 4.

Steamship *Pacific* founders, 200 lives lost,

Wellesley College, Mass. (for women) opens.

1876 Emperor Dom Pedro of Brazil arrives in New
York, May 7.

Centennial Exposition in Phil. op., May 10.

Massacre of Custer's troops by Sitting Bull,
June 25. [July 4.

Centenary of Am. Independence celebrated,

1876 Centennial International Medical Congress at Philadelphia.

Silver " trade dollar " no longer a legal tender, July 22.

Library Association of U. S. organized.

Colorado (38th State) admitted, Aug. 1.

Congress appropriates $200,000 to complete Washington Monument, Aug. 2.

Statue of Lafayette unveiled in N. Y., Sept. 6.

" Hell Gate," New York, blown up, Sept. 24.

Twelve American whaling-ships lost in arctic ice, Oct. 12. [Dec. 5.

Brooklyn Theatre burned, 295 lives lost,

First body cremation in U. S., at Washington, D.C., Dec.

Railroad accident at Ashtabula, O.; many killed, Dec. 29. [Jan. 29.

1877 Presidential Electoral Com. Act approved.

Wrought-iron girder bridge over the Ohio at Cincinnati built.

Prof. A. Graham Bell exhibits his telephone at Salem, Mass., Feb. 12.

Kentucky River bridge completed, Feb. 20.

R. B. Hayes inaug. president, March 5.

" Molly Maguires " hanged in Pa., June 21.

Civil service order issued by Pres. Hayes, June 22. [July 16.

Great strike on Baltimore and Ohio Railroad.

Anti-Chinese riot in San Francisco.

War with the Nez Percés Indians, Sept. 30.

1877   New phonograph announced by Edison; improved, Nov., 1888.

Fisheries Commission awards $5,500,000 to be paid by U. S. to Gt. Britain, Nov. 23.

U. S. sloop-of-war *Huron* wrecked off coast of N. Car.. about 100 lives lost, Nov. 24.

1878   Bland silver bill passed over veto, Feb. 28.

William M. Tweed ("Tweed Ring") dies in jail, April 12.

Trial trip on elevated railroad N. Y. City, April 29.

Electric lighting introduced by T. A. Edison and others.

Yellow fever in Southern States, July.

First resident embassy of China to the United States, Sept. 28.

Railroad accident at Wollaston, Mass., many lives lost, Oct. 8.

Gold at par in Wall Street, N. Y., Dec. 17.

1879   U. S. gov. resumes specie payment, Jan. 1.

Women permitted to practise before U. S. courts, Feb. 15.

Salvation Army corps established in Phil.

Bill to restrict Chinese immigration vetoed, March 1.   [March 3.

National Board of Health author. by Cong.,

Archæological Institute of Amer. organized at Boston, May 17.

Jeannette sails for arctic regions, July 8.

J. B. Hood, Confed. gen., d. Aug. 30; b. 1831.

1879 Henry C. Carey, political economist, dies Oct. 13; b. Dec. 15, 1793.   [Mass., Nov. 15.

French Atlantic cable landed at N. Eastham,

1880 Denis Kearney, "sand-lots" agitator, imprisoned, March 15.

U. S. steamer *Constellation* carries food to sufferers in Ireland, March 30.

Dr. Tanner fasts for 40 days, June 8–Aug. 7.

Egyptian obelisk "Cleopatra's Needle" arrives in New York, July 20.

Presidential election, Nov. 2: James A. Garfield, Republican; Winfield S. Hancock, Democrat; James B. Weaver, Greenback; Neal Dow, Prohibition. Garfield elected.

Amer. Society of Mechanical Engineers org.

Broadway, New York, lighted by electricity, Dec. 20.

1881 Clan-na-Gael, Irish secret society, formed.

Intn'l Sanitary Congress at Wash., Jan. 5.

Christian Endeavor Society formed by F. E. Clark, Feb. 2.

President vetoes "Funding Act," March 3.

James A. Garfield inaug. president, Mar. 4.

Am. Association of Red Cross org., June 9.

Arctic steamer *Jeannette* crushed in ice, June 12.

Pres. Garfield shot by C. J. Guiteau, July 2.

Lieut. A. W. Greely sails for polar reg., July 7.

President Garfield dies, Sept. 19.

Vice-pres. Arthur sworn as pres., Sept. 20.

1881 International Cotton Exposition at Atlanta,
Ga., Oct. 5. [b. 1832.

Dr. I. I. Hayes, arctic explorer, d. Dec. 17;

1882 Bodies of arctic explorers, De Long and
eleven of his men, found, March, 23.

Jesse James killed by the Ford Bros., Apr. 3.

Elephant Jumbo arrives in New York from
England, April 9. [28.

Survivors of *Jeannette* arrive in N. Y., May

Star-Route trial begins, June 1.

Guiteau hanged at Washington, June 30.

1883 Lot M. Morrill d. Jan. 10 ; b. May 3, 1813.

Great flood in Ohio River, Feb. 15. [24.

N. York and Brooklyn bridge opened, May

Remains of John Howard Payne brought to
America, June 9.

Great strike of telegraph operators, July 19,

Northern Pacific railroad completed, Sept. 9.

Corean ambassadors arrive in N. Y., Sept. 18.

University of Texas, at Austin, opens.

First electric street railway in U. S., at Balt.

Florida University, Lake City, incorporated.

Dr. J. Marion Sims dies Nov. 13 ; b. 1813.

Standard railroad time in U. S., adopted,
Nov. 18.

1884 Steamer *City of Columbus* wrecked off Gay
Head, Mass., Jan. 18 ; many lives lost.

Unparalleled series of tornadoes over Western and Southern States, Feb. 9.

Great floods in the Ohio valley, Feb. 14.

1884   Financial crisis in New York City, May 14.
Lieut. A. W. Greely and six others rescued,
      June 22.
National Bureau of Labor estab., June 27.
Bureau of Navigation created, July 5.
Paul Morphy, famous chess-player, d. July
      10, aged 47.
North Dakota University opens.   [Pa.
Natural gas as fuel introduced in Pittsburg,
Amer. Institute of Electrical Engineers org.
Marble first quarried at Rutland, Vt.
Tulane University of Louisiana chartered.
Presidential election : Cleveland and Hen-
      dricks, Dem. ; Blaine and Logan, Repub. ;
      Butler and West, Greenback ; St. John
      and Daniel, Prohib.   Cleveland and Hen-
      dricks elected.   [Dec. 16.
Industrial Cotton Centennial at New Orleans,
1885   Dedication of Washington Monu., Feb. 21.
Emigrant alien labor bill passed, Feb. 26.
Stephen Grover Cleveland inaugurated pres.,
      March 4.   [May 15.
Revised version of Old Testament published,
Apache Indian war in New Mexico, May 17.
Niagara Falls reservation made a New York
      State Park, July 15 ; Queen Victoria Nia-
      gara Falls Park on Canadian side opened,
      May 24, 1888.
Dakota University at Mitchell opens, Sept.
Massacre of Chinese in Wyoming, Sept. 2.

1885 Yacht *Puritan* wins America's cup, Sept. 14.

Nebraska Central College opens.

World's Industrial and Cotton Exposition at
New Orleans. [1811.

William Page, artist, d. Oct. 1 : b. Jan. 23,

John McClosky, first American cardinal,
dies Oct. 10 ; born March 10, 1810.

Gen. Newton blows up Flood Rock, Hell
Gate, Oct. 10.

H. W. Shaw ("Josh Billings") dies Oct. 14 ;
born April 21, 1818. [1837.

John McCulloch, actor, d. Nov. 8 ; b. Nov. 2,

American Exposition opened at New Orleans, Nov. 10.

Elizur Wright, abol., d. Nov. 22 ; b. 1804.

Farmers' Cong. org. at Indianapolis, Dec. 3.

W. H. Vanderbilt d. Dec. 8 ; b. May 8, 1821.

Robert Toombs d. Dec. 15 ; b. July 2, 1810.

1886 "King's Daughters" organized in New York,
Jan. 18.

Act providing for presidential succession,
Jan. 19. [Feb. 7–9.

Anti-Chinese riots in Washington Territory,

Horatio Seymour d. Feb. 12 ; b. May 31, 1810.

Great Knights of Labor strike on railroads
begins, March 6 ; ends, May 4.

Anarchist riot in Chicago, May 4.

Street-car strike in New York, June 5.

Judge David Davis d. June 26 ; b. Mar. 9,
1815.

1886 Incorporation of nat'l trades unions legalized, June 29.

Congress authorizes 1, 2, and 5 dollar silver certificates, Aug. 4. [20.

Chicago anarchists convicted of murder, Aug.

Great earthquake at Charleston, S.C., Aug. 31.

Yacht *Mayflower* wins America's cup, Sept. 7.

Disastrous gale in Gulf of Mexico, 250 lives lost, Oct. 12. [28.

Bartholdi's statue of Liberty unveiled, Oct.

American Federation of Labor formed at Columbus, O., Dec. [completed.

1887 Kentucky and Indiana bridge over the Ohio

John Roach, shipbuilder, d. Jan. 10; b. 1813.

Remnant of Table Rock at Niagara falls, Jan. 12. [Feb. 23.

Importation of opium from China prohibited,

Agricultural experiment stations established, March 2.

Tenure of Office Act repealed, March 3.

Jno. B. Eads, eng., d. Mar. 8; b. May 23, 1820.

Railroad accident at Roslindale, Mass., many killed, March 14.

Improved process reduces aluminum from $1 per ounce to $7 per pound.

Ex-vice-pres. Wm. A. Wheeler d. June 4; b. June 30, 1819.

Gold first discovered at Silver Bay, Alaska.

Jennie Collins, working-girls' friend, d. July 20, aged 59.

1887 University of Wyoming opens, September.

Yacht *Volunteer* wins America's cup, Sept. 27.

Women vote for school officers in Kansas.

Chicago anarchists hanged, Nov. 11.

1888 Asa Gray, bot., dies Jan. 30; b. Nov. 18, 1810.

D. R. Locke ("Petroleum V. Nasby") d. Feb. 15; b. Sept. 20, 1833.

Great "blizzard" in Eastern States, many lives lost, March 11–14.

Chief-justice M. R. Waite d. Mar. 23; b. Nov. 29, 1816.

Lick observatory transferred to University of California, June 1.

Linotype type-casting machine perfected.

National Dep't of Labor estab., June 13.

Centennial exhibition at Cincinnati, July 4.

Gen. J. M. Schofield, com. of army, Aug. 14.

Chinese immigration prohibited, Sept. 13.

Presidential election: Cleveland and Thurman, Dem.; Harrison and Morton, Repub.; Fiske, Prohibition; Streeter, Union Labor; Cowdry, United Labor; Curtis, American. Harrison and Morton elected.

Highway bridge over Harlem River built at New York.

Poughkeepsie bridge over the Hudson opens.

1889 Department of Agriculture created, Feb. 9.

United States steamships *Trenton* and *Vandalia* wrecked at Samoa, March 16.

Oklahoma opened for settlement, April 22.

1889 Bursting of reservoir causes great flood in Johnstown, Penn., May 31; about 8,000 lives lost.

Pan-American Congress meets in Washington, D.C., Oct. 2.

North and South Dakota (39th and 40th States) admitted, Nov. 2.

Maritime exhibition at Boston, Nov. 4.

Montana (41st State) admitted, Nov. 8.

Washington (42d State) admitted, Nov. 11.

Great fire in Lynn, Mass., Nov. 26. [Dec. 2.

Thos. B. Reed elected Speaker of H. of R.,

The "grip" appears in U. S., Dec. 21.

1890 W. D. Kelley, oldest member of U. S. House of Representatives in term of service (since 1860) and in years, dies Jan. 9; born April 12, 1814. [Jan. 23.

Woman's Christian Temperance League org.

Part of Great Sioux reservation opened for settlement, Feb. 10.

Chicago selected for World's Columbian Exposition, Feb. 24. [April 2.

Australian ballot system introduced in R. I.,

Pension Bill for disabled Union soldiers and sailors passed, June 27.

Idaho (43d State) admitted, July 3.

Wyoming (44th State) admitted, July 10.

Act authorizing purchase of silver, July 14.

First execution by electricity at Auburn prison (New York), Aug. 6.

1890 People's Party convenes at Topeka, Kan.,
Aug. 13.

National Military Park established at Chickamauga, Aug. 19.   [1822.

Dion Boucicault, dramatist, d. Sept. 18; b.

McKinley Tariff Bill approved, Oct. 1.

Polygamy abolished by Mormons in Utah,
Oct. 6.   [Oct.

"Ghost dance" excitement of Sioux Indians,

B. P. Shillaber ("Mrs. Partington") dies
Nov. 25; born 1814.

Sitting Bull, Indian chief, killed, Dec. 15.

Gen. F. E. Spinner, U. S. ex-treasurer 1861–
75, dies Dec. 31; born Jan. 21, 1802.

Cincinnati iron truss railway bridge across
the Ohio completed.

1891 International Monetary Conference at Washington, Jan. 7.

Free coinage bill adopted, Jan. 14.

Sec. of Treas. Windom d. Jan. 29; b. 1827.

Strike of 10,000 miners in coke regions,
Penn., Feb. 9.

Appropriation by Congress for artificial
rain-making, March 3.

Registry of certain foreign-built vessels
granted, March 3.

International copyright act approved, Mar. 3.

Massacre of Italians in the parish prison,
New Orleans, March 14.

Montana University opens at Helena.

1891 Century Dictionary published.

Eben Tourgée, founder N. E. Conservatory of Music, dies April 12; b. June 1, 1834.

Transmississippi Commercial Congress at Denver, May 19.   [1892.

Lieut. Peary's arctic expedition, June–Sept..

B. J. Lossing. hist., d. June 3; b. Feb. 12,1813.

Agreement with Great Britain in regard to seal fisheries, June 15.   [June 23.

Rain-making experiments begin in Texas.

Weather Bureau transferred to Department of Agriculture, June 30.   [July 25.

Smokeless powder used for first time in U.S.,

Removal of restrictions on importation of American pork in Germany. Sept. 3; in Denmark, Sept. 8; in Italy, Oct. 21; in France, Dec. 6.   [ment. Sept. 18.

Indian lands in Oklahoma opened to settle-

Leland Stanford University opens, Oct.

Am. sailors mobbed in Valparaiso, Oct. 16.

James Parton dies Oct. 17; b. Feb. 9, 1822.

Southern States exposition opens at Augusta, Ga., Nov. 2.

First World's Convention of the Woman's Christian Temp. Union at Boston, Nov. 10.

1892 First Continental Congress of Daughters of American Revolution, Feb. 22.

Behring-sea dispute referred to arbitration. Feb. 29; treaty ratified, May 9. [April 2.

Treaty for suppressing slave-trade signed,

1892 Indian lands in Dakota, Oklahoma, etc., opened to settlement, April 11.   [May 5.
Bill prohibiting coming of Chinese approved,
Wm. Bradford, painter, d. Apr. 25; b. 1827.
400th anniversary of dis. of Am., June 29.
Great strike of miners at Cœur d'Alene, Id.,
    July 11.
Survivors of Indian wars pensioned, July 27.
Army nurses of civil war pensioned, Aug. 5.
Great railroad strike at Buffalo, N.Y., begins,
    Aug. 14.
Continental Congress of Salvation Army in
    New York, Nov. 21.

1893 Proclamation of amnesty to Mormons, Jan. 4.
Great Northern railroad completed, Jan. 6.
L. Q. C. Lamar, ex-Confederate, dies Jan. 23;
    born Sept. 1, 1825.   [Feb. 22.
Inman steamers transferred to Am. registry,
Stephen Grover Cleveland inaug. pres., Mar. 4.
Temple at Salt Lake City dedicated, April
    6; 40 years building.
Spanish caravels arrive in N. Y., April 24.
John M. Corse, gen., dies April 27; born
    April 27, 1835.   [April 27.
Columbian naval review in N. Y. Harbor,
Columbian exposition formally opened at
    Chicago, May 1.   [June 5.
Extradition treaty with Russia promulgated,
Floor of Ford's Theatre in Washington falls;
    many clerks killed and injured, June 9.

1893 Many failures among banks, July–Sept.

Severe hurricane in Southern States, Aug. 28.

Pan-American Medical Congress opens at Washington. D.C., over 1,000 physicians present, Sept. 5.   [Sept. 11.

World's Parliament of Religions at Chicago,

A daughter born to Lieut. and Mrs. Peary in the arctic regions, Sept. 12.

Great storm on Gulf of Mexico, 2,000 lives lost, Oct. 2.

Yacht *Vigilant* wins America's cup, Oct. 13.

World's Colum. Exposition closes, Oct. 30.

Wilson Silver Bill approved, Nov. 1.

Chinese Exclusion Bill approved, Nov. 3.

1894 Nicaragua Canal Co. incorporated in Vt.

Fire destroys buildings in World's Fair grounds, Chicago, Jan. 8.

Wilson Tariff Bill passes Congress.

Growth of the American Protective Association (A. P. A.), organized in Iowa, 1887.

Reciprocity treaties abrogated.

Electrical measurement established.

Dr. C. H. Parkhurst active in reform work in New York.   [dor Reef, Feb. 2.

U. S. corvette *Kearsarge* wrecked on Ronca-

George W. Childs, publisher, dies Feb. 3; born May 12, 1829.

Federal Election Laws repealed, Feb. 8.

Rioting in South Carolina resulting from Dispensary Law, March.

1894 John Y. McKane sent to Sing Sing for election frauds, March 1.

William F. Poole. librarian, dies March 1; born Dec. 24, 1821.

Coxey's "army" starts for Wash., March 25.

President Cleveland vetoes the Bland Silver Bill, March 29.

H. W. Slocum, general, dies April 14; born Sept. 24, 1827.

Monument to the mother of Washington unveiled, May 10.

William D. Whitney, philologist, dies June 7; born Feb. 9, 1827.

Pullman Car Co. boycotted, June 26.

Labor Day made a legal holiday, June 28.

Great railroad strike from Ohio to the Pacific coast begins, June 29; ends, Aug. 5.

Interstate Irrigation Congress meets at Omaha, Neb.   [1808.

A. Pleasanton, gen., d. July 26; b. Aug. 18,

Charter of the Louisiana State Lottery expires; not renewed.

Joseph Holt, dies Aug. 1; born Jan. 1807.

F. H. Underwood, projector of *Atlantic Monthly*. dies Aug. 7; born Jan. 12, 1825.

Republic of Hawaii recognized, Aug. 8.

Wilson-Gorman Tariff Bill becomes a law, Aug. 31.

Josiah P. Cooke, chemist, dies Sept. 3; born Oct. 12, 1827.

1894   George Stoneman, general, dies Sept. 5; born
Aug. 8, 1822.

James McCosh, ex-president Princeton College, dies Nov. 16; born April 1, 1811.

New treaty with Japan, Nov. 23.

Eugene V. Debs, labor leader, imprisoned,
Dec. 14.

Philological Cong. at Philadelphia, Dec. 27.

National Military Park est. at Shiloh, Dec. 28.

1895   Frederick Douglass, colored orator, dies Feb.
20, aged 78.

Largest refracting telescope in the world
made by Alvan G. Clark at Cam., Mass.

John J. Almy, admiral, dies May 16; born
April 25, 1814.

Important gold discoveries in Utah.

W. Q. Gresham, d. May 28; b. Mar. 17, 1832.

Monument to Confederate soldiers dedicated
in Chicago, May 30.

Atchison, Topeka, and Santa Fé railroad
sold at auction for $60,000,000.

E. W. Bull, originator Concord grape, dies
Sept. 26; born March 4, 1806.

First Eucharistic Congress (Catholic) in
America, in Washington, Oct. 1.

Gettysburg National Military Park estab.

Wesley Merritt, com. major-gen., born 1836.

Miss Helen Culver gives $1,000,000 to the
biological department of University of
Chicago, Dec. 14.

1895 Allen G. Thurman, statesman of Ohio, dies; born Nov. 13, 1813.

A lockout of 4,000 tailors begins in New York, Dec. 16. [question, Dec. 17.

Special message of president on Venezuelan

Great strike of motormen and conductors on Phil. trolley cars, Dec. 17 ; settled, Dec. 23.

Rev. Dr. Josiah Tyler, 40 years missionary among the Zulus, dies Dec. 20.

John De Haven White, "Father of American dentistry," dies Dec. 25, aged 80.

Numerous strikes of labor organizations during the year.

1896 President Cleveland appoints Venezuelan commissioners, Jan. 1.

Utah (45th State) admitted, Jan. 4.

Cardinal's beretta bestowed on Mgr. Satolli, Jan. 5.

Francis C. Barlow dies Jan. 11; born Oct. 19, 1834. [1829.

Thomas Ewing, gen., d. Jan. 21 ; b. Aug. 7,

Meeting of Free Silver advocates in Washington, Jan. 22.

Mint directors ordered to prepare to coin standard silver dollars, Jan. 24.

William H. Furness, div., d. Jan. 30, a. 94.

Protestant Episcopal bishops protest against Turkish atrocities, Jan. 31.

The name of Columbia College changed to Columbia University.

1896 John Gibbons, general, dies Feb. 6, aged 69.

Prize-fighting prohibited in the Territories, Feb. 7. [Feb. 8.

Sealing-treaty with Great Britain ratified, George M. Bache, com., dies Feb. 11, a. 56.

System of free lodgings in New York police stations abolished, Feb. 15.

Edgar W. Nye ("Bill Nye") dies Feb. 22; born Aug. 25, 1850.

General Garcia and other Cuban leaders arrested in New York, Feb. 25.

Dense fog in New York causes serious disasters to shipping, Feb. 29.

Charles C. Coffin ("Carleton") dies March 2; born July 26, 1823.

Ground broken for American University in Washington, D.C., March 9.

Fire destroys records in Census Office, Washington, D.C., March 22.

Mississippi exempts factories from taxation for 10 years, March 23. [ates, Mar.

All disabilities removed from ex-Confeder-Augustus Hoppin, art., dies April 2, aged 68.

The Raines law (liquor) rigorously enforced in New York City and Brooklyn, April 5.

Double-turreted *Monitor* launched, April 15.

"Greater New York" bill signed, May 11.

Lucius Fairchild d. May 23; b. Dec. 27, 1831.

College of New Jersey changed to Princeton University, May 27.

1896   Benj. H. Bristow, d. June 22; born June 20,
       1832.   [1813.

      Lyman Trumbull, d. June 25; born Oct. 12,

      Sectarian Indian schools to be abolished
      after July 1. 1897.

      William J. Bryan nominated Democratic
      candidate for president, July 10.

      William E. Russell, ex-governor of Mass.,
      dies July 15; born Jan. 6, 1857.

      President Cleveland issues a warning to
      Cuban sympathizers, July 30.

      Intense heat in N.Y., many deaths, Aug. 8–14.

      Mary Abigail Dodge (" Gail Hamilton ")
      dies Aug. 17; born 1833.

      " Flag Day " observed in many cities, Oct. 31.

      Great Britain yields to the demand of the
      U. S. for arbitration in Venezuelan boun-
      dary dispute, Nov.   [ver, Nov. 24.

      W. J. Bryan begins a campaign for free sil-

      Retaliatory tonnage tax imposed on German
      vessels ordered, Dec. 5.

      Daughters of American Revolution incorp.

      Treaty with Choctaws of Indian Territory,
      Dec. 19.

1897   Francis A. Walker, pres. Mass. Institute of
      Technology, d. Jan. 5; b. July 2, 1840.

      General arbitration treaty with Great Britain
      signed, Jan. 11.

      Treaties with Orange Free State and Argen-
      tine Republic ratified, Jan. 28.

1897 Alaska boundary line settled, Jan. 30.

Treaty with Japan ratified, Feb. 1. [2.

State Capitol of Penn. destroyed by fire, Feb.

Darius N. Couch d. Feb. 12 ; b. July 23, 1822.

John C. Robinson, gen., d. Feb. 18 ; b. April 10, 1817.

Wm. McKinley inaug. president, March 4.

A great storm along the Atlantic coast, March 7.

Wm. T. Adams ("Oliver Optic") d. March 27 ; b. July 30, 1822. [4, 1827.

John H. Russell, admiral, d. April 1 ; b. July

Tomb of Gen. Grant dedicated at Riverside, April 27. [1.

Tennessee Centennial Exposition opens, May

Anglo-American arbitration treaty rejected by Senate, May 5.

Governor Black signs charter of Greater New York, May 5. [May 5.

Universal Postal Congress meets at Wash.,

Horatio King d. May 20 ; b. June 21, 1811.

Congress votes $50,000 to aid suffering Cubans, May 20. [May 26.

Bradford's Pilgrim Journal pres. to Mass.,

Shaw monument unveiled in Boston, May 30.

Snow falls in many States, June 1.

Alvan G. Clark d. June 9 ; b. July 10, 1832.

Treaty for annexation of Hawaii signed by president, June 16. [June 16.

Intense heat in Chicago, many prostrations,

1897 Severe earthquake shocks in Cal., June 20.

Extensive strikes among coal and iron miners, June—July; ends, Sept. 13.

Christian Endeavor Society in session at San Francisco, July 7.

Klondike miners arrive in California with gold, July 15.

Monument to General Logan dedicated in Chicago, July 22.

Dingley Tariff Bill goes into effect, July 24.

Submarine torpedo-boat *Plunger* launched, Aug. 7.   [Aug. 20.

Cash wheat passes the dollar mark in N. Y.,

Yellow fever appears in Southern States, Sept.

Many lives lost in Texas hurricanes, Sept. 14.

Henry George nominated for mayor of New York, Sept. 27.

John L. Worden, adm., d. Oct. 18, aged 79.

Geo. M. Pullman d. Oct. 19, aged 66.

Justin Winsor, librarian of Harvard, d. Oct. 22; b. Jan. 2, 1831.

T. L. Clingman d. Nov. 3 ; b. July 27, 1812.

Sealing treaty with Russia and Japan signed, Nov. 6.

Dr. Geo. H. Houghton, rector of "Little Church round the Corner,"d. Nov. 17, a. 77.

Joseph F. Green, admiral, dies Dec. 9 ; born Nov. 24, 1811.

Appropriation of $175,000 for relief in Klondike region, Dec. 16.

1898 City gov. of Greater New York inaug., Jan. 1.

North Atlantic squadron assembles near Tortugas, Jan. 1–12.

Maine sails for Havana, Jan. 24.

Pres. Dole of Hawaii arr. in Wash., Jan. 26.

Silver defeated in H. R., Jan. 31.

Heavy fall of snow in Boston, Feb. 1.

Dupuy De Lome, Spanish minister at Wash., resigns, Feb. 8; Luis Bernabe succeeds, Feb. 14.

Spanish cruiser *Viscaya* visits N. Y., Feb. 18.

Secretary Long calls for more ships, Feb. 26.

Reindeer for Alaska arrive in N. Y., Feb. 27.

Wm. A. Rogers, astronomer, d. March 1 ; b. Nov. 13, 1832. [11.

War dep't begins mobilization of army, Mar.

Battleship *Oregon* sails from San Francisco, March 12.

Seacoast defences manned, March 12. [14.

Government decides to arm ocean liners, Mar.

Battleships *Kearsarge* and *Kentucky* launched, March 24.

Com. Sampson succeeds Sicard, March 24.

Com. Schley com. flying squadron, Mar. 24.

House of Representatives defeats Cuban recognition, April 18.

Geo. P. Lathrop d. April 19 ; b. Aug. 25, 1851.

Congress orders intervention in Cuba by force, April 19.

Pres. signs intervention resolution, Apr. 20.

1898 President sends ultimatum to Spain, Apr. 20.

Bernabe, Spanish minister, asks for passports, April 20.

Spanish gov't sends Minister Woodford his passports at Madrid, April 21.

Sampson's fleet sails for Cuba, April 22.

President issues a call for 125,000 volunteers, April 23. [23.

Massachusetts naval reserve ordered out, Apr.

Cong. declares the existence of war, Apr. 25.

John Sherman resigns from cabinet, Apr. 25.

Day becomes secretary of state, April 26.

Com. George Dewey sails from Hong Kong for Manila, Apr. 27. [28.

New England coast patrolled by a fleet, Apr.

Dewey wins naval victory at Manila, May 1.

Fitzhugh Lee and Joseph Wheeler made major-generals, May 4.

May wheat $1.91 in New York, May 10.

Dewey made acting rear-admiral, May 11.

Flying squadron leaves Hampton Roads, May 13.

Battleship *Alabama* launched, May 18. [25.

Pres. calls for 75,000 more volunteers, May

Oregon arrives at Key West, May 26.

U. S. flag raised over the Ladrones, June 21.

Hawaii annexed to the U. S., July 7. [1819.

Daniel Ammen, adm., d. July 11 : b. July 7.

Spain asks for terms of peace, July 26.

Peace protocol signed at Wash.. Aug. 12.

1898 Pres. McKinley orders cessation of fighting,
Aug. 12.   [Aug. 12.
Sampson and Schley made rear-admirals,
Rear-admiral Kirkland d. Aug. 12; b. 1828.
Manila surrenders, Aug. 13.   [20.
Imposing naval parade in N. Y. harbor, Aug.
American peace commis. named, Aug. 26.
Boston subway opened entire length, Sept. 3.
16,000 Odd Fellows par. in Boston, Sept. 21.
Thomas F. Bayard dies Sept. 28; born Oct.
29, 1828.
Peace commissioners meet at Paris, Oct. 1.
Battleship *Illinois* launched, Oct. 4.
Rear-admiral Febiger dies, Oct. 9.
Yellow fever in Mississippi, Oct. 10.
Serious labor riots in Illinois, Oct. 12.
Chicago peace jubilee begins, Oct. 17.
White Pass and Yukon railway in operation,
Oct.   [Oct.
Outbreak of Pillager Indians at Leech Lake,
South Dakota adopts "initiative and refer-
endum" plan, Nov.   [Nov.
Maria Teresa, capt. Spanish cruiser, wrecked,
David A. Wells d. Nov. 5; b. June 17, 1828.
Theodore Roosevelt elected governor of New
York, Nov. 8.
Ultimatum to Spaniards at Paris, Nov. 21.
Battleship *Wisconsin* launched, Nov. 26.
Great storm on Atl. coast, vessels wrecked
worth $2,500,000, Nov. 27.

1898   Steamship *Portland* lost, with all on board, Nov. 27.

Spain acc. terms of peace, at Paris, Nov. 28.

Peace treaty signed at Paris, Dec. 10.

[For events of war in Cuba, etc., see *Spanish America*.]

Cuban Junta in U. S. dissolves, Dec. 21.

Justin S. Morrill d. Dec. 28 ; b. Apr. 14, 1810.

Southern Union Station, Boston, Mass., dedicated, Dec. 30.

Anglo-American commission closes its hearings in Behring-sea case, Dec.

1899   Formal cession of Spanish sovereignty in Cuba to United States, Jan. 1.

Canadian-American commission in session.

Nelson Dingley, Congressman, d. Jan. 13, a. 67.

Disastrous storm on Atlantic coast.

John R. Young, librarian of Congress, dies Jan. 15, aged 57.   [Washington.

Canadian-Am. comm. resumes its sessions in

George Dewey made admiral. March 3.

Joseph Medill, editor Chicago *Tribune*, dies Mar. 16 ; born in New Brunswick, 1823.

Hotel Windsor, New York, burned; many lives lost, March 17.

MEXICO.

1503   Montezuma emperor.

1521   Cortez captures city of Mexico.

1522   Mexico constituted a kingdom.

1535 Mendoza, first viceroy of New Spain, establishes a mint.

1821 Mexico becomes independent, Aug. 23.

1822 Mexico becomes an empire, Iturbide emperor.

1823 Federal Republic proclaimed, Oct. 4.

1829 Expulsion of the Spaniards decreed, March.

1833 Santa Aña president, May 11.

1835 Texas declares her independence, March 2.

1836 Independence recognized by Spain.

1838 Declaration of war against France, Nov. 30; war terminates, March 9, 1839.

1846 Gen. Mejia issues a proclamation of hostility to the United States, March.

Battle of Palo Alta, May 8.

Battle of Resaca de la Palma, May 9.

Gen. Taylor occupies Matamoras, May 18.

Mex. Cong. dec. war against U. S., May 23.

Monterey surr. to Gen. Taylor, Sept. 25.

1847 Sequestration of church property to raise funds, Jan. 7.

Battle of Buena Vista, Feb. 22, 23.

Siege and bomb. of Vera Cruz, Mar. 22–26.

Vera Cruz surrenders to Gen. Scott, Mar. 29.

Battle of Cerro Gordo, Gen. Scott defeats Santa Aña, April 18.

Com. Perry captures Tuspan, May 18.

Battle of Contreras, Aug. 19–20.

Scott def. Santa Aña at Churubusco, Aug. 20.

El Molino del Rey capt. by Amer., Sept. 8.

Chapultepec taken by storm, Sept. 13.

1847 Gen. Quitman military governor of city of
Mexico. Oct.   [May 24.

1848 Treaty of peace ratified by Mexican Senate,
U. S. flag on palace at Mexico replaced by
Mexican, June 12.

1856 Property of clergy sequestrated, March 31.

1857 New constitution established, Feb. 5.
Beginning of Reformed Church.   [11.

1858 Constitution annulled by church party, Jan.
Benito Juarez president, Feb. 11.
Civil war, Aug.–Nov.

1859 Miramon nominated pres. by Junta, Jan. 6.
Juarez confiscates church property. July 13.

1860 Civil war between Zuloaga and Miramon.

1861 Juarez made dictator.
Troubles with England. France, and Spain.

1862 Mexican monarchy for Maximilian disap-
proved by England and Spain. Feb.

1863 Mexico occupied by French under Bazaine,
June 5.

1864 Maximilian accepts crown from Mexican
deputation, April 10.

1865 Emperor Maximilian proclaims war ended,
Oct. 2.   [Oct. 16.
Juarist generals taken prisoners and shot,
U. S. protest against French occupation.

1866 Napoleon III. agrees to withdraw his troops,
April.

1867 Maximilian. Miramon, and Mejia tried and
shot, June 19.

1867 City of Mexico taken, and republic re-established, June 21.

Juarez inaugurated president about Dec. 25.

1871 Civil war and insurrections.

1872 Benito Juarez d. July 18, aged about 68.

1874 Religious orders suppressed, Dec.

1876 Santa Aña, ex-president, d. June 20.

1880 Gonzalez elected president, July 11.

1883 Ancient city discovered in Sonora.

1884 Porfirio Diaz inaugurated president, Dec. 1.

1892 Diaz re-elected president, July 11.

1893 Destructive storm in Gulf of Mexico, about 1,000 lives lost, Oct. 2.

1896 Porfirio Diaz inaug. pres. for 5th time, Dec. 1.

Law enacted to provide a uniform system of education, Dec. 19.

1897 Attempt to assassinate Pres. Diaz, Sept. 16.

CENTRAL AMERICA.

COSTA RICA.

1502 Discovered by Columbus.

1523 Bruselas founded by Hernandez.

1530 Indian tribes subdued by Alvarado.

1539 Badajos founded.

1568 Rivera founded on the west coast.

1605 Talamanca founded.

1610 Santiago burned by Indians.   [ish.

1611 The Talamanca Indians massacre the Span-

1630 Alvarado subdues the Indians.

1665 Great depredations by pirates.

1709 Indian slaves in the gold-mines rise, and massacre Spaniards.

1797 A period of prosperity begins.

1812 The Spanish constitution promulgated.

1821 Declaration of independence. Sept. 15.

1822 Union with Mexico proclaimed.

1823 The imperialists revolt, April.

Joins the federation of Central American States, July 1.

1824 First congress meets, Sept. 8; Juan Mora president.

1840 Becomes an independent state.

1856 Wm. Walker, American filibuster, attempts revolution.   [president, 1877.

1876 Revolution. Gen. Thomas Guardia becomes

1882   Constitution adopted, April 26.   [15.

1890   Declares against a Cent. Amer. confed., Feb.
      Rodriguez president.

1891   A revolution breaks out, suppressed by gov't;
      breaks out again; suppressed in 1893.

1894   Another revolution breaks out.
      Rafael Inglesias becomes president.

1897   Inglesias re-elected, for term of four years,
      1898–1902.

1898   "Greater Republic" of Central America
      breaks up, Dec. 1.

GUATEMALA.

[From its conquest by the Spaniards until the struggle for Independence in 1821, the history of Guatemala is similar to that of the other Central American States, — a succession of conflicts with the natives, and of struggles between rival officials, — and presents no especial events of general interest.]

1773   Santiago destroyed by an earthquake, June 7.

1774   Old Guatemala destroyed by the Volcan de
      Agua.

1821   Independence declared.

1823   Withdraws from the Mexican Confederation.

1824   Joins Confed. of Central American States.
      Slavery abolished.

1829   Subjugated by San Salvador.

1851   Regains its independence under Carrera.

1854   Invaded by American filibusters under Ken-
      ny and Walker.

1854 Carrera appointed president for life.

1863 War with San Salvador.

1865 Carrera dies, and is succeeded by Gen. Cerna.
Cerna deposed by Granados.

1871 The Jesuits exiled for political intrigues.

1872 Alliance with Honduras against San Salvador.
Property of the Jesuits confiscated.

1873 Alliance with San Salvador.
Barrios elected president.

1876 War with Honduras and San Salvador.

1884 Work begun on the Interoceanic railroad.

1886 Torture prohibited as punishment.

1889 Cholera rages; over 1,000 deaths.

1890 War with San Salvador.
Guatemala joins Union of Central Am. States.

1893 Brit. legation attacked by rioters, Jan. 23.

1894 Pres. Lainfiesa proclaims himself dictator.

1897 Prospero Morales incites a revolution; subdued, October.

1898 President Barrios assassinated, Feb. 8.

HONDURAS.

1502 Discovered by Columbus.

1526 Cortez founds Truxillo and Puerto Caballos.

1540 Comayagua founded by Carceres.

1821 Honduras declares its independence of Spain.

1822 Becomes part of the Central Amer. Confed.

1839 Withdraws from Cent. Amer. Confederation.

[Civil wars follow for nearly twenty years.]

1855 President Cabaños defeated and exiled.

1856 Pres. Guardiola makes peace with Guatemala.

1860 Wm. Walker, Am. filibuster, invades Honduras; is captured, and executed at Truxillo,
Sept. 12.

1861 Insurrection instigated by the clergy.

1862 Guardiola assassinated.

1863 Montes president. [ernment.
Medina deserts Montes, and usurps the gov-

1872 Don Celeo Arias deposes Medina, and takes
the presidency.

1875 Marco Aurelio Soto ap. provisional governor.
A new constitution adopted.

1876 Soto appointed president for four years.

1883 Louis Bogran president, Nov. 27.

1890 Insurrection, headed by Gen. Sanchez.

1891 Gen. Pariano Leista elected pres., Nov. 10.
Bonilla proclaimed president, Dec. 12.

1892 Civil war begins in May and continues.

1893 Insurrection in South Honduras.
Gen. Vasquez elected president, Sept. 20.
Policarpo Bonilla elected president, Dec. 24,
for four years.

1894 War with Nicaragua.
Bonilla, leader of insurgents, assumes the
presidency, Jan. 5.
President Vasquez repulses the insurgents.

BRITISH HONDURAS.

[The Bay of Honduras was a favorite resort for the English
buccaneers during the English and Spanish wars. After the
decline of freebooting, the more industrious of the buccaneers
turned to the pursuit of cutting mahogany, dyewoods, etc.,
which brought on conflicts with the Spaniards.]

1725 Spaniards attempt to expel English wood-
cutters; fail.

1754 Wood-cutters defeat Spaniards.

1763 Treaty between England and Spain relating
to wood-cutters.   [defined.

1783 Limits of Belize and rights of wood-cutters

1796 Spain attempts to expel men of Belize, but
fails.

1840 Alexander McDonald, superintendent, sets
aside local laws, and proclaims supremacy
of English law.   .

1845 Eng. gov't assumes control of the territory.

1850 Belize excluded from conditions of British-
American treaty.

NICARAGUA.

1502 Discovered by Columbus.

1521 Gil Gonzalez Davila explores the country.

1524 Granada founded by Cordova.

1550 Unsuccessful revolt against Spain.

1610 Leon founded.

1685 Dampier, English buccaneer, sacks Leon.

1821 Independence declared.

1823 Joins Confederation of Central Amer. States.

1826 First survey for ship-canal route.

1847 Boundary trouble with Great Britain.
Great Britain seizes San Juan del Norte, Dec.

1850 Independence recognized by Spain.
Clayton-Bulwer treaty arranged at Greytown.

1856 Walker, American filibuster, burns Granada;
he is driven from Central America, 1857.
President Rivas claims the Mosquito Coast.

1859 T. Martinez elected president.

1860 England cedes the protectorate of the Mosquito Coast to Nicaragua.

1885 The United States government procures surveys of a ship-canal route.
Concessions for 100 years granted to the Nicaragua Canal Company.   [fields.

1894 Gen. Cabeza hoists Nicaraguan flag at Blue-Mosquito country organized under laws of Nicaragua.

1897 Death penalty abolished, May 9.
Important concessions to syndicate of American capitalists.

SAN SALVADOR.

1524 Conquered by Alvarado.

1821 Independence of Spain proclaimed.

1824 Joins the Central American Union.

1839 Becomes independent.

1853 A constitution adopted.

1854 Great earthquake in San Salvador, April 16.

1856 Becomes a republic, Castillo president.

1860 Gen. Barrios president, Feb. 1; overthrown, Oct., 1863.

1865 General Duenas president, April.

Barrios executed, Aug.

1872 Gonzalez president, Feb. 1.

1876 Zaldivar president, May.

1885 Francisco Menendez president, June.

1887 Revolution. Menendez deposed, June.

1890 Gen. Carlos Ezeta president, Sept. 11.

War with Guatemala; peace ratified, Sept. 22.

1894 Gen. Gutierrez president, June 5.

Revolution; Ezeta defeated; provisional government formed, June 26.

BERMUDA.

[Discovered at the beginning of the 16th century by Juan Bermudas.]

1609 Sir George Somers lands in Bermuda.

1612 Virginia Company sell the islands to members of their body.

Richard Moore, a ship's carpenter, the first governor.

1620 The first representative assembly meets.

1725 Bishop Berkeley attempts to found a college in Bermuda; unsuccessful.

1775 Ships gunpowder to assist Americans.
1784 Ships fitted out to follow the whale-fishery.
1824 Convicts sent to construct dockyards.
1834 Slavery abolished.

[No important events have transpired in recent years.]

WEST INDIES.

1492 Columbus discovers Hayti.
1623 St. Kitt's receives its first English settlers.
1624 English settle in Barbados. [Cruz.
1625 Eng. and Dutch take joint possession of Santa
 First regular French colony in West Indies,
 at St. Kitt's.
1628 Nevis and Barbuda settled by the English.
1630 Hayti seized by French buccaneers.
1632 St. Eustatius and Tobago set. by the Dutch.
 Antigua and Montserrat settled by English.
 Three hundred French settlers in Dominica.
1635 Guadaloupe and Martinique col. by French.
1638 English take possession of St. Lucia, driven
 out by Caribs, 1641.
1640 Tortuga a buccaneers' station.
1648 French set. St. Bartholomew and St. Martin.
1650 French colonization spreads to St. Lucia.
1650 French settlement established at Santa Cruz.
 Barbados adheres to the Royalists of Eng.
1652 Barbados submits to the Commonwealth.
1655 Jamaica taken by Cromwell's forces.
1660 Dutch introduce slaves into Barbados.

1670 British possession of Jamaica secured.

1671 The Danes occupy St. Thomas.

1692 Great earthquake in Jamaica; Port Royal destroyed.   [hamas.

1718 Capt. Rogers puts down piracy in the Ba-

1719 Danish colonists occupy St. John.

1733 Danes buy Santa Cruz from the French.

1738 Settlem't of the Maroon troubles in Jamaica.

1755 Kingston made the seat of gov't of Jamaica.

1760 Slave insurrection in Jamaica.

1763 Great Britain secures St. Vincent.

1784 St. Bartholomew transferred to Sweden.

1791 Negroes of Hayti revolt against France.

1795 The last Maroon war in Jamaica occurs.

1801 Toussaint l'Ouverture founds republic in St. Domingo, May 9.   [France, 1803.

1802 Toussaint surrenders to the French; dies in

1803 French quit Hayti.

1804 Dessalines proclaims massacre of all whites in Hayti, March 29.

1831 Great hurricanes in the West Indies.

1838 Slavery abolished in the British West Indies.

1844 The "Dominican republic" proclaimed in Hayti, Feb.   [April 18.

1852 Hayti proclaimed an empire under Solouque,

1858 Republic proclaimed in Hayti, Dec. 22.

1861 Reunion of St. Domingo with Spain.

1865 Insurrection in Jamaica, sup. by Gov. Eyre.

1873 Turk's Island annexed to Jamaica.

[See *Spanish America*, etc.]

SOUTH AMERICA.

ARGENTINE REPUBLIC.

1516 Juan Dias de Solis lands on north coast.

1527 Sebastian Cabot establishes a settlement named San Espiritu.

1535 Buenos Ayres founded, Feb. 2.

1573 City of Santa Fé founded.

1620 Buenos Ayres separated from Asuncion.

1776 Buenos Ayres becomes the capital of a vice-royalty. [June 27.

1806 Gen. Beresford (Brit.) capt. Buenos Ayres,

1807 Sir Samuel Auchmuty takes Montevideo.

1809 Argentines refuse to acknowledge Napoleonic dynasty in Spain.

1810 Political independence of the country begins.

1814 Montevideo captured by the revolutionary army of Buenos Ayres. [clared.

1816 Separation of the country from Spain de-

1817 Spaniards defeated at Chacabuco; at Maypu in 1818.

1824 War of independence ended.

1825 A national constitution decreed for the federated States. [the country.

Great Britain acknowledges independence of

Rivadavia elected president.

Political parties take names of Unitarians and Federals.

1826 Vicente Lopez, Federalist, president.

1827 Dorrego, Federalist, president.

1828 Unitarians rebel, and defeat the Federalists.

1829 Rosas, chief of the Federal party, rules.

1838 Buenos Ayres blockaded by a French fleet.

1840 Lavalle, Unitarian, invades province of Buenos Ayres, but is defeated by Federalists under Pacheco.

1845 England and France intervene in the civil war, and blockade Buenos Ayres.

1847 Blockade of Buenos Ayres raised.

1852 Brazilians invade Buenos Ayres and defeat Rosas.   [director.
A new constitution proclaimed, with Urquiza

1853 Civil war rages ; province of Buenos Ayres becomes an independent state, with Obligado governor.
Parana becomes capital of the 13 provinces.

1859 Buenos Ayres rejoins the confederation.

1865 Paraguayans invade Argentine territories.

1867 A rebellion breaks out in the northwest.

1868 Rebellion suppressed, Nov.

1870 Urquiza murdered.

1873 Treaty with Brazil.

1874 Insurrection of Mitre at Buenos Ayres, Sept.; suppressed, Dec. 2.

1880 Gen. Roca becomes president, Oct.
Buenos Ayres to be definitive capital.

1890 Insurrections and severe street-fighting.
Great financial crisis.

1891 Riots at Cordova, Feb.

Banks suspend payment.

Bank of the Argentine Nation opened, Dec. 1.

1892 Jewish settlements prospering, Jan.

Dr. Luiz Saens-Peña elected president, June.

Insurrections in different provinces.

1893 Continued insurrections and revolutions.

1894 General financial embarrassment.

Destructive earthquake in San Juan, Oct. 27.

1895 Pres. Saens-Peña resigns, Jan. 22.

Sen. Uriburu becomes president, Jan. 23.

1898 Gen. D. Julio A. Roca inaug. pres. Oct. 12.

Concession to Herr Schiflner for construction of a complete network of railways.

BOLIVIA.

1825 Upper Peru becomes an independent state, and takes the name of Bolivia, Aug. 11.

1826 First Congress meets, May 25; Gen. Sucre governs.

1828 Santa Cruz rules until 1839.

1836 Slavery abolished.

1839 Velasco president.

1841 José Ballivian president.

1848 General Belzu president until 1855.

1853 Free trade proclaimed.

1855 General Cordova president.

1859 José Maria Linares, dictator, March 31.

1860 Cordova constitutional president.

1861 Linares deposed, and Dr. José M. de Acha chosen president, May.

1862 Treaty of peace and commerce with U. S.

1864 Melgarejo defeats troops of De Acha, Dec. 28.

1865 Melgarejo becomes dictator of republic, Feb. Belzu revolts; is defeated by Melgarejo, Mar.

1866 Melgarejo defeats Arguedas at Viacha, and proclaims an amnesty, Jan. 24.

1869 Melgarejo becomes dictator until 1871.

1871 Morales president; said to have been murdered, 1873.

1874 Dr. Tomas Frias president. Corral's insurrection suppressed, Sept.

1876 Gen. Hilarion Daza president.

1879 Bolivia joins Peru in war against Chile, Apr.

1880 Daza deposed; Campero becomes president.

1883 Peace with Chile; conditions finally settled, Dec.

1888 Aniceto Arce, president, suppresses a revolt.

1892 Mariano Baptista declared president, Aug. 8.

1898 Civil war in progress against Pres. Alonzo.

BRAZIL.

1499 Brazil discovered by Vincent Yañes Pinçon.

1500 Cabral erects an altar on Easter Day (April) at Port Seguro, and claims the country for Portugal.

1504 Brazil explored by Amerigo Vespucci.

1531 De Souza founds first colony at S. Vincente.
1548 Jews banished from Portugal to Brazil.
1555 French Protestants occupy Bay of Rio.
1580 Brazil becomes subject to Spain.
1594 The French establish a colony at Maranham.
1615 The French expelled.
1630 The Dutch seize the coast.
1661 Dutch give up Brazil.
1693 Gold-mining begins.
1710 The French capture Rio Janeiro.
1758 Jesuits expelled.   [neiro.
1763 Capital transferred from Bahia to Rio Ja-
1808 Royal family of Portugal arrive, March 7.
1815 Brazil becomes a kingdom.
1821 Dom Pedro regent.
1822 Brazil declares its independence, Sept. 7.
     Pedro I. crowned emperor, Dec. 1.   [29.
1825 Independence recognized by Portugal, Aug.
1831 Revolution; abdication of Dom Pedro, Apr. 7.
1840 Pedro II. declared of age, July 23.
1850 Steamship line to Europe commenced.
1852 Suppression of the slave-trade.
1861 Difficulties with British government on ac-
     count of plundering a wrecked British
     ship, June.
1863 Dispute settled by arbitration of king of the
     Belgians in favor of Brazil, June 18.
1864 Confederate steamer *Florida* seized by U. S.
     Wachusett while under protection of Brazil.
     Sec. Seward apologizes, Dec. 26.

1865 War with Uruguay.

Amicable relations with England restored.

Treaty betw. Brazil, Uruguay, and the Argentine Republic against Paraguay, May 1.

1866 War continues with indecisive results for four years.

1870 Paraguay subdued; treaty of peace, June 20.

1874 German emigrants called ·· Muckers " attempt to convert their neighbors by force. July 21–26.   [Sept.

1885 Bill for gradual abolition of slavery passed,

1888 Slavery totally abolished; 700,000 slaves freed.

1889 Revolution at Rio Janeiro; republic proclaimed, and the emperor forcibly conveyed to the Alagoas.

Decree banishing the emperor and his family, Dec. 20.   [28.

Sudden death of the empress at Oporto, Dec.

1890 The republic recognized by the United States, Jan. 29; by Great Britain about Oct. 20.

First Congress of the republic meets, Nov. 15.

1891 About 25,000 Polish emigrants said to arrive, Jan.   [Feb. 5.

Reciprocal treaty of commerce with the U. S., Deodoro da Fonseca elected pres., Feb. 25.

Fonseca assumes the dictatorship, Nov. 4.

Insurrection breaks out in Rio Grande, Nov. 10.

1891   Ex-emp. Dom Pedro II. dies at Paris, Dec. 5.
1892   Revolutions and insurrections continue.
        Solimoes, armor-clad, founders, May 21.
        Deodoro da Fonseca dies Aug. 23.
1893   Naval revolt led by Adm. de Mello, Sept. 7.
        Rio bombarded, many killed, Sept. 11–25.
        Nictheroy bombarded, Oct. 27 *et seq.*
        Renewed bombardment of Rio, Dec. 28.
        Adm. da Gama joins the insurgents, Nov. 7.
1894   Shots fired between Da Gama and American
            Admiral Benham, Jan. 29; Benham's con-
            duct approved by U. S. gov.
        Prudente de Moraes elec. president, Mar. 1.
        Unconditional sur. of Da Gama, Mar. 13.
        De Mello's squadron sur. to Argentine Re-
            public, April 16.   [suppressed.
1895   Renewal of war in Rio Grande, Feb. 28;
        Da Gama killed at Santa Aña, June 24.
1896   Revolt of " Fanatics."
1898   Campos Salles elected president, March 2.

CHILE.

1433   Peruvian Inca Yupanqui conquers Chile.
1533   Rule of Peruvian Incas cease.
1535   Spanish invasion, led by Diego Almagro,
            repulsed.
1541   Valdivia enters Chile, and founds Santiago.
1563   The Araucanians (Chileans) defeat Valdivia
            about this time.

[War continues between the Araucanians and Spaniards for 180 years.]

1722 Treaty between Chileans and Spaniards; boundary established.

1810 Mateo de Toro the last Spanish governor.
Chileans depose the Spanish governor, and assert their independence, July.

1813 Reconquered by Spain.   [buco.

1817 The Chileans defeat the Spaniards at Chaca-Independence of Chile secured.

1826 Peace with Spain.

1833 Present constitution formed, May 22.

1864 Trouble with Bolivia over "Guano Islands," March 1.

1865 Religious toleration enacted.
Chile declares war against Spain, Sept. 29.

1866 Spaniards bombard Valparaiso.

1879 War with Peru and Bolivia.
Naval battle; Chileans defeated. May 21, 23.
Peruvian and Bolivian army defeated about Nov. 27.

1880 War continues with varying results.

1881 Treaty of peace with Spain confirmed, Sept.
Domingo Santa Maria becomes president, Sept. 18.

1882 Treaty of peace with Bolivia, Jan. 25.
Peace protocol between Chile and Peru, Mar.
War resumed; Peruvians defeated, July.

1883 Peruvians def. with great loss, July 10, 19.
Treaty of peace with Peru signed, Oct. 20.

1886 Señor don José Manuel Balmaceda president, Sept. 18.

1891 Congress deposes the pres. for treason, Jan. 1.
Civil war with varying results.
Itata surrenders to American cruisers, June 4.
Battle of Placilla, Balmaceda totally defeated, Aug. 28.
The Great Powers recognize the Congressists, Sept. 16.
Balmaceda commits suicide, Sept. 19.
Egan, U. S. minister, charged with breach of neutrality, Oct.   [16.
Mob at Valparaiso assaults U. S. sailors, Oct.
Señhor Jorge Montt elected pres., Nov. 4.

1892 Rioters punished for assaulting U. S. sailors, Jan.   [U. S., Aug.
Egan concludes convention bet. Chile and

1894 Arbitration com. awards U. S. $240,564 damages for assault against sailors of *Baltimore*.

1895 Congress House at Santiago burned, May 18.
Gold standard adopted, June 3.

1896 Treaty of amity with Bolivia, May.
Señor Errazuriz elected president, June.
Deneira heads a rebellion ; is def., June 1.
Chile reasserts ownership of Juan Fernandez, Sept.

COLOMBIA.

1499 Visited by Alonso de Ojeda.
1502 Columbus touches at Veragua.
1508 Territory granted to Ojeda and Nicuessa.
         A presidency erect., and called New Grenada.
1718 Raised to the rank of a viceroyalty.
1811 Insurrection against the home government.
1819 Union of N. Grenada and Veneza., Dec. 17.
1821 The Royalists defeated, June 24.
1824 Bolivar named dictator, Feb. 10.
1825 Independence recognized, June.
1826 Bolivar president, Aug. ; dictator, Nov. 23.
1828 Padilla's insurrection, April 9.   [25.
         Conspir. of Santander against Bolivar, Sept.
1829 Venezuela separates from New Grenada, Nov.
1830 Bolivar resigns, April 4 ; dies Dec. 17.
1871 The republic named Colombia.
1872 Manuel Murillo Toro president, April 1.
1874 Santiago Perez president, April 1.
1876 Aquileo Parra president, April 1.
1878 Trujillo president, proclaimed, April 1.
1880 R. Nuñez president, Apr. 1 ; again in Sept.,
         1883, and Aug. 7, 1886.
1885 Insurrection and civil war, Jan. ; ends, July.
1894 President Nuñez dies Sept. 18.   [restored.
1895 Civil war breaks out ; crushed, and peace
         Construction on Panama Canal in progress.
1896 President Caro resigns, March 6.
         General Quinto Calderon president.

ECUADOR.

280 Foreign tribes said to have founded a kingdom at Quito which lasted 1,200 years.

1460 Tupac Yupanqui, Inca of Peru, invades Quito, which is subsequently conquered by his son Huaina-Capac.

1533 Conquered by Pizarro.
Made a presidency of Peru.

1710 Attached to viceroyalty of Santa Fé.

1722 Restored to Peru.

1809 Attempts to throw off the Spanish yoke fail.

1822 Independence secured.

1828 Invaded by Peru; peace restored, 1829.

1830 Separates from the Colombian Confederation.
Gen. José Flores first president.

1835 Vicente Rocafuerte president.

1839 Flores pres.; again in 1843; suc. by Roca, who joins with England against slave-trade.

1850 Diego Noboa president, recalls the Jesuits.

1856 Francisco Robles president, secures adoption of French system of coinage, weights, and measures.

1859 Robles abdicates, and leaves the country.

1861 Dr. Gabriel Garcia Moreno elected president.

1865 Moreno retires from office.
Geronimo Carrion president; Spanish subjects banished.

1868 Xavier Espinosa president.
Great earthquake, many towns destroyed.

1869   Revolution, Moreno elected pres. for 6 years.
1875   Moreno assassinated in Quito, Aug. 14.
1876   Dr. Borrero president, Sept.
        Insurrection breaks out, Dec., under Veinte-
            milla, who becomes president.
1877   Eruption of volcano Cotopaxi, June 25.
1883   Alfaro dictator, Jan.   [12.
1884   José Maria Placido Caamano president, Feb.
1886   Revolution at Esmeraldas, Nov. 4.
1888   Antonio Flores president, June 30.
1892   Luis Cordero president, June 30.
1895   Epidemic of yellow fever at Guayaquil, Feb.
        Alfaro organizes a government, June 10,
            and proclaims a general amnesty.
1896   Conspiracy against Alfaro; crushed, Aug. 12.
        Jesuits expelled from the country, Nov.
1898   Pres. Alfaro assumes dictatorship, Dec. 1.

GUIANA.

BRITISH GUIANA.

1504   Vasco Nuñez lands on the coast.
1580   Dutch said to have settled near River Po-
            meroon.   [Dorado.
1595   Raleigh ascends the Orinoro in search of El
1613   A colony of Zealanders on the banks of the
            Essequibo.
1652   The English return to Paramaribo.
1662   The colony granted to Lord Willoughby.

1669 Dutch Guiana covers all the territory now divided into British, Dutch, and French.

1712 French attack the settlement, and exact a contribution. [General.

1732 Berbice receives a constitution from States-

1763 Formidable insurrection of negro slaves.

1781 English admiral Rodney takes possession.

1783 The colonies restored to Holland.

1796 Surrendered again to the British.

1802 The Dutch resume authority.

1803 British Guiana finally acquired.

DUTCH GUIANA.

1580 Dutch visit the coasts. [Dutch citizens.

1614 The States-General grant monopolies to

1674 The country confirmed to the Dutch by the treaty of Westminster.

1675 Sommelsdijk governor of the colony; assas. in a mutiny of soldiers, June 17, 1688.

Troubles with the bush negroes and slaves continue for many years. [plete.

1786 Pacification with the negroes and tribes com-

1804 The English take possession of the colony.

1807 The slave-trade abolished.

1815 Dutch authority restored.

1828 Surinam joined to Dutch West Indies.

1832 Incendiary negroes publicly burned alive.

1845 Surinam separated from West Indies.

Baron von Raders governor.

[The suppression of slavery and the organization of immigration are the main events of the recent history of the colony.]

FRENCH GUIANA.

1626 Traders from Rouen settle on the Sinnamary.

1634 Settlers take up their quarters at Cayenne.

1674 Colony passes under direct control of the crown.

1763 Choiseul, prime minister, sends out 12,000 volunteer colonists from Alsace and Lorraine ; but 918 are alive in 1766.

1800 Victor Hugues appointed governor.   [ish.

1809 Successful invasion of Portuguese and Brit-

1814 Territory nominally restored to France, really surrendered by the Portuguese, 1817.

1823 Attempt to settle French agriculturists; frustrated by fevers.

[The principal events of recent years have been the discovery of gold-fields and the introduction of convict establishments.]

PARAGUAY.

1528 Sebastian Cabot builds a fort called Santo Espiritu.

1537 Asuncion founded, Aug. 15.

1542 First Christian missions established.

1620 Paraguay separated from Buenos Ayres.

1776 Placed under jurisdiction of Buenos Ayres.

1811 Declares itself independent of Spain.

1814 A despotism in the hands of Dr. Francia.

1840 Vibal succeeds.

[From 1814 to 1844 the country was rigidly closed against foreigners.]

1844 C. A. Lopez president.

1862 Francis S. Lopez president.

1864 Hostilities between Paraguay and Brazil.

1865 Lopez invades Argentine Republic; def. Sept.

1869 Provisional government installed, Aug. 17.

1870 Lopez killed near the Aquidaban, Mar. 1.
Peace signed with Brazil and Argentine
Republic. [Dec. 12.

1871 Salvador Jovellanos elect. pres. for 3 years,

1874 Juan Bautista Gill president, Nov. 25.

1877 The president assassinated, April.
Higinio Uriarte president, April 12.

1878 Candido Bareiro elec. pres. for 4 yrs., Nov. 25.

1882 Gen. B. Caballero president.

1890 J. Gonzales president.

1891 Revolutionary attempt by Vera sup., Oct. 24.

1893 Establishment of a Socialistic settlement by
emigrants from Australia to be named
"New Australia," July.

1894 *Coup d'état*, Marinigo pres., June 11.
Señor Egusguiza elected president, Sept. 26.

PATAGONIA.

1520 Discovered by Magellan.

1577 Drake passes through the strait of Magellan.

1669 Taken possession of by Sir John Narborough.

1832 Visited by Charles Darwin, the great scientist.

1873 Explored by Moreno; 1877 by Rogers;
1878–80 by Lista; 1880 by Moyano.

1881   Eastern Patagonia comes under the jurisdiction of the Argentine Republic; Chile retains the western portion.

[See *Argentine Republic*.]

PERU.

1527   The great Inca, Huayna Ccapac, dies.
       Pizarro reaches the coast at Tumbez; returns, 1528.   [15.
1532   Pizarro and his army enter Caxamarca, Nov.
1533   Re-enforced by Amalgro.
       The Inca Atahualpa murdered.   [24.
1534   Manco, son of Huayna Ccapac, crowned, Mar.
1535   The city of Lima founded, Jan. 18.
1536   The Peruvians besiege the Span. in Cuzco.
       Amalgro raises the siege.
1538   Fight between Amalgro and Pizarro; Amalgro defeated and executed.
1541   Pizarro assassinated at Lima, June 26.
1542   Vaca de Castro governor.
       De Castro defeats Amalgro the Lad, who is beheaded at Cuzco, Sept.
       Blasco Nuñez de Vela the first viceroy. [28.
1544   Gonzalo Pizarro rebels, and enters Lima, Oct.
1546   Battle of Anaquito, the viceroy kill'd, Jan. 18.
1547   Pedro de la Gasca defeats Pizarro near Cuzco, and executes him on the field, April 8.
1551   Don Antonio de Mendoza 2d viceroy.

1554 Insurrection of Giron, who is defeated and executed, Dec. 7.

1555 Andres H. de Mendoza 3d viceroy, July 6.

[The cultivation of wheat, vines, and olives, and European domestic animals introduced, good priests provided, and schools established, during Mendoza's administration.]

1561 Conde de Nieva viceroy ; 1564-69, Lope Garcia de Castro governor.

1569 Don Francisco de Toledo governor, Nov. 26.

1571 Tupac Amaru, the last of the Incas, behead.

1581 Between this date and 1776, 59 heretics burned at Lima, principally Europeans.

1780 Insur. of Peruvians under Tupac Amaru.

1814 Mateo Garcia Pumacagua, a Peruvian chief, raises the cry of independence, is defeated and executed, March 12, 1815.

1821 San Martin proclaims ind. of Peru, July 28.

1824 War against Spain.
Bolivar made dictator, Feb.
Mariano Prado president, Nov. 28.
Independence secured, Dec. 9.

1829 War with Colombia, treaty of peace, Feb. 28.

1845 Ramon Castilla president.

1860 New Constitution adopted.

1864 Spanish admiral Pinzon takes Chincha isles (guano), April 14.
American congress at Lima, Nov.

1865 Chincha islands restored, Feb. 3.

1866 Joins Chile in war against Spain.
Spanish quit Peruvian waters, May 10.

1868 Severe earthquakes, Aug. 13–15.

1872 Military insurrection ; Gutierrez, minister of war, imprisons President Balta ; is himself killed, and hanged to a lamp-post, July 26.

Manuel Pardo elected president, Aug. 2.

1873 Armed riots in Lima, May.

1874 British ship *Talisman* seized and condemned as a prize, Nov., for supplying rebels.

1876 Mariano I. Pardo president, Aug. 2.

1877 Nicolas de Pierolas sails away with iron-clad *Huascar*, May 29 ; is forced by Brit. warships to sur. at Lima ; Peruvians resent Brit. interf. and threaten reprisals, June.

Pierolas and his adherents amnestied, Aug.

1878 Ex-president Pardo assas. at Lima, Nov. 16.

1879 War declared against Chile, April 2. [See *Chile.*]

Revolution at Lima, Pierolas dictator, Dec. 22 *et seq.*

1881 Lima occupied by the Chileans, Jan. 17.

Anarchy in Lima, March.

1882 Pierolas quits Peru, April 10.

1883 Lima evacuated by the Chileans, Oct. 23.

[Constant civil wars for twelve years.]

1892 Great fire at Callao, Aug. 21.

1894 General Caceres president, Aug. 10.

1895 Revolution ended by compromise, Candamo president, March 19.

Gen. Nicola Pierola elected pres., July 10.

Caceres inaugurated president, Sept. 8.

1896   A revolt breaks out under Col. Seminarios, May.

Gold mines of great value discovered.

A serious Indian uprising in Nov.; crushed.

1897   Coinage of silver suspended, April 9.

Negotiations for reciprocity with United States are begun, Dec. 2.

Civil marriage-law promulgated, Dec. 24.

URUGUAY.

1512   Visited by Juan Diaz de Solis.

1516   Solis slain by Charruas in Colonia.

1603   Natives destroy a veteran force of Spaniards.

1729   Spaniards estab. themselves in Montevideo.

1814   Montevideo taken by Gen. Alvear (Buenos Ayres).

1828   Becomes a free and independent state.

1830   Republic formally constituted.

1856   G. A. Pereyra president.

1860   B. P. Berro president.

[Revolutions and insurrections for the next thirty years.]

1894   Don Juan Idiarte Borda president.

1897   President Borda assassinated, Aug. 25.

VENEZUELA

1498   First main land in Amer. seen by Columbus.

1550   The territory becomes a Spanish captain-generalcy.

1811 Proclaims its independence; war ensues for ten years.

1845 Independence recognized by Spain; civil wars follow. [Sept.

1876 Renunciation of papal authority announced,

1886 Gen. A. Guzman Blanco elected pres. Sept. 14.

1888 Disputes with Great Britain begin, Feb.

[Civil wars rage for many years.]

1894 Gen. Crespo assumes office, March 14. [7.

1895 French and Belgian consuls dismissed, Mar.

Revolutionary plots against President Crespo, July–March. 1896.

Expatriated citizens return, April.

1896 Venezuela adopts the gold standard.

1897 Boundary treaty with Great Britain ratified, April 5.

Ignacio Andrade elected president, Sept.

1898 Hernandez' insurrection subdued, May 19.

EUROPE.

AUSTRIA.

[Anciently Noricum and part of Pannonia, inhabited by the
Taurisci (or Norici), a Celtic race, who were conquered by the
Romans 14 B.C. In the 5th and 6th centuries it was overrun
by various Teutonic and Asiatic tribes, and finally became a
margraviate under Leopold I., whose dynasty ruled the country 263 years.]

1246 Frederick II. killed in battle, June 15.

1308 Albert I. assassinated by his nephew, May 1.

1315 Austrians defeated by Swiss at Morgarten,
Nov. 16.

1363 Tyrol acquired by Austria.

1437 Albert V. elected emp. of Germany. [Jan. 6.

1453 Frederick III. creates Archduchy of Austria,

1477 Low Countries accrue to Austria.

1496 Philip I. acquires Aragon and Castile.

1526 Bohemia and Hungary united to Austria.

1529 Austria har. by Turkish invasions until 1515.

1556 Charles V. reigns over Austria.   [1583.

1634 Wallenstein assassinated, Feb. 25; b. Sept.

1683 John Sobieski raises siege of Vienna, Sept. 12.

1701 War of the Spanish Succession until 1714.

1732 Joseph Haydn b. Mar. 31; d. May 31, 1809.

1740 Charles VI., last sovereign of the male line
of House of Hapsburg, dies Oct. 20.
Maria Theresa empress of Austria.

1748 Peace of Aix-la-Chapelle.

1756 Seven Years' War until 1763

1792 War with France until 1797.

1797 Franz Schubert born ; dies 1828.

1804 Francis I., emperor of Austria, Aug. 11.

1809 Vienna captured by the French, May 13.

1815 Treaty of Vienna, Feb. 25.

1835 Ferdinand I. emperor, March 2.

1848 Insurrection at Vienna, March 13.

Revolution in Hungary, Sept. 11.

Francis Joseph emperor, Dec. 2.

1854 Austrians enter Danubian principalities, Aug.

Alliance with England and France, Dec. 2.

1859 War with France and Sardinia, April.

Austrians defeated at Montebello, May 20 ;
at Magenta, June 4; at Melegnano, June
8 ; at Solferino, June 24 ; treaty of peace,
Nov. 10.

Prince Metternich dies June 11, aged 86.

1860 Jewish disabilities removed, Jan., Feb.

1861 New constitution for Austrian monarchy,
Feb. 26.

Civil and political rights granted to Protestants, Apr. 8.   [Nov. 18.

1862 Amnesty to political offenders in Hungary,

1864 Joins Prussia in war with Denmark, Jan.

1866 War with Prussia and Italy, June.

Battle of Königgrätz, or Sadowa, July 3.

Archduke Albrecht defeats Italians at Custozza, June 24.   (See *Prussia*.)

1867 Autonomy for Hungary announced, Feb. 7.

Czechs protest against absorption, May–July.

1867 Emperor and empress crowned king and queen of Hungary at Buda, June 8.

Von Beust, chancellor, dies Oct. 24, 1886.

1868 Civil marriage bill becomes law, May 25.

1870 Concordat with Rome suspended, July 30.

1871 New German empire recognized, Jan.

Count Andrassy, min. of Foreign Affairs, Nov. 13.

1873 Reichsrath changed into national representative assembly, March 10.

1875 New bed of Danube opened, May 30.

1878 Austrians enter Bosnia, July 29.

1882 600th anniv. of House of Hapsburg, Dec. 27.

1883 Slavonic agitation against Germans and Magyars, Aug.–Sept.

1886 Army put on a war-footing of 1,500,000 men.

1889 Crown Prince Rudolph dies Jan. 30.

1890 Count Andrassy dies Feb. 18.

1891 Triple alliance renewed, June 28.   [6.

1894 Commercial treaty with Russia ratified, July

1895 Death of Archduke Albrecht, Feb. 18; born 1817.

Richard Metternich, diplomatist, d. Mar. 1.

Charter of Vienna suspended, May (granted in 1278).

Remarkable application of telephone to commercial purposes.

The Anti-Semitic agitation assumes vast proportions.

Young Czechs carry the Bohemian Diet, Nov.

1895   Discovery of " X rays " announced by Prof. Wilhelm Conrad Röntgen of Würzburg University, Dec.

1896   Archduke Karl Ludwig, heir to the throne, dies May 19.

" The Iron Gates " barring the egress of the Danube removed, Sept. 27 (one of the great engineering feats of the century).

Liberal party win in Hungary, but are defeated in Lower Austria, Oct.

Millennial exposition in Buda-Pesth.

1897   Crushing defeat of the Liberals in the Reichsrath.

University of Vienna confers degree of M. D. upon a woman first time in its history.

Stormy scenes in the Chamber, Sept. 27.

Agreement between Austria and Hungary (" Ausgleich ") prolonged for a year, Oct.

Riotous scenes continue in the Reichsrath.

Francis Joseph's semi-centennial Dec. 2.

1898   Empress of Austria assassinated by an anarchist at Geneva, Sept. 10.

Outbreak of bubonic plague in Vienna, Oct.

[See *Germany, Hungary, France, Italy*, etc.]

BAVARIA.

895   Margrave Leopold the first duke.

1071   Guelf I., an illustrious warrior, duke.

1154   Henry the Lion, duke.

1231 Otho the Illustrious, duke, assassinated.

1596 Maximilian the Great, first elector.

1726 Charles Albert, duke; elected emperor, 1742.

1796 The French capture Munich.

1806 Maximilian-Joseph I., king, deserts Napoleon.

1848 Maximilian-Joseph II., king.

1866 Supports Austria against Prussia.

1869 International exhibition at Munich, July 20.

1870 Joins Prussia in the war with France.

Becomes part of German empire, Nov. 22.

1871 Dr. Döllinger opposes Papal infallibility.

1872 "Old Catholic" ch. opens at Munich, Sept.

1879 International exhibition at Munich, July 19.

1886 Prince Luitpold regent, June 10.

King Otho drowns himself, June 13.

[See *Germany, Austria*, etc.]

BELGIUM.

[Belgium, the original seat of the tribes of the Belgæ, was finally conquered by Julius Cæsar about 54 B.C. It was included in Gaul, and was known as Gallica Belga. In the 5th and 6th centuries it was under the rule of the Franks. It was afterwards divided into a number of independent principalities, and subsequently passed under the dominion of Austria, Spain, France, and Holland. In 1830 a revolution broke out, when the history of modern Belgium begins.]

1830 Revolution begins at Brussels, Aug. 25.

Provisional government declares ind., Oct. 4.

1831 Leopold of Saxe-Coburg accepts the crown, July 12.

1831 War with Netherlands begins, Aug. 3.

1839 Treaty of Holland and Belgium at London, April 19.

1864 Dissensions of Catholics and Protestants.

1865 Leopold I. dies Dec. 10; Leopold II. king.

1868 International Congress of Workingmen at Brussels, Nov. 6–13.

1874 International Conference at Brussels on rights of neutrals, July 27.

1875 Popular opposition to religious processions. Conf. on hygiene at Brussels, Sept. 27.

1878 Gigantic weir for water-distribution inaugurated, July 28.   [cation.

1879 Roman Catholic hierarchy oppose mixed edu-

1880 Permanent International Exhibition opens at Brussels, June 1.   [June 28.
Diplomatic intercourse with Vatican susp.,

1883 Parliamentary reform bill passed, Aug. 17.
Henri Conscience, national poet and novelist, dies Sept. 9, aged 73.   [Oct. 19.

1884 Communal elections, great liberal majority,

1885 Leopold proc. sov. of Congo Free State, May 2.

1889 Great colliery strike at Charleroi, Dec. 21.

1890 Castle of Laeken burned; valuable works of art and historical documents lost, Jan. 1.

1891 Wide-spread strikes of colliers and metallurgists.   [3, a. 69.

1892 Emile de Laveleye, eminent publicist, d. Jan.

1893 Universal suffrage adopted, April 21.

1895 Congo State annexed by government, Jan. 4.

1895 Anarchists sentenced to penal servitude for
life, Feb. 9.

Labor Bureau established by decree, Apr. 30.

Religious teaching made compulsory in
schools, Sept. 17.

Brussels declared a seaport, Oct. 19.   [Jan.

1897 Importation of American cattle prohibited,

Cattle to be identified by disk in lobe of ear.

Strike of about 12,000 miners, June.

Americans exempted from military service
by treaty.

BOHEMIA.

[Bohemia was the seat of the Boii, a Celtic race, who were
driven from the country by the Marcomani, who were subsequently supplanted by the Slavonic race.]

550 Czechs (Slavonians) conquer Bohemia.

795 City of Prague founded.

894 Christianity introduced.

1041 Bohemia conquered by Emperor Henry III.

1198 Ottocar I., first king of Bohemia.

1253 Ottocar II. rules over Austria; killed at
battle of Marchfeld, Aug. 26, 1278.

1346 King John (blind) slain at Crécy.   [heresy.

1415 John Huss, reformer, burned at Prague for

1416 Jerome of Prague burned for heresy.

1419 Ziska, leader of the Hussites, takes Prague.

1424 Ziska dies of the plague.

1437 Albert of Austria receives the crown.

1440 Ladislas of Poland king.

1458 George Podiebrad king.

1527 Ferdinand of Austria king.

1620 Battle of Prague, Nov. 9.

1648 Bohemia secured to Austria by treaty.

1744 Prague taken by the Prussians.

1757 Prussians defeat Austrians at Prague.

1775 The peasantry revolt.

1848 Insurrection at Prague, July 12.

1866 The Prussians enter Bohemia.

1867 Agitation of the Czechs.   [Germans.

1890 Settlement of disputes between Czechs and

1891 The "Young Czechs" victorious in the
elections.

1892 Fire in the great silver mine at Birkenberg,
many deaths, May 31.

[See *Austria, Germany*, etc.]

BULGARIA.

[The Bulgarians were originally a people of Ungrian or Finnish extraction, and appear for the first time in history about 120 B.C., when they settled on the banks of the Araxes. About 660 a portion of them crossed the Danube, and settled in Mœsia, and subjugated the Slavonic population. After prolonged struggles with the Byzantines, Hungarians, and Tatars, they were finally subjugated by the Turks.]

1396 Annexed to the Ottoman empire.   [13.

1878 Constituted an autonomous principality, July

1879 Alexander of Hesse elected prince, April 29.

1885 Reunited with Roumelia, Oct.
War with Servia; peace, 1886. [July 7.
1887 Ferdinand of Saxe-Coburg elected prince,
1891 M. Beltcheff, minister of finance, assassinated, March 27.
1892 First Bulgarian exhibition opened, Aug. 27.
1893 First Bulgarian steamship company inaugurated, Aug. 29.
1895 Rupture with Turkey.

[See *Turkey*, *Servia*. *Roumelia*, etc.]

DENMARK.

B.C.
60 Skiold, alleged first king.

A.D.
935 Gorm the Old, first authentic king.
1016 Canute the Great conquers Norway.
1168 Valdemar I. subjugates the Wends.
1202 Valdemar II. king; loses the family conquests.
1375 Margaret the Great regent and queen until 1412.
1397 Denmark, Sweden, and Norway united.
1440 Copenhagen made the capital.
1448 Accession of Christian I.
1527 Lutheranism introduced.
1545 Tycho Brahe, b. Dec. 9; d. Oct. 13, 1601.
1629 Christian IV. head of the Protestant league.
1665 Crown made hereditary and absolute.
1716 Ferdinand IV. drives Swedes from Norway.

1728 Copenhagen nearly destroyed by fire.

1767 Abolition of serfage begun: completed 20 years later.

1801 Copenhagen bombarded by Nelson, April 2.

1844 Albert Bertel Thorwaldsen, sculptor, dies Mar. 24; born Nov. 15. 1770.

1848 Insurrection in Schleswig-Holstein, Mar. 23. Danes defeated by the Prussians near Danna-werke, April 23. [10.

1849 Victory over Holsteiners and Germans, Apr.

1850 Separate peace with Prussia, July 2. [18.

1852 Integrity guaranteed by Great Powers, Feb.

1855 New constitution adopted, Oct. 1.

1861 Decimal coinage adopted.

1862 Agitation for union with Sweden, June.

1863 Princess Alexandra marries Prince of Wales, March 10. [Greece, June 6. Prince William George accepts crown of Accession of Christian IX., Nov. 15. War with Prussia and Austria.

1864 German troops enter Holstein, Jan. 21. [9. Danes gain naval battle off Heligoland, May Duchies resigned to the Germans, Oct. 30.

1866 Princess Dagmar marries Alexander of Russia, Nov. 9.

1867 Proposals to sell W. I. to U. S., Oct. 25.

1892 Celebration of King Christian's golden wedding, May 26.

[No important event in recent years.]

FRANCE.

A.D.

418	Franks settle in Gaul.
496	Clovis embraces Christianity.
511	Salique law proclaimed.
714	Charles Martel rules.
732	Martel defeats the Saracens, Oct. 10.
752	Pepin the Short reigns.
800	Charlemagne crowned emperor of the West.
911	Invasion and settlement of Normans.
987	Hugh Capet reigns.
996	Paris made capital of all France.
1146	Louis VII. joins the Crusades.
1163	Albigenses persecuted.
1224	Louis VIII. frees his serfs.
1249	Louis IX. goes to the Holy Land.
1307	Knights Templars suppressed.
1314	Union of France and Navarre.
1328	The House of Valois reigns.
1346	English invasion; battle of Crécy, Aug. 26.
1356	Battle of Poictiers, Sept. 19.
1407	France under Papal interdict.
1415	Battle of Agincourt, Oct. 25.
1429	Siege of Orleans raised, May 8.
1431	Joan of Arc burned at Rouen, May 30.
1475	Edward IV. of England invades France.
1509	John Calvin b. July 10; d. May 27, 1564.
1520	"Field of the Cloth of Gold;" tournament of Francis I. and Henry VIII. of Eng.
1530	Persecution of Protestants begins.

1531   Royal printing-press established.
1532   Brittany annexed to France.
1572   Massacre of St. Bartholomew, Aug. 24.
1576   " Holy Catholic League " established.
1589   Henry III. assassinated, Aug. 1.
1590   Battle of Ivry, March 14.
1593   Henry IV. becomes a Roman Catholic.
1596   Descartes born Mar. 31; dies Feb. 11, 1650.
1598   Edict of Nantes promulgated, April 13.
1606   Pierre Corneille born June 6; d. Oct., 1684.
1610   Henry IV. murdered by Ravaillac, May 14.
1613   La Rochefoucauld born; dies 1680.
1620   Navarre annexed to France.
1623   Blaise Pascal b. June 19; d. Aug. 19, 1662.
1624   Administration of Richelieu.
1628   Siege of Rochelle.
1634   *Académie de France* org. by Richelieu.
1636   Boileau-Despreaux born Nov. 1; dies Mar. 13, 1711.
1639   Racine born Dec. 21; dies April 26, 1699.
1642   Death of Cardinal Richelieu, Dec. 4, a. 58.
1643   Accession of Louis XIV., aged 4, May 14.
1648   Civil wars of the Fronde.
1672   War with Holland.
1685   Edict of Nantes revoked, Oct. 22.
1689   War with William III. of England.
1694   Voltaire born Feb. 20; dies May 30, 1778.
1697   Peace of Ryswick, Sept. 20.
1701   War of the Spanish Succession.
1704   Battle of Blenheim, defeat of French, Aug. 2.

1706	French defeated at Ramillies, May 23.
1707	Buffon b. Sept. 7; d. April 16, 1788.
1712	Rousseau born June 28; dies July 2, 1778.
1713	Peace of Utrecht, April 11.
	Dissensions of Jesuits and Jansenists, Sept.
1715	Accession of Louis XV., Sept. 1. [schemes.
1716	Disastrous results of George Law's financial
1743	French defeated at Dettingen, June 16.
1748	Peace of Aix-la-Chapelle, Oct. 18.
1762	Jesuits banished from France.
1768	Chateaubriand b. Sept. 14; d. July 4, 1848.
1778	France assists America in its struggle.
1780	Béranger born Aug. 19; dies July 16, 1857.
	Torture abolished in French Judicature.
1783	Peace of Versailles with England, Sept. 3.
	Montgolfier bros. ascend in a balloon, June 5.
1785	Diamond Necklace affair.
1789	Destruction of Bastille, Rev. begins, July 14.
1790	France declared a limited monarchy, July 14.
1791	Death of Mirabeau, April 2.
1792	First coalition against France, June.
	Massacre in Paris, 100 priests slain, Sept. 2–5.
	Republic proclaimed, Sept. 22.
1793	Louis XVI. beheaded, Jan. 21. [Feb. 1.
	War with England and Holland declared,
	War in La Vendée, March.
	Charlotte Corday stabs Marat, July 13.
	Marie Antoinette beheaded, Oct. 16.
	Worship of Goddess of Reason, Nov. 10.
1794	Danton ex. April 5; Robespierre, June 4.

1795 Louis XVII. dies in prison, June 8.
French Directory chosen, Nov. 1.

1796 Napoleon Bonaparte's campaigns in Italy.
Isidore Comte b. Jan. 19; d. Sept. 5, 1857.

1799 European coalition against France.
Napoleon declared First Consul, Nov. 10.

1800 Napoleon defeats the Austrians at Marengo,
June 14.
Bank of France founded.

1802 Peace of Amiens, March 25–27.
Legion of Honor instituted, May 19.
Napoleon made Consul for life, Aug. 2.

1804 Duc d'Enghien executed, March 21.
Napoleon proclaimed emperor, May 18.

1805 Napoleon crowned king of Italy, May 26.
Battle of Austerlitz, French victory. Dec. 2.

1806 French defeat Prussians at Jena, Oct. 14.

1807 French defeat Russians at Eylau, Feb. 8.

1808 War in the Spanish Peninsula.

1809 Napoleon divorced from Josephine, Dec. 16.

1810 Napoleon marries Maria Louise of Austria,
April 1.

1811 King of Rome, Napoleon II., born March 20.

1812 War with Russia; battle of Borodino, Sept. 7.
Disastrous retreat of French army from
Russia, Oct.

1813 War with Russia. Austria, and Prussia, Mar.

1814 Paris surrenders to the Allies, March 31.
Abdication of Napoleon, April 5.
Bourbon dynasty restored, May 3.

1814 Napoleon arrives at Elba, May 4.   [Mar. 1.
1815 Napoleon leaves Elba, and arrives at Cannes,
Napoleon abolishes the slave-trade, Mar. 29.
French defeated at Waterloo, June 18.
Abdication of Napoleon, June 22.
Napoleon arrives at St. Helena, Oct. 15.
Marshal Ney shot, Dec. 7.
1821 Death of Napoleon at St. Helena, May 5.
1824 Louis XVIII. dies; Charles X. king, Sept. 16.
1830 Algiers taken by the French, July 5.
Revolution, July 27.
Abdication of Charles X., Aug. 2.   [7.
Louis Philippe, Duke of Orleans, king, Aug.
1831 Abolition of hereditary peerage in France,
      Dec. 27.   [Strasburg, Oct. 29.
1836 Louis Napoleon attempts insurrection at
1838 Talleyrand dies May 20; born 1754.
Daguerreotype process discovered.
1840 Body of Napoleon deposited in Hôtel des
      Invalides, Dec. 15.
1844 War with Morocco, May.
1846 Louis Napoleon escapes from fortress of
      Ham, May 25.
1848 Abdication of Louis Philippe, Feb. 24.
Republic proclaimed, Feb. 26.
Rise of the Red Republicans, June.
Louis Napoleon elected president, Dec. 11.
1851 Electric telegraph between France and Eng-
      land, Nov. 13.
Coup d'état of Louis Napoleon, Dec. 2.

1852 Louis Napoleon declared emperor, Dec. 2.

1853 Marriage of Louis Napoleon and Eugénie,
   Jan. 29.   [1786.
   Francis Arago, astronomer, dies Oct. 2 ; born

1854 War declared against Russia, March 27.

1855 Industrial exhib. at Paris opened, May 15.
   Attempted assassination of emperor, Sept. 8.

1856 Birth of the Prince Imperial, March 16.
   Peace with Russia signed, March 30.

1858 Mlle. Rachel, tragédienne, dies Jan. 4, a. 38.
   Orsini conspiracy, Jan. 14.

1859 War with Austria, May 12 ; battle of Montebello, May 20 ; Palestro, May 30, 31 ; Magenta, June 4 ; Melegnano, June 8 ; Solferino, June 24 ; peace, July 12.

1860 Commercial treaty with Eng. signed, Jan. 23.

1862 Great distress caused by civil war in America, Dec.

1864 Marshal Pelissier dies May 22 ; born 1794.

1865 Proudhon dies, Jan. 19 ; born 1809.

1867 International Exhibition opened, April 1.
   Imprisonment for debt abolished, July 18.

1869 Lamartine dies, Feb. 28 ; born Oct., 1792.
   French Atlantic tel. cable laid, July 23.
   Père Hyacinthe protests against Papal infal-
   libility, Sept. 20.

1870 France declares war against Prussia, July 17.
   Battles of Woerth and Forbach, Aug. 6.
   Battle of Mars-la-Tour, Aug. 16.
   Battle of Gravelotte, Aug. 18.

1870 Battle of Sedan, Sept. 1.

Republic proclaimed, Sept. 4.

Siege of Paris begins, Sept. 15. [Oct. 7.

Gambetta escapes from Paris in a balloon,

Surrender of Metz, Oct. 27.

Alexandre Dumas dies Dec. 10, aged 67.

1871 King William proclaimed Emperor of Germany at Versailles, Jan. 18.

Capitulation of Paris, Jan. 28.

Germans enter Paris, March 1. [28.

Communist revolution at Paris, Mar. 18–May

Vendôme Column pulled down, May 16.

Peace between France and Germany ratified,

May 18. [31.

M. Thiers appointed pres. of Republic, Aug.

Mont Cenis Tunnel opened, Sept. 17.

1873 Napoleon III. dies at Chiselhurst, Jan. 9.

Marshal MacMahon president, May 26.

Last instalment of Prussian indemnity paid,

Sept. 5.

Bazaine sentenced to death; commuted to 20

years' imprisonment, Dec. 12.

1874 Vendôme Column restored, Aug. 31.

M. Guizot dies Sept. 12; born Oct. 4, 1787.

M. Ledru-Rollin dies Dec. 31; born 1808.

1877 M. Thiers dies Sept. 3, aged 80.

1879 F. P. Jules Grévy elected president, Jan. 30.

Prince Louis Napoleon killed in Zululand,

June 1.

1880 Tahiti controlled by France, June 29.

1882 Louis Blanc dies Dec. 6 ; born 1813.

M. Leon Gambetta dies Dec. 31, aged 44.

1883 Statue of Lafayette unveiled at Lepuy,
Sept. 6. [unveiled at Par., July 4.

1884 Bartholdi's statue of Liberty (pres. to U. S.),

1885 Victor Hugo dies May 22, aged 83.

1887 M. Sadi-Carnot elected president, Dec. 3.

General Boulanger arrested, Oct. 14.

1888 Louis Pasteur introduces cure for hydropho-
bia, July 7.

1889 M. Chevreul, chemist, dies April 9, a. 102.

Universal exhibition opened, May 6.

Rochefort and Boulanger sentenced to de-
portation, Aug. 14.

1890 War with Dahomey, Feb.–May.

1892 Ernest Renan, scholar, d. Oct. 2, aged 69.

Panama Canal scandals, Nov. 25 *et seq.*

1893 H. A. Taine, author, dies, March 5, a. 64.

Henri Guy de Maupassant, novelist, dies
July 6 ; born 1850.

Marshal MacMahon dies Oct. 17, aged 85.

M. Gounod, musical composer, dies Oct. 18 ;
born 1818.

1894 Pres. Carnot assassinated at Lyons, June 24.

M. Casimir-Perier elected president, June 27.

Comte de Paris dies Sept. 8. [1805.

Ferdinand de Lesseps d. Dec. 7 ; b. Nov. 19,

Capt. A. Dreyfus sentenced to perpetual imprisonment for betraying military plans,
Dec. 23.

1895 Pres. Casimir-Perier resigns, Jan. 15.
M. Felix Faure elected pres., Jan. 17 ; d. 1899.
Marshal Canrobert dies Jan. 28, aged 86.
Important reform in criminal law, May.
War against the Hovas in Madagascar, Sept.
Prof. Louis Pasteur dies Sept. 28, aged 73.

1897 Great fire at Charity Bazar in Paris, May 4.
Duel between Prince Henri d'Orleans and
Prince Victor Emmanuel of Savoy ; Prince
Henri wounded, Aug. 15.
Deputies fix ten hours as a day's work for
railway employees, Dec. 17.
Panama Canal scandal trials begin, Dec. 18.
Alphonse Daudet dies Dec. 16, aged 57.
Bill for annexation of Tahiti passed, Dec. 23.

1898 Trial of M. Zola begins, Feb. 7 ; found guilty,
and sentenced to imprisonment, Feb. 23.
Revision granted in Dreyfus case, Nov. 15.

GERMANY.

9 Hermann, or Arminius, defeats Varus; assassinated, 19.

450 Great irruption of Germanic tribes into Gaul.

772 Charlemagne subdues and Christianizes
Saxons.

800 Charlemagne emperor of West, Dec. 25.

839 Louis (le Debonnaire) sep. Ger. from Fr.

911 German princes assert independence.

918 Henry I. (the Fowler) defeats Huns, etc.

962	Otho I. crowned emperor.
978	Otho II. conquers Lorraine.
1042	Henry III. conquers Bohemia.
1077	Henry IV. humiliated at Canossa.
1140	Guelph and Ghibelline feuds begin.
1154	Frederic Barbarossa emperor; drowned in Syria, June 10, 1190.
	Teutonic order of knighthood established.
1245	Hanseatic League established.
1273	Rudolph of Hapsburg emperor. [monk.(?)
1320	Invention of gunpowder, by Schwarz, a Ger.
1356	Charles IV. issues edict called "Golden Bull."
1414	Sigismund of Bohemia emperor.
1437	Albert of Austria emperor.
1439	Pragmatic Sanction settles empire.
1442	John Faust establishes a printing-office at Mentz. (?) [type existing.
1454	Earliest specimen of printing from movable
1455	John Gutenberg invents cut metal type.
1457	First book with a printed date, by Schöffer.
1462	First Latin Bible by Faust and Schöffer.
1471	Albert Dürer born May 20; d. April, 1528.
1483	Martin Luther b. Nov. 10; d. Feb. 18, 1546.
1497	Hans Holbein (the Younger) born; dies 1543.
1502	Peasants' wars; also in 1514, 1524.
1517	Lutheran Reformation.
1519	Charles V. emperor.
1521	Luther excom. by Diet of Worms, April 17.
1522	German Bible published by Luther.
1530	Confession of Augsburg published, Jan. 25.

1531	Protestant League of Smalcalde, Dec. 31.
1535	Anabaptist war; John Leyden slain, 1536.
1555	Charles V. abdicates, Oct. 25.
1570	Hungary joined to empire.
1618	Thirty Years' War begins; ends 1648.
1630	Ger. invaded by Gustavus Adolphus, June.
1646	Baron Leibnitz b. July 6; d. Nov. 14, 1716.
1674	War with France.
1697	Peace of Ryswick, Sept. 20.
1702	Battle of Blenheim, Aug. 13, 1704.
1713	Peace of Utrecht, April 17.
1722	Pragmatic Sanction, settling the succession of the Empire in the House of Austria.
1724	Immanuel Kant b. Apr. 26; d. Feb. 12, 1804.
1745	Francis I. emperor.
1749	Goethe born Aug. 28; dies March 22, 1832.
1756	Seven Years' War between Austria and Prussia begins. [1791.
	Wolfgang A. Mozart b. Jan. 27; d. Dec. 5,
1759	Johann von Schiller born Nov. 10; dies May 9, 1805.
1765	Joseph II. emperor.
1766	Lorraine ceded to France.
1788	War with Turkey.
1793	Wars with France until 1803.
1806	German empire dissolved, July 12. [1847.
1809	Felix Mendelssohn-Bartholdy b.; d. Nov. 4,
1810	North Germany annexed to France.
	Robert Schumann born; dies 1856.
1813	Battle of Leipsic, Oct. 16-19.

1813 Richard Wagner born; dies 1883.

1814 Congress of Vienna, Nov. 1; 2d, May 25, 1815.

1815 Germanic Confederation formed, June 8.

1818 Zollverein formed.

1830 Revolution at Brunswick, Sept. 7.

1848 Insurrections throughout Germany.

1849 Treaty of Vienna, agreement of Austria and Prussia, Sept. 30.

1850 Treaty of Munich for revision of German Confederation, Feb. 27.

1863 War with Denmark. (See *Denmark.*)

1866 War between German States.   [June 25.

1868 Inauguration of Luther Monument at Worms,

1870 War with France. (See *France.*)

1871 German empire restored; William of Prus. proclaimed emp. at Versailles, Jan. 18.
First Reichstag, or imperial council. Mar. 21.
Prince Bismarck chancellor, May 12.

1872 Jesuits expelled from empire.

1875 Civil-marriage bill passed, Jan. 25.

1877 Attempted assassination of emp. by Hödel, May 11.   [June 2.

1878 Emperor wounded by Nobiling, a socialist, Decree for expulsion of Socialists issued. Nov.

1879 Emperor's golden wedding kept, June 11.

1882 German colonization society formed, Dec. 6.

1883 Germania, colossal statue, uncovered by emperor, Sept. 28.   [June 8.

1884 Foundation of new Parliament House laid,

1886 Leopold von Ranke, hist., d. May 23, a. 90.

1887 Treaty of alliance with Aus. and It., Mar. 13.
1888 Emperor William I. dies March 9, aged 91.
Frederick III. emperor, March ; d. June 15.
William II. emperor.
1889 Great strike of coal miners in Westphalia,
May. [men passed, May 24.
Bill to provide assistance for aged working-
1890 Resignation of Bismarck, chancellor, Mar. 18.
Heligoland trans. to Ger. by Eng., Aug. 9.
International Socialist Congress at Halle,
Oct. 12–18.
1891 Field-Marshal Von Moltke d. Apr. 24, a. 90.
Triple alliance renewed, June 28. [2.
Strike of printers throughout Germany, Nov.
1892 Rioting at Berlin and other cities through
distress, Feb. 25 *et seq.*
Cholera rages at Hamburg, Aug.–Oct.
1893 Seven weeks' drought closed, July 11.
Anti-Jesuit law of 1872 repealed, Dec. 1.
1894 Von Sybel's " The Founding of the German
Empire " completed ; first vol. pub. 1889.
Commercial treaty with Russia for 10 years.
Hermann von Helmholtz dies Sept. 8, a. 73.
New parliament-house opened at Ber., Dec. 5.
1895 The Reichstag favors bi-metalism, Feb. 16.
Gustav Freytag, author, d. Apr. 30 ; b. 1816.
North Sea and Baltic canal opened, June 20.
Rudolf von Gneist, statesman, dies July 21 ;
born 1816. [1816.
Tauchnitz, eminent publisher, d. Aug. 13 ; b.

1895 Congress of Social Democrats at Breslau, Oct. 6.

Restrictions imposed on American insurance companies. [Nov.

1896 Convention of Christian Socialists at Erfurt, Codification of the civil code for the empire completed. [22.

1897 Statue of William I. unveiled at Berlin, Mar.

1898 Defeat of the Agrarian League party (protectionist), June. [1813.

Otto Bismarck-Schoenhausen d. July 30; b.

The emperor visits Constantinople and Jerusalem, Oct.

GREAT BRITAIN AND IRELAND.

B.C.

55 Cæsar invades Britain.

A.D.

43 Expedition of Claudius to Britain.

47 London founded by A. Plautius.

. 51 Caractacus carried captive to Rome.

61 Insurrections of the Britons under Boadicea.

78 Agricola commands in Britain.

95 Danes and Normans invade Ireland.

120 Hadrian visits Britain.

208 Invasion of Caledonia by Severus.

284 Revolt of Carausius in Britain.

289 Victory of Carausius over Maximian.

296 Britain recovered by Constantius. [Scots.

367 Theodosius aids Britons against Picts and

396 War of Britons with Picts and Scots.

418 Final withdrawal of the Romans.

448 Arrival of St. Patrick in Ireland. (?)

449 Landing of the Angles in Britain.

457 Kingdom of Kent founded by Hengist.

477 Landing of South Saxons in Britain.

495 Cerdic and West Saxons land in Britain.

593 Kingdom of Northumbria founded.

597 Arrival of St. Augustine in England.

604 See of London founded.

664 Cædmon the great English poet flourishes.

735 Death of the Venerable Bede.

795 Danes and Normans invade Ireland.

800 Dublin and other cities built by Danes.

827 Egbert "overlord" of all England.

843 The Picts subdued by Kenneth M·Alpin.

849 Alfred the Great born ; d. Oct. 21, 901.

878 Alfred defeats the Danes ; peace of Wedmore.

959 Dunstan archbishop of Canterbury; d. 988.

975 Edward the Martyr, king of England.

1004 Feudal system established in Scotland.

1013 Sweyn, king of Denmark, conquers England.

1014 Brian Boroimhe defeats Danes in Ireland.

1016 Edmund II. ("Ironside") king of England.

1017 Canute the Dane king of England.

1039 Macbeth murders Duncan king of Scotland.

1040 The Danes driven out of Scotland.

1042 Edward the Confessor king of England.

1054 Macbeth, king of Scotland, defeated at Dunsinane ; killed, 1056.

1066 Harold II. last of the Saxon kings.
Battle of Hastings, defeat of Harold, Oct. 14.
William the Norman king of England.
1070 Lanfranc archbishop of Canterbury.
1080 Anglo-Saxon language introd. into Scotland.
1087 William II. (Rufus) king of England.
1100 Henry I. king of England.
1107 Alexander I. king of Scotland.
1117 War with France and Anjou.
1124 David I. king of Scotland.
1129 Earthquake in England.
1135 Stephen of Blois king of England.
1138 David, king of Scotland. invades England.
1153 Malcolm IV. king of Scotland.
1154 Henry II. (Plantagenet) king of England.
1155 Pope Adrian IV. authorizes invasion of Ire.
1165 William I. ("the Lion") king of Scotland.
1167 War between England and France.
1170 Assassination of Thomas à Becket.
1171 Henry II. invades Ireland.
1174 Henry II. does penance at à Becket's tomb.
1175 The bull of Adrian IV. promulgated in Ire.
1177 Ireland partitioned by English invaders.
1189 Richard I. king of England. Massacre of
Jews.
1190 King Richard sets out for the Crusade.
1204 France conquers Normandy from the Eng.
1208 Eng. placed under interdict by Innocent III.
1210 English laws introduced into Ireland.
1214 Roger Bacon born ; dies 1294.

1215	Magna Charta signed by King John.
1216	Henry III. king of England.
1218	Trial by ordeal abolished in England.
1228	Stephen Langton, archb. of Canterbury, dies.
1249	Alexander III. king of Scotland.
	University of Oxford founded.
1252	English laws introduced into Wales.
1272	Edward I. king of England.
1286	Margaret of Norway queen of Scotland.
1290	Expulsion of Jews from England by Edw. I.
1292	Baliol and Bruce contend for throne of Scot.
	John Baliol king of Scotland.
1295	Final organization of English parliament.
1296	Conquest of Scotland by Edward II.
1297	The Great Charter confirmed by Edward I.
1301	Title of Prince of Wales first conferred on king's son (afterwards Edward II.)
1304	Scotland submits to England.
1305	Wm. Wallace executed by the Eng., Aug. 23.
1306	Robert Bruce crowned king of Scotland.
1307	Edward II. king of England.
1314	Battle of Bannockburn, June 24.
1323	Thirteen years' truce between Eng. and Scot.
1324	John Wycliffe born; dies Dec. 31, 1384.
1327	Edward II. deposed and murdered.
	Edward III. king of England.
1329	David II. (Bruce) king of Scotland.
1332	Edward III. invades Scotland.
1333	Battle of Halidon Hill; defeat of Scots.
1339	Edward III. invades France.

1344 First English gold coinage (the florin).

1350 Order of the Garter instituted.

1362 Use of English in law pleadings.

1370 Robert II. (first Stuart) king of Scotland.

1376 Death of the Black Prince.

1377 Richard II. king of England.

1378 Appearance of Halley's comet.

1380 Wycliffe's English New Testament completed; Bible completed, 1384.

1381 Revolt of the peasantry under Wat Tyler.

1388 Battle of Chevy Chase between Percy and Douglas.

Battle of Otterburn, Douglas killed, Aug. 19.

1390 Statute for uniformity of weights and measures in England.

1399 Richard II. deposed; assassinated.

Henry IV. king of England.

1400 Death of Chaucer, Oct. 25; born 1340 (?).

1402 Scots defeated at Homildon by Hotspur.

1403 Battle of Shrewsbury, Hotspur killed, July 23.

1406 James I. of Scot. captured by Eng., Mar. 30.

1407 John Risby, Lollard preacher, burned in Scotland.

1413 Henry V. king of England.

1414 Lollards persecuted in England.

1418 Sir John Oldcastle hung in chains.

1422 Henry VI. king of England and France.

1424 James I. king of Scotland; murdered, 1437.

1436 War bet. Eng. and Scot.; 9 years' truce, 1438.

1440 Eton College founded.

1443 King's College, Cambridge, founded.
1450 Insurrection of Jack Cade.
1451 St. Andrew's University, Glasgow, founded.
1455 Wars of the Roses begin.
1460 James III. king of Scotland.
1461 Edward IV. king of England.
1465 Irish adopt surnames.
1470 Henry VI. restored by Warwick.
1471 Return of Edward IV.; battles of Barnet and Tewkesbury, deaths of Warwick and Henry VI.
Cardinal Wolsey born; dies Nov. 29, 1530.
1473 Chevalier Bayard born; dies 1524.
1475 Edward IV. invades France.
1476 Caxton sets up printing-press at Westminster.
1480 War between England and Scotland.
1483 Edward V. king of England; murdered.
Richard III. king of England.
1485 Battle of Bosworth; king Richard killed.
Henry VII. (house of Tudor) king of Eng.
1488 James IV. king of Scotland.
1492 Henry VII. invades France.
1494 University of Aberdeen founded.
1495 " Perkin Warbeck," impostor, invades England; executed, 1499.
1505 John Knox born; dies Nov. 24, 1572.
1509 Henry VIII. king of England.
1512 War between England and France.
1513 Battle of Flodden Field, Sept. 9; James IV. of Scotland killed.

1515 Roger Ascham born; dies 1568.

1526 Tyndale's New Testament published.

1528 James V. of Scot. banishes the Douglases.

1531 Gypsies expelled from England.

1534 Great rebellion of the Fitzgeralds in Ireland.
Papal power in Eng. abrogated by Parlia't.

1535 Coverdale's English Bible published.

1536 Incorporation of Wales with England.
Dissolution of monasteries begins.

1538 Use of English Bible in churches enjoined;
the *Great Bible* published.

1540 Order of Knights of St. John suppressed.

1542 Mary Queen of Scots born, Dec. 7; beheaded, Feb. 8, 1587.

1544 Edinburgh and Leith burnt by the English.
First cannon cast in England. [drew's.

1546 Cardinal Beatoun assassinated at St. An-
Christ's Church, Oxford, and Trinity College,
Cambridge, founded.

1547 Edward VI. king of England.

1549 Act of Uniformity passed in England.

1550 Rise of Protestantism in England.

1552 Edmund Spenser born; dies 1599.
Sir Walter Raleigh b.; exec., Oct. 29, 1618.

1553 Mary queen of England.
Lady Jane Grey executed, Feb. 12, 1554.

1554 Sir Philip Sidney b. Nov. 29; d. Oct. 7, 1586.

1556 Ridley and Latimer burnt at Oxford.

1558 Elizabeth queen of England.

1559 English Book of Common Prayer first used.

1560 The Reformation estab. by Scots Parlia't.
1561 Francis Bacon b. Jan. 22; dies Apr. 19, 1626.
Rebellion of Shane O'Neal, Earl of Tyrone, in Ireland.
Tobacco introduced into Great Britain.
1562 African slave-trade begun by Hawkins.
1563 Thirty-nine Articles of Eng. Church settled.
1564 Shakespeare b. April 23; d. April 23, 1616.
1566 Rizzio murdered in Scotland, March 9.
1567 Murder of Darnley in Edinburgh, Feb. 10.
1568 Flight of Queen Mary to England.
1569 Revolt of Catholic earls in England, Nov.
1570 Assassination of Regent Murray of Scotland.
1571 Universities of Oxford and Cambridge incor.
1572 Inigo Jones, architect, born; dies 1652.
First English translation of " Euclid " pub.
1574 Ben Jonson, dramatist, born; dies 1637.
1576 John Fletcher, dramatist, born; dies 1625.
1578 William Harvey, physician, born April; dies June, 1657.
1580 Archbishop Ussher b. Jan. 4; d. Mar. 1656.
Rise of the Brownists in England.
1581 Morton, regent of Scot., executed, June 3.
1582 University of Edinburgh founded.
1585 Francis Beaumont, dramatist, b.; d. 1616.
1587 John Foxe, martyrologist, dies; b. 1517.
1588 Spanish armada defeated, July.
Thomas Hobbes, philosopher, b.; dies 1679.
1592 Presbyterianism established in Scotland.
1593 Izaak Walton b. Aug. 9; d. Dec. 15, 1683.

1593 George Herbert born ; dies 1632.

1594 Rebellion of Tyrone in Ireland.

1600 English East India Co. chartered, Dec. 31.

1601 Earl of Essex executed, Feb. 25.

1602 *Hamlet* published.

1603 James I. king of England, March 24.
Union of crowns of England and Scotland.

1605 Gunpowder Plot of Guy Fawkes, Nov. 5.

1608 John Milton b. Dec. 9 ; d. Nov. 8, 1674.

1611 King James's Bible published.

1614 Logarithms invented by Napier.

1615 Richard Baxter b. Nov. 12; d. Dec. 8, 1691.

1616 Circulation of the blood disc. by Harvey.

1620 Pilgrim Fathers sail in *Mayflower*, Sept. 6.
John Evelyn, diarist, b. Oct. 31 ; d. 1706.

1621 Eng. Commons claim freedom of discussion.

1623 Shakespeare's works, first folio. published.

1625 Charles I. king of England, March 27.

1628 John Bunyan b.; d. Aug. 31, 1688.

1631 John Dryden born Aug. 9 ; d. May 1, 1700.

1632 John Locke b. Aug. 29 ; d. Oct. 28, 1704.
Samuel Pepys, diarist, b. Feb. 23; d. May 26, 1703.
Christopher Wren b. Oct. 20; d. Feb. 1723.

1636 John Hampden resists imposition of ship-money.

1638 Solemn League and Covenant pub., Mar. 1.

1640 Long Parliament meets, Nov. 3.

1641 Abolition of Star Chamber.
Rebellion in Ire.; great massacre, Oct. 23.

1641 Terms "Roundhead" and "Cavalier" first used.

1642 Civil war breaks out in England.
Battle of Edgehill, Oct. 23.   [1727.
Sir Isaac Newton b. Dec. 25; d. March 20,

1643 John Hampden killed in battle, June 24.
Battle of Newbury, Sept. 20.

1644 Battle of Marston Moor, July 2.
William Penn born Oct. 11; dies 1718.

1645 Archbishop Laud beheaded, Jan. 10.
Battle of Naseby, June 14.

1646 Charles I. surrenders to Scots May 5.

1647 Charles I. given up by Scots to English Parliament, Jan. 30.
George Fox, Quaker, begins to preach.

1649 Charles I. executed, Jan. 30.
England declared a Commonwealth, May 19.
Cromwell captures Drogheda.

1650 John Churchill, Duke of Marlborough, b.; d. 1722.

1651 Prince Charles Stuart invades England.
Victory of Cromwell at Worcester, Sept. 3.
Scotland united to Eng. by Cromwell, Sept.

1652 War between the English and Dutch.
Irish rebellion suppressed, May.   [20.

1653 Expulsion of the "Rump" by Cromwell, Apr.
Cromwell made Protector, Dec. 16.

1654 Peace between England and Holland, Apr. 5.

1656 General Post-Office, London, established.

1658 Oliver Cromwell d., Sept. 3; b. Apr. 25, 1599.

1658 Richard Cromwell, Protector: retires May 25, 1659.

1660 Charles II. proclaimed king, May 8. [1661. Episcopacy restored in England; in Scot., The Royal Society of London founded.

1661 Charles Rollin, historian, born; dies 1741.

1665 The Great Plague in London.
The *London Gazette* established.

1666 Great Fire in London, Sept. 2–6.

1667 " Paradise Lost " published.
Jonathan Swift b. Nov. 30; d. Oct. 19, 1745.

1668 Triple Alliance between England, Holland, and Sweden, Jan. 23, April 25.

1669 Reflecting telescope constructed by Newton.

1670 Hudson's Bay Company incorporated.

1672 Addison born May 1; dies June 17, 1719.

1674 Isaac Watts born; dies 1748.

1675 St. Paul's Cathedral begun; completed, 1710.
Greenwich Observatory founded.

1676 Motion of the sun proved by Halley.   [13.

1678 Popish plot invented by Titus Oates, Aug.
Bunyan's " Pilgrim's Progress " published.

1679 Terms " Whig " and " Tory " come into use.
Archbishop Sharp murdered, May 3.
Habeas Corpus Act passed.

1682 Chelsea Hospital founded.

1683 Lord William Russell executed. July 21.
Algernon Sidney executed, Dec. 7.

1685 James II. king of England. Feb. 6.
Battle of Sedgemoor, July 6.

1685 Monmouth beheaded, July 15.

1688 Prince of Orange lands at Torbay, Nov. 5.

Catalogue of the stars made by Flamsteed.

English Revolution.   James II. deposed.

Alexander Pope b. May 22 ; dies May, 1744.

1689 William and Mary declared king and queen, Feb. 13.

Siege of Londonderry, April 20.   [July 27.

Battle of Killiecrankie, death of Dundee,

1690 Sea-fight off Beachy Head, June 30.

Battle of the Boyne, July 1 (N. S., July 12).

1691 Capitulation of Limerick, Oct. 3.

1692 Massacre of Glencoe, Feb. 13.

1694 Queen Mary dies Dec. 28.

Bank of England incorporated.   [1705.

1696 Greenwich Hospital begun by Wren ; fin.,

1697 William Hogarth born ; dies Oct. 26, 1764.

1702 Anne queen of Great Britain, March 8.

War against France and Spain, May 4.

1703 John Wesley born June 17 ; d. March, 1791.

1704 Gibraltar taken by Admiral Rooke, July 24.

Battle of Blenheim, Aug. 13.

1705 Newcomen's steam-engine patented.

Composition of light discovered by Newton.

1707 Henry Fielding b. April 22 ; d. Oct. 8, 1754.

Act of Union of England and Scotland, May 1.   [July.

National flag of Great Britain appointed,

First Parliament of Great Britain meets, Oct. 23.

1708 William Pitt, Earl of Chatham, born Nov. 15; dies May 11, 1778.

1709 Samuel Johnson b. Sept. 18; d. Dec. 13, 1784.

1710 South Sea Company founded.

1711 David Hume born April 26; d. Aug., 1776.

1712 Duty on advertisements; abolished 1855.

1713 Clarendon Press, Oxford, established.

1714 George I. king of England, Aug. 1.
George Whitefield born; dies Sept. 1770.

1715 Jacobite rebellion; James III. (Pretender) proclaimed.
Battle of Sheriffmuir (Dunblane), Nov. 13.
Battle of Preston, Nov. 12–13.
Pope's "Homer's Iliad" published.

1716 Mississippi Scheme projected by Law.
David Garrick, actor, b. Feb. 20; d. Feb. 1779.
Thomas Gray, poet, born; dies July, 1771.

1717 Triple Alliance between France, England, and Holland, Jan. 4.

1718 England declares war against Spain, Dec. 27.

1719 "Robinson Crusoe," by Daniel Defoe, pub.
Watts's "Psalms of David" published.

1720 The South Sea Bubble causes finan. distress.

1721 Tobias George Smollett, b.; dies Oct., 1771.

1722 Jacobite plot in England, May.   [1792.

1723 Sir Joshua Reynolds born July 16; d. Feb.,
Sir William Blackstone b. July 10; d. 1780.

1724 Fahrenheit's thermometer invented.

1726 "Gulliver's Travels" published.
John Howard, philan., born; dies 1790.

1727 George II. king of England, July 10.
Aberration of light discovered by Bradley.
Thomas Gainsborough born; d. Aug., 1788.

1728 Rise of Methodism.
Oliver Goldsmith b. Nov. 10; d. Apr. 4, 1774.
John Hunter, physician, born; dies 1793.

1730 Edmund Burke b. Jan. 1; dies July 9, 1797.
Josiah Wedgwood, potter, born; dies 1795.

1731 Eng. language to be used in courts of justice.
William Cowper, poet, born Nov. 26; dies
April 25, 1800.

1735 Harrison's first timepiece constructed, for
determining longitude at sea.

1736 Steam-vessel patented by Hulls.
James Watt, born Jan. 19; dies Aug., 1819.

1737 Edward Gibbon, historian, b.; d. Jan., 1794.

1738 Sir William Herschel born Nov. 15; dies
Aug., 1822.

1739 Foundling Hospital, London, established.

1742 Händel's " Messiah " produced.

1743 William Paley, theologian, born; dies 1805.

1744 Sea-fight with French and Spanish fleets off
Toulon, Feb. 22.

1745 Charles Edw. Stuart lands in Scot., July 23.
Battle of Prestonpans, Sept. 21.

1746 Battle of Culloden, Apr. 16; end of rebellion.
Henry Grattan b. July 3; d. May 14, 1820.
Highland dress prohibited by Parliament,
Aug. 12.   [1794.
Sir Wm. Jones, phil., b. Sept. 28; d. Apr. 27,

1747 Naval victories of Anson and Hawke, May, Oct.

Shakers appear about this time.

1748 Jeremy Bentham b. Feb. 15 ; d. June 6, 1832.

1749 Charles James Fox, statesman, born Jan. 24 ; dies Sept. 13, 1806.

1750 Westminster Bridge, London, opened.

1752 New style calendar adopted in Great Britain, omitting 11 days after the 2d of September, making the next day the 14th.

Thomas Chatterton, poet, b. ; d. Aug., 1770.

1753 British Museum founded.

Wesley's " Hymns " published.

1754 Society of Arts, London, founded.

1755 Johnson's " Dictionary " published.   [1831.

Mrs. Siddons, actress, born July ; dies June 8,

1758 Horatio Nelson b. Sept. 29 ; d. Oct. 21, 1805.

1759 Rob. Burns b. Jan. 25 ; dies July 21, 1796.

1760 George III. king of Great Britain.

Eddystone lighthouse completed by Smeaton.

1763 Latent heat discovered by Black.

1765 Stamp Act passed by British Parl., March 22.

Blackstone's " Commentaries " published.

1766 Death of the " Old Pretender," Jan. 2.

" Vicar of Wakefield " published.

1767 " Nautical Almanac " first published.

1768 Royal Academy of Arts, London, founded.

1769 Letters of " Junius " begin to appear, Jan.

Duke of Wellington born May 1 ; dies Sept. 14, 1852.

1769 Sir Thos. Lawrence b. May 4 ; d. Jan. 7, 1830.

1770 Wm. Wordsworth b. Apr. 7 ; d. Apr. 24, 1850.

1771 Sir Walter Scott b. Aug. 15 ; d. Sept. 21, 1832.
Sydney Smith born ; dies Feb. 22, 1845.

1772 Samuel T. Coleridge born Oct. 21 ; dies July 25, 1834.

1774 Boston Port Bill passed, March.
Oxygen discovered by Priestley.
Daniel O'Connell b. Aug.; d. May 15, 1847.

1775 Walter Savage Landor born Jan. 30; dies Sept. 17, 1864.
Charles Lamb born Feb.; dies 1834.
Charles Kemble, actor, b.; d. Nov. 12, 1854.
Joseph M. W. Turner born ; dies 1851.

1776 Adam Smith's " Wealth of Nations " pub.

1777 Thomas Campbell, poet, born ; dies 1844.

1778 Sir Humphry Davy b. Dec. 17 ; d. May, 1829.

1779 Thomas Moore, poet, born ; d. Feb. 26, 1852.
Lord Henry Brougham born Sept. 19 ; dies May 7, 1868.   [cent, Jan. 16.

1780 Sea-fight with Spaniards off Cape St. Vin-
Dr. Chalmers b. March 17 ; d. May 31, 1847.
Lord George Gordon riots in London, June 2.
Elizabeth Fry, phil., born ; d. Oct. 12, 1845.
Vaccination suggested by Edward Jenner.

1781 Sunday-schools originated by Robert Raikes.

1782 The *Royal George* sinks at Spithead, Aug. 29.

1783 Gabriel Rossetti born ; dies 1854.

1784 Bramah lock patented.
Lord Palmerston b. Oct. 20 ; d. Oct. 18, 1865.

1785 Royal Irish Academy incorporated.

1786 Warren Hastings impeached; acquitted Apr.
23, 1795.

Thos. De Quincey b. Aug. 15; d. Dec. 8, 1859.

1787 Society for suppression of slave-trade formed.

Edmund Kean, actor, born; dies 1833.

1788 First publication of *London Times*, Jan. 1.

Lord Byron b. Jan. 22; dies April 18, 1824.

Sir Robert Peel b. Feb. 5; d. July 2, 1850.

George III. insane; Prince of Wales regent.

1789 Herschel's great telescope completed.

1791 Michael Faraday born; dies Aug. 25, 1867.

1792 Gas first used for lighting.

John Keble b. April 25; d. March 29, 1866.

Sir John Herschel born; dies May 11, 1871.

Percy Bysshe Shelley b. Aug. 4; d. July, 1822.

Lord John Russell b. Aug. 18; dies May 28,
1878.

1793 Dionysius Lardner born; d. April 29, 1859.

1794 Thomas Arnold b. June 13; d. June 12, 1842.

1795 Maynooth College, Ireland, founded.

Thomas Carlyle b. Dec. 4; d. Feb. 4, 1881.

1796 John Keats, poet, born; dies Feb. 24, 1821.

1798 Rebellion in Ireland breaks out, May 23.

Battle of the Nile, victory of Nelson, Aug. 1, 2.

1800 Legislative union of G. B. and Ire., July 2.

Thomas B. Macaulay born Oct. 25; dies
Dec. 28, 1859.   [meets, Jan. 22.

1801 First Imperial Parlia't of United Kingdom
Victory of Nelson over Danish fleet, Apr. 2.

1802 Robert Chambers, pub., b.; d. Mar. 17, 1871.
Sir Edwin Landseer born March 7; dies Oct.
1, 1873.
Hugh Miller born Oct. 10; d. Dec. 24, 1856.

1803 Rising in Ire. under Rob. Emmett, July 23.
Atomic theory propounded by Dalton.
Douglas Jerrold born; dies June 8, 1857.
Robert Stephenson, engineer, born Oct.; dies
Oct. 12, 1859.

1804 British and Foreign Bible Society estab.
Savings banks originated.
Richard Cobden b. June; dies Apr. 2, 1865.

1805 Bulwer Lytton born May; dies Jan., 1873.
Victory and death of Nelson at Trafalgar,
Oct. 21.
Benjamin D'Israeli, Lord Beaconsfield, born
Dec. 21; dies April 19, 1881.

1806 John Stuart Mill b. May; dies May 8, 1873.

1807 Abolition of slave-trade in British Empire,
March 25.
Cardinal York, last of the Stuarts, d. July 13.

1808 Cardinal Manning born; dies Jan. 14, 1892.

1809 Elizabeth (Barrett) Browning born; dies
June 29, 1861.
Alfred Tennyson born; dies Oct. 6, 1892.

1811 Great comet visible for four months.
Daniel Maclise born; dies April 25, 1870.
William M. Thackeray b.; d. Dec. 24, 1863.
John Bright b. Nov. 16; d. March 27, 1889.

1812 War with the U. S.; peace, Feb. 17, 1815.

1812 Charles Dickens b. Feb.; dies June 9, 1870.
Robert Browning born; dies Dec. 12, 1889.

1813 Electric light discovered by Davy.

·1815 Safety lamp invented by Davy.

1816 Electric telegraph invented by Ronalds.
Charlotte Brontë b. Apr. 21; d. Dec. 19, 1848.

1817 Waterloo Bridge, London, opened.
The kaleidoscope invented by Brewster.

1818 The stethoscope invented by Laennec.
James A. Froude b. Apr. 23; d. Oct. 20, 1894.

1819 Princess Victoria born May 24.
Marian Evans ("George Eliot") born Nov.
22; dies Dec. 22, 1880.
Prince Albert born Aug.; dies Dec. 14, 1861.
John Ruskin born Feb. 8.

1820 George IV. king of England, Jan. 29.
Astronomical Society of London founded.
John Tyndall b. Aug. 21; dies Dec. 4, 1893.
Herbert Spencer born April 27.
Florence Nightingale born May.

1822 Matthew Arnold b. Dec. 24; d. Apr. 15, 1888.
Calculating machine invented by Babbage.

1823 British Antislavery Society founded.

1825 First voyage by steam from Eng. to India.
Thomas H. Huxley born; d. June 29, 1895.

1826 Zoölogical Society of London founded.

1828 Test Act and Corporation Act repealed.
Dante Gabriel Rossetti b.; d. Apr. 9, 1882.
New corn-law in England.
London University opened.

1829 Roman Catholic Emancipation Act passed,
Apr. 13.
William M. Rossetti born Sept. 25.
1830 William IV. king of England.
Robert Cecil, Marquis of Salisbury, born.
Christina Rossetti born Dec. 5.   [Nov.
1831 First appearance of Asiatic cholera in Eng.,
1832 Lord John Russell's reform bill passed.
June 7.   [Aug. 1.
1834 Emancipation of slaves in British colonies.
Charles H. Spurgeon born; d. Jan. 31, 1892.
1837 Punishment by pillory abolished.
Father Mathews' temperance missions begin.
Algernon Charles Swinburne born April 5.
1838 Queen Victoria crowned, June 28.
International copyright act passed.
National Gallery, London, opened.   [lantic.
First voyage of *Great Western* across the At-
1839 Anti-corn-law League formed, March 20.
1840 Penny postage in G. B. comes into operation.
Queen Victoria m. to Prince Albert, Feb. 10.
1841 Prince of Wales born Nov. 9.
"Young Ireland" party formed.
1842 Income and Property tax imposed in G. B.
1843 Disruption of the Church of Scotland.
Daniel O'Connell arrested, Oct. 11.
The Thames Tunnel opened.
1844 Bank of Eng. Charter Act passed, July 19.
1845 Sir John Franklin sails to the Arctic, May 23.
Maynooth College incorporated, June 30.

1845 Failure of potato crop in G. Brit. and Ire.
Gun-cotton invented.

1846 Repeal of English corn-laws, June 26.
Evangelical Alliance formed.
Planet Neptune discovered Sept. 23.
Charles Stewart Parnell b.; d. Oct. 6, 1891.

1847 Roman Catholic hierarchy established in
England, Oct.   [10.

1848 Great Chartist demonstration in Eng., Apr.
Insur. in Ire. under Smith O'Brien, July 29.

1850 First submarine telegraph bet. Eng. and Fr.

1851 London Great Exhibition opened, May 1.

1853 Cholera breaks out in England, Sept. 4.
Advertising vans prohibited.

1854 Declaration of war against Russia, Mar. 28;
treaty of alliance with France, April 10.
Armstrong gun manufactured.

1855 Newspaper stamp abolished in G. B., June 15.
Bessemer's process for manufacture of steel
patented.

1858 First message over Atlantic cable, Aug. 20.
Government of India transf. to crown, Sept. 1.

1859 Darwin's "Origin of Species" published.

1860 *Great Eastern* crosses Atlantic, June 17–27.

1861 Paper duty in G. Brit. abolished, June 12.
Spectrum analysis applied in astronomy.
Post-Office Savings Banks opened in Eng.

1862 International Exhibition opened at South
Kensington, May 1.   [July 29.
Alabama (Confederate) sails from Liverpool,

1862 Cotton famine in Lancashire at its height,
Dec. [mark, March 10.

1863 Prince of Wales marries Alexandra of Den-

1864 Appearance of the Fenians in Ireland.
Rudyard Kipling born.

1865 Rinderpest in England, July–Oct.
Arrest of Fenian leaders in Ireland, Sept. 15.

1866 Suspension of Bank of England Charter
Act, May 11.
Successful laying of Atlantic cable, July 27.

1870 Irish Land Act passed, Aug. 1.

1871 Trial of Tichborne case begins, May 11.

1873 Payment of Alabama indemnity by England,
Sept. [May 1.

1876 Queen Victoria proclaimed Empress of India,

1877 Statue of King Alfred unveiled, July 14.

1882 Queen Victoria shot at, March 10.
Charles R. Darwin dies April 19, aged 73.

1883 Fenian dynamite explosions.

1884 Prince Leopold dies March 28.

1886 Colonial and Indian Exhibition at South
Kensington, May 4.

1887 Queen's Jubilee. [Aug.–Dec.

1889 Great labor strikes throughout the country,

1890 H. M. Stanley returns from Africa. [26.
Empress Dock at Southampton opened, July

1893 Duke of York marries Princess May, July 6.
Behring Sea arbitration of G. Britain, Aug.

1894 Manchester ship-canal opened, Jan. 1.

1895 Gladstone retires from political life, July 3.

1895 Duke of Cambridge, commander-in-chief of British army, retires, Oct. 31.

1896 Alfred Austin appointed poet laureate, Jan. 1.

Thomas Hughes d. Mar. 22; b. Oct., 1823.

Ancient and Honorable Artillery Company of Boston, Mass., arrives in London, July 8.

Sir John Everett Millais d. Aug. 13; b. 1829.

1897 Queen Victoria's Diamond Jubilee celebrated, June 22.

Blackwell Tunnel opened, May 22.

William Morris, poet, dies Oct. 3, aged 62.

1898 *Formidable*, reported largest war-ship afloat, launched, Nov. 17.

Imperial penny-postage on half-ounce letters announced, Dec. 25.   [1809.

Wm. E. Gladstone d. May 19; b. Dec. 29,

Irish local government bill passed.

Vaccination bill, modifying compulsory vaccination, passed.

GREECE.

B.C.   [Early dates conjectural.]

2042 Uranus arrives in Greece.

1910 Inachus king of the Argives.

1856 Kingdom of Argos begun.

1773 Sacrifices to the gods introduced.

1764 Deluge of Ogyges.

1700 Pelasgi in the Peloponnesus; succeeded by the Hellenes, 1500.

1582 Chronology of the Arundelian marbles begins.

Cecrops arrives from Egypt.

1504 The Areopagus established.

1503 Deluge of Deucalion.

1495 Panathenæan games instituted.

1493 Cadmus, with the Phœnician letters, settles
in Bœotia, and founds Thebes.

1453 First Olympic games at Elis.

1356 Eleusinian mysteries institut. by Eumolpus.

1326 Isthmian games instituted.

1263 Argonautic expedition of Jason.

Pythian games begun by Adrastus.

1235 Theseus reigns in Athens for 30 years.

1213 Amazonian war.

1198 Abduction of Helen.

1193 Beginning of Trojan war; Troy taken, 1184.

1044 Settlement of the Ionians in Asia Minor.

Royalty abolished in Athens.

1000 Homer, epic poet, flourishes.

916 The Rhodians begin navigation laws.

884 Lycurgus, lawgiver, flourishes.

869 Pheidon, eminent sculptor, flourishes.

800 Hesiod, epic poet, flourishes.

776 The first Olympiad.

743 The Messenian wars; continue until 669.

664 First sea-fight on record, which took place
between the Corinthians and Corcyrans.

657 Byzantium built.

638 Solon, Athenian legislator, born; d. 558.

621   Laws of Draco published.

619   Æsop, fabulist, born; dies 564.

600   Spherical form of the earth taught by Thales.

590   Seven sages of Greece (Solon, Periander, Pittacus, Chilo, Thales, Cleobulus, and Bias) flourish.

560   Anacreon, lyric poet, born; dies 478.

527   Pisistratus, the tyrant, seizes Athens.

525   Æschylus, tragic poet, born; dies 456.

514   Themistocles, Athenian gen. and statesman, born; dies 449.

510   The law of ostracism established.

500   Miltiades, Athenian general and statesman, born; dies 489.

490   Battle of Marathon, def. of Persians, Sept. 28.
       First appearance of Aristides; d. about 468.

484   Herodotus, historian, born; dies 420.

483   Aristides, "the Just," banished.

480   Euripides, tragic poet, born; dies 406.
       Athens taken by Xerxes the Persian.
       Myron, eminent sculptor, flourishes.
       Leonidas defends pass of Thermopylæ.
       Battle of Salamis, defeat of Persians, Oct. 20.

479   Battle of Platæa; Persian fleet destroyed at Mycale.
       Themistocles banished.

471   Thucydides, Athenian historian, b.; d. 401.

470   Pythagoras teaches the doctrine of celestial motions.

469   Pericles takes part in public affairs; d. 429.

460 Democritus, "the Laughing Philosopher," b. ;
    dies 361.   [flourishes.

450 Polygnotus, first portrait and historic painter,
    Alcibiades, Athenian orator, born ; dies 404.

448 The sacred war begun ; ended by Philip, 346.

445 Xenophon, historian and general, b. ; d. 355.

444 Agesilaus II., king of Sparta, born ; dies 361.
    Aristophanes, comic poet, born ; d. 380.

442 Phidias, greatest of Grecian sculptors, flour.

440 Apollodorus, Athenian painter, born.

436 Isocrates, Athenian orator, born ; dies 338.

431 Peloponnesian war ; lasts until 404.

429 Plato b. ; founds the Academy, 388 ; d. 347.

412 Diogenes, cynic philosopher, born ; d. 323.

411 Governm't of the "Four Hundred" in Athens.

403 Rule of the "Thirty Tyrants" in Athens.

400 Retreat of the 10,000 under Xenophon.
    Zeuxis and Parrhasius, em. painters, flourish.

399 Death of Socrates ; born 468.

385 Demosthenes, Athenian orator, born ; d. 322.

384 Aristotle, philosopher, born ; dies 322.

370 Rise and fall of the Theban power (in 360).

362 Battle of Mantinea, death of Epaminondas.

360 Praxiteles, eminent sculptor, flourishes.

350 Pausias of Sicyon, inv. of encaustic, flourishes.

342 Epicurus, philosopher, born ; dies 270.

341 Menander, dramatic poet, flourishes.

340 Athens and allies declare war against Philip ;
    defeated, 338.

336 Assassination of Philip of Macedon.

336 Alexander subdues the Athenians.

330 Apelles, eminent painter, flourishes.

328 Lysippus, eminent sculptor, flourishes.

323 Death of Alexander the Great; born 356.
    Euclid, geometer, flourishes.

319 Antipater, regent of Macedonia, dies.

288 Chares, eminent sculptor, flourishes.

277 Greece invaded by the Gauls.

212 Archimedes observes solstices.

160 Hipparchus disc. precession of equinoxes.

147 Greece made a Roman province.

86 Athens conquered by Sylla, Roman general.

70 Dionysius of Halicarnassus, hist., flourishes.

A.D.

50 Plutarch, biographer, flourishes.

95 Dionysius the Areopagite, Athenian judge,
    flourishes.

100 Clemens, Church Father, dies.

115 Ignatius, Church Father, dies.

130 Irenæus, Saint, born; dies 202.

169 Polycarp, Church Father, dies.

253 Origen, Church Father, dies.

296 Athanasius, Church Father, born; dies 373.

336 Arius, founder of Arianism, dies.

340 Eusebius, Church Father, dies.

347 Chrysostom, Church Father, born; dies 407.

395 Rise of *Eastern Empire,* which see.

1456 Turks under Mahomet II. conquer Athens.

1466 The Venetians hold Athens.

1770 Struggle for independence, helped by Rus.

1790   Marco Bozzaris, patriot, born; killed Aug. 10, 1823.

1821   Missolonghi taken by Greeks, Nov.

1822   Independence of Greece proclaimed, Jan. 27. Siege of Corinth by the Turks, Jan.

1829   Greek National Assembly opens at Argos, July 23.   [of Greece, Sept. 14. The Porte acknowledges the independence

1832   Othô of Bavaria king of Greece, May 7.

1837   University at Athens established.

1843   Bloodless revolution at Athens; new constitution established.

1863   Prince William of Denmark becomes king with title of George I., Oct. 31.

1864   Alexander Mavrocordato, patriot, d. Aug. 18.

1870   Decree suppressing brigandage issued, Oct.

1878   Thessaly ceded to Greece, May 24, 1881.

1882   Cutting of Isthmus of Corinth begins, May 5.

1883   Coumoundouros, statesman, dies March 9.

1885   Railway between Athens and Corinth opens, April 15. Great discovery of statuary at Athens.

1886   Electoral reform bill passed, June 17.

1888   National Industrial Exhib. at Athens, Nov. 1.

1890   Formation of "Young Greek" party at Athens, Aug.

1893   Corinth canal opened, Aug. 6.

1894   Destructive earthquake at Thebes, April 20.

1896   Olympic games revived, April. Revolt of Cretans against Turkey.

1897 Greece makes war against Turkey; defeated, April–May; treaty of peace signed, Dec. 4.

1898 Revolt of students at Athens, Jan.

Attempt to assassinate King George, Feb. 26.

THE EASTERN EMPIRE.

[After the division of the Roman Empire the influence and energy of the Greeks will be found manifested in the fortunes of the Eastern Empire, which came to an end by the taking of Constantinople by Mahomet II. May 29, 1453.]

381 Nestorius, first patriarch of Constantinople, July 9.   [of the East.

395 The Roman empire divided, Arcadius emp.

413 Alaric the Goth ravages the empire.

431 First Council of Ephesus; 2d, 449.

451 Council of Chalcedon.

529 Justinian code published.

War with Persia; victorious career of Belisarius, dies 565, aged 84.

537 Dedication of St. Sophia.

632 Saracens invade the empire.

770 The monasteries dissolved.

1203 The Crusaders take Constantinople, July 19.

1204 Baldwin, earl of Flanders, elected emperor.

1261 The empire re-established by Michael Palæologus, July 25.

1361 The Sultan Amurath takes Adrianople.

1390 All the Greek possessions in Asia lost.

1402 Greek empire tributary to Timour the Tatar.

1448 Constantine XIII. the last emperor.

1453 Mahomet II. takes Constantinople.

[See *Italy, Turkey.*]

HANOVER.

[The country at present included in the kingdom of Hanover was occupied in remote ages by Saxon tribes, who submitted to Charlemagne, and embraced Christianity. The emperor Ludvig incorporated it in the Duchy of Saxony, and it subsequently passed to the family of the Guelphs.]

1535 Protestantism permanently established.

1714 Elector becomes king of England as Geo. I.

1745 University of Göttingen founded. [lie.

1793 Hanoverian troops act against the Fr. repub-

1810 Becomes a part of kingdom of Westphalia.

1814 Elevated to the rank of a kingdom.

1837 Ernest Augustus, Duke of Cumberland, king.

1848 Liberal constitution adopted.

1851 George V., king ; opposed to reforms.

1866 Becomes part of the German empire.

[See *Germany*.]

HERZEGOVINA.

[Herzegovina, originally a part of Croatia, was united with Bosnia in 1326, and made the Duchy of St. Saba by the emperor Frederic III. in the following century. It was ceded to Turkey in 1699 at the peace of Carlowitz. In December, 1861, an insurrection against the Turks broke out, fostered by the Prince of Montenegro. It was subdued ; and on Sept. 23, 1862, Tucatovitch, chief of the insurgents, surrendered to Kurschid Pacha, and an amnesty was granted.]

1875 Insurrection against the Turks, July 1. [22.
European powers attempt to mediate, Aug.
Insurgents demand full and real freedom,
Sept. 12. [sults, Sept. Nov.
Sanguinary engagements, with various re-

1876 Insurgents defeated near Trebinje, Jan. 18–20.

1878 Occupied by the Austrians, July 13.

1882 Insurrection against Austria, Jan. 16–31; suppressed, Oct. 26.

[See *Austria, Turkey*.]

HESSE.

[Hesse, the original seat of the Catti, formed part of the empire of Charlemagne. It was joined to Thuringia until about 1263, when Henry I. became landgrave of Hesse.]

1530 Philip the Magnanimous signs the Augsburg Confession.   [stadt.

1567 Divided into Hesse-Cassel and Hesse-Darm-

1803 Hesse-Cassel becomes an electorate.

1806 Hesse-Darmstadt becomes a grand duchy.

1807 Hesse-Cassel incorporated with Westphalia.

1866 Hesse-Cassel annexed to Prussia.

[See *Germany, Prussia*.]

HOLLAND (NETHERLANDS).

[The oldest inhabitants of Holland were of Celtic origin. In Cæsar's day the whole district between the Rhine and the Scheldt was occupied by Belgæ, while the Betaw (the Insula Batavorum) was peopled by a portion of the Germanic tribe of the Chatti (the Batavi). The Frisians occupied the whole northern portion. From 28 to 47 A.D. a struggle went on between the Romans and the Frisians, which ended in the complete reduction of the tribe. The Batavi and Frisians subsequently became auxiliaries of Rome.]

70 Rome dismisses her Batavian cohorts.

70 Claudius Civilis attacks the Romans; after an exhaustive struggle, peace made on easy terms.

481 Clovis, chief of the Franks, possesses Hol.

695 Willibrord, first bishop of the Netherlands.

[From the 10th to the 15th century the country was governed by counts under the German emperors.]

1299 Holland united to Hainault.

1347 Civil war bet. "Hooks" and "Codfish."

1416 Holland united to Brabant.   [flourishes.

1438 Lourens Coster, a reputed inv. of printing,

1477 Annexed to Austria.

1555 Philip II. establishes the Inquisition.

1576 Union of North and South Provinces.

1577 Peter Paul Rubens born; dies 1640.

1584 Assassination of William of Orange, July 10.

1586 Battle of Zutphen, Sir Philip Sidney killed, Sept. 22.

1587 Maurice, famous gen., becomes stadtholder.

1599 Van Dyck born; dies 1641.

1605 Albert Cuyp born; dies 1691.

1608 Paul Rembrandt born; dies 1669.

1609 Independence of United Provinces estab.

1610 David Teniers born; dies 1694.

1613 Gerard Douw born; dies 1680.

1617 Sir Peter Lely born; dies 1680.

1618 Synod of Dort; persecution of Arminians.

1619 Execution of Barneveldt, May 14.

1639 Victories of Van Tromp over Spanish fleet.

1647 William II. stadtholder.

1652 War with Eng. ; De Ruyter def. by Blake, Oct. 22.

Van Tromp sails through British Channel with broom at his masthead, Nov. 29.

1659 Victorious war with Sweden.

1665 War with England ; indecisive sea-fights.

1668 Triple All. of England, Holland, and Sweden.

1671 French overrun Holland ; the sluices opened.

1672 Murder of Cornelius and John De Witt, Aug. 20.

William III. stadtholder.

1677 William of Orange marries Mary of England.

1678 Peace with France (Nimeguen).

1689 William becomes king of England.

War with France ; ends, 1696.

1697 Peace of Ryswick, Sept. 20.

1702 War against France and Spain.

1713 Peace of Utrecht, April 11.   [*tria.*

1743 Holland supports Maria Theresa. (See *Aus-*

1748 Peace of Aix-la-Chapelle, Oct. 18.

1781 War with England for naval supremacy.

1787 Civil war in Low Countries.

1793 French Republicans march into Holland.

1795 Batavian Republic established.

1799 Texel fleet surrenders to British, Aug. 30.

1806 Louis Bonaparte king of Holland, June 5.

1810 Louis abdicates, July 1.

Holland united to France, July 9.

1813 Restored to house of Orange, and Belgium annexed, Nov. 17.

1813 William Frederic, Prince of Orange, declared sovereign prince of United Neth., Dec. 6.

1831 Belgium separated from Holland, July 12.

1840 William II. king, Oct. 7.

1849 William III. king, March 17.

1853 Re-establishment of Roman Catholic hierarchy, Mar. 12.

1861 Great inundations; 40,000 acres submerged, Jan.–Feb.

1863 Slavery ceases in Dutch West Indies, July 1.

1868 Fortifications of Luxemburg razed, May.

1869 International Exhibition at Amsterdam.

1871 Possessions in Guinea ceded to Gr. Br., July 7.

1872 Death of De Thorbecke, statesman, June 4.

1876 Canal between North Sea and Amsterdam opened, Oct. 4.

1883 International Exhibition at Amsterdam.

1890 Death of King William III., Nov. 23.
Wilhelmina queen (b. 1880), under queen-regent.

1894 Insurrection in Dutch East Indies, Aug. 25.

1898 Queen Wilhelmina reigns, Sept. 5.
Wilhelmina betrothed to Prince William of Wied, Oct.

HUNGARY.

890 Settled by the Ungri and Magyars.

997 Stephen, first king, establishes Christianity.

1061 Poles overrun Hungary.

1174 Bela III. introduces Greek civilization.

1241 Ravaged by the Tatars.

1301 Andrew II. dies; end of Arpad dynasty.

1344 Victories of Louis the Great in Bulgaria, etc.

1437 Albert of Austria becomes king of Hungary.

1442 Victories of John Hunniades over the Turks.

1444 King Ladislas defeated and slain at Varna.
       John Hunniades becomes regent.

1526 Buda taken by Solyman II.
       Battle of Mohatz, Aug. 29, Louis II. killed.
       Hungary subject to Austria.

1683 John Sobieski defeats the Turks. Nov. 12.

1686 The Duke of Lorraine retakes Buda.   [19.

1691 Prince Louis of Baden def. the Turks, Aug.

1697 Prince Eugene gains battle of Zenta.

1722 Pragmatic Sanction, authorizing female suc-
       cession to the throne.

1740 Hungarians support Maria Theresa.

1790 Independence of Hungary guaranteed.

1811 Franz Liszt born; dies 1868.

1848 Rebellion against Austria.

1849 Hungary declares itself a free state; Louis
       Kossuth supreme governor.
       Russia assists the Austrians.   [10.
       Defeat of Hungarian army by Haynau, Aug.
       Louis Batthyany, patriot, shot, Oct. 6.

1851 Count Andrassy sentenced to death, Feb. 23;
       subsequently prime minister of Austria.

1861 Liberal constitution promulgated, Feb. 26.

1866 Hungarian legions join the Prussian army.

1867 Restoration of the constitution of 1848.

1868 Congress of Hungarian Jews, Dec. 14.
1873 Buda-Pesth constituted the capital.
1876 Francis Deak, patriot, dies Jan. 28.
1883 Violent anti-Jewish riots, July, Aug.
1885 National exhibition at Buda-Pesth, May 2.
1889 Count Julius Andrassy dies Feb. 18.
1892 General Klapka, hero of Komorn, dies about
    May 17.
1894 Kossuth dies at Turin, March 20; b. 1802.

[See *Austria, Turkey*.]

ITALY.

ROME.

B.C. [Early dates conjectural.]

753 Romulus builds Rome.
750 Romans seize the Sabine women.
747 Rome taken by the Sabines.
716 Romulus said to have been killed by senators.
    Calendar of 10 mos. reformed and made 12.
710 Priesthood, augurs, and vestals instituted.
615 The Capitol founded.
510 Rape of Lucretia by Tarquin.
509 Tarquin II. expelled for tyranny.
    Junius Brutus and Tarquinius first consuls.
507 The Capitol dedicated to Jupiter Capitolinus.
501 Titus Lartius first dictator.
496 Battle of Lake Regillus; defeat of Latins.
494 Secession of Plebeians to Sacred Mount.

491 Coriolanus besieges Rome.
486 First agrarian law passed.
458 Victory of Cincinnatus over the Æquians.
456 Mount Aventine allotted to the Plebeians.
451 Virginius kills his daughter Virginia.
434 War with the Etruscans.
390 The Gauls under Brennus sack Rome.
343 First Samnite war.
340 Latin war.
339 Equal political rights granted the Plebeians.
304 Second Samnite war ; the Samnites sub., 291.
265 Rome supreme in Italy.
264 The first Punic war.
260 First Roman fleet built.
254 Plautus born ; dies 184.
235 Temple of Janus closed.
234 Cato the elder born ; dies 149.
225 The Gauls invade Rome.
213 The Macedonian wars begin.
207 Second Punic war.
185 Death of Scipio Africanus the elder.
    Terence born ; dies 159.
168 Macedon annexed.
167 First public library erected at Rome.
149 Third Punic war begins.
132 Plebeian consuls chosen.
100 Cornelius Nepos flourishes about this time.
 98 Lucretius born ; dies 55.
 94 Catullus born ; dies 54.
 86 Sallust born ; dies 34.

79 Sylla defeats Marius; becomes dictator.
73 Revolt of Spartacus the gladiator.
70 Virgil born; dies 19.
65 Horace born; dies 8.
63 The Catiline conspiracy suppressed by Cicero.
60 First triumvirate, — Cæsar, Pompey, Crassus.
59 Livy born; dies 17 A.D.
58 Cæsar's campaigns in Gaul.
54 Tibullus born; dies 19.
50 War between Pompey and Cæsar.
46 Cato kills himself at Utica; born 95.
    Julius Cæsar reforms the calendar.
44 Cæsar killed in the Senate House, March 15.
43 Ovid born; dies 17 A.D.   [dus.
    Second triumvirate, — Octavius, Antony, Lepi-
    Cicero killed, proscribed by Antony; b. 106.
42 Battle of Philippi, death of Brutus and Cassius.
27 Octavius emperor, as Augustus Cæsar.
 4 The empire at peace with all the world; the
       Temple of Janus shut; Jesus Christ born.
 3 Seneca born; dies 65 A.D.

A.D.
14 Tiberius emperor.
23 Pliny the elder born; dies 79.
35 Quintilian born; dies 96.
37 Caligula emperor; murdered by a tribune.
38 Juvenal born; dies 120.
39 Lucan born; dies 65.
40 Martial born; dies 104.   [wife.
41 Claudius I. emp.; poisoned by Agrippina, his

54 Nero emperor; kills himself, 68.

55 Tacitus b. about this time; d. after 117 (?).

61 Pliny the younger born; dies 115.

62 St. Paul arrives in Rome in bonds.

64 Rome burnt under Nero.

67 Peter and Paul said to have been put to death.

68 Galba emperor : slain by the prætorians.

69 Otho emperor; stabs himself.
Vitellius emperor; put to death by Vespasian.
Vespasian emperor.

72 Suetonius born; dies 140.

75 Coliseum founded by Vespasian.

79 Titus emperor.

81 Domitian, last of the 12 Cæsars, assassinated.

86 Dacian war begins; continues 15 years.

96 Nerva emperor.

98 Trajan emperor; Trajan's column erected, 114.

102 Pliny proconsul in Bithynia.

117 Adrian, or Hadrian, emperor.

138 Antoninus Pius emperor.

161 Marcus Aurelius emperor.

188 The Capitol destroyed by lightning.

222 The Goths are paid tribute.

250 Invasion of the Goths.

269 Great victory over the Goths; 300,000 slain.

284 The era of the martyrs, or of Diocletian.

312 Constantine the Great favors the Christians.

321 Seat of empire removed from Rome to Byzantium.

325 First general council of Christians at Nice.

330	Constantine orders the heathen temples to be destroyed.
334	Revolt of 300,000 Sarmatian slaves.
361	Julian, emperor, abjures Christianity.
364	Empire divided into Eastern and Western. (See *Eastern Empire.*)
410	Rome taken by Alaric.
455	Pillaged by Genseric.
475	Boetius born; dies 525.
476	Odoacer takes Rome.
536	Empire recovered for Justinian by Belisarius.
600	Rome at her lowest state.
728	Independent under the popes.
896	Taken by Arnulf and the Germans.
962	Otho I. crowned at Rome.
1084	City taken by Emperor Henry IV.
1155	Arnold of Brescia put to death as a heretic.
1309	The pope removes to Avignon.
1347	Nicola di Rienzi, tribune, establishes a repub.
1377	Papal court returns to Rome.
1474	Ludovico Ariosto b. (in Reggio); dies 1533.
1483	Raphael Sanzio born (at Urbino); dies 1520.
1494	Correggio born; dies March 5, 1534.
1503	Julius II. conquers the Romagna. [May 6.
1527	Rome captured by Constable de Bourbon,
1581	Domenichino Zampieri born; dies 1641.
1626	St. Peter's dedicated, Nov. 18; begun, 1150.
1693	Barometer invented by Torricelli.
1773	The Jesuits expelled from Rome.
1792	Gioacchimo Rossini b. Feb. 29; d. Nov., 1868.

1798 The French proclaim the Roman Republic, March 20.   [of Italy, May.

1808 Rome annexed by Napoleon to the kingdom

1814 Inquisition re-established, Aug. 7.

1831 "Young Italy" party establ. by Mazzini.

1846 Pius IX. elected pope, June 16.

1848 Insurrection at Rome, Nov. 16.   [24.
The pope escapes from Rome to Gaëta, Nov.

1849 Rome capitulates to the French, June 30.
Re-establishment of the pope's authority, July 15.   .

1855 Important concordat with Austria.

1860 Tuscan volunteers enter the Papal States, May 19.

1864 Encyclical letter of the pope, censuring 80 errors in religion, philosophy, and politics, Dec. 8.

1865 The pope denounces secret societies, Sept. 25.

1866 Law prohibiting Protestant worship enforced, Dec. 31.   [troops, Sept. *et seq.*

1867 Conflicts between Garibaldians and Papal

1868 The pope summons an Œcumenical Council, Dec. 8.

1869 Œcumenical Council opens. Dec. 8.   [18.

1870 Dogma of Papal infallibility adopted, July
The Italian troops enter Rome, Sept. 20.
Rome and its provinces incorporated with the kingdom of Italy, Oct. 9.

1861   Assembly of first Italian parliament, Feb. 26; Victor Emmanuel declared king of Italy, March 14.   [15.

The pope protests against the kingdom, Apr.

Count Cavour dies June 6, aged 52.

1862   Triumphant progress of Garibaldi through Italy, March; taken prisoner, Aug. 29; receives amnesty, Oct. 5.   [mont, June 1.

1863   Cavour canal opened for irrigation of Pied-

1864   Franco-Italian convention signed; Florence to be the capital of Italy, Sept. 15.

1865   600th anniversary of Dante's birth celebrated, May 14.

Bank of Italy established, Nov. 7.

1866   Alliance with Prussia, May 12.

War declared against Austria, June 18.

Italian army defeated at Custozza, June 24.

Venetia ceded to France by Austria, July 3.

Naval bat. near Lissa; Italians def., July 20.

Treaty of peace with Austria, Oct. 12.

1867   Garibaldi invades Roman territories; defeated and captured, Sept. *et seq.*

Italian troops enter Papal territory, Oct. 30.

1868   Prince Humbert marries his cousin Margherita, April 22.

1870   Mazzini arrested, Aug. 14; included in general amnesty to political offenders, Oct. 16; dies March 10, 1872.

1870 Rome declared the capital of Italy, Dec. 5.

1871 The king and ministers remove to Rome, July 1, 2.   [Oct.

1872 Great inundations in the valley of the Po,

1873 Jesuits expelled from Italy, Oct. 20.

1874 Secret assassination societies prevalent.

1875 Garibaldi takes his seat in the Chamber of Deputies, Jan. 24.   [Aug.

Synod of Italian Catholic Church at Naples.

1876 Discovery of a " black book " recording misdeeds of many officials, June.

1878 Victor Emmanuel II. dies Jan. 9 ; buried in the Pantheon at Rome. Jan. 17.

Humbert succeeds to the throne.

Pope Pius IX. dies Feb. 7 ; Leo XIII. elected, Feb. 20.

Attempted assassination of the king, Nov. 17.

1882 Garibaldi dies at Caprera, June 2 ; b. 1807.

1883 International fine art exhibition at Rome. Jan. 21.

1884 Sig. Sella, great finan. minister, d. Mar. 14.

1885 Heavy snowstorms in Piedmont, many villages destroyed, and great loss of life, Jan. 16–28.

War with Abyssinia.   [10.

1886 Marco Minghetti, ex-prime-minister, d. Dec.

1887 Destructive earthquakes at Calabria, etc., Feb. 23 ; Dec. 4.

Defensive treaty of alliance with Austria-Hungary and Germany signed, March 13.

1887 M. Crispi becomes prime minister, Aug.

1888 Fall of vast avalanches in Northern It., Feb.

Capital punishment abolished, June.

1889 Father Gavazzi, church reformer, dies Jan. 9, aged 80.

Benedetto Cairoli, patriot, d. Aug. 8, a. 63.

Treaty with Abyssinia ratified, Oct. 2.

1890 Duke of Aosta dies Jan. 18, aged 44.

1891 Treaty with Great Britain in relation to East Africa signed, April 15.

The Triple Alliance renewed, June 28.

1892 Gen. Cialdini, patriot, dies Sept. 8, aged 81.

1893 The pope's jubilee at Rome, Feb.

1894 Anarchist riots in Carrara, Jan. 16 *et seq.*

1895 Att. Gen. Celli of Milan assassinated, Jan. 7.

Tri-centenary of the death of Tasso celebrated, April 25.

Humbert bridge over the Tiber op., Sept. 22.

1896 Peace concluded with Abyssinia, Oct. 26.

1897 Attempt to assas. King Humbert, Apr. 22.

Pope issues encyclical on Manitoba school question, Dec. 24.

1898 Twentieth anniversary of coronation of Leo XIII., March 1.   [Apr. 4.

Pope offers to mediate in Cuban question,

Bread riots in many places, April–May.

FLORENCE.

[Florence, a portion of the ancient Etruria, formed a part of the Lombard kingdom conquered by Charlemagne. The most important of the Tuscan cities gradually asserted their independence, and were governed by rulers of their own selection, until finally absorbed by Florence.]

1198 Becomes an independent republic.

1215 Wars of the Guelphs and Ghibellines.

1240 Giovanni Cimabue born; dies about 1302.

1265 Dante Alighieri born May 14; dies 1321.

1266 Arts or guilds established.

1276 Giotto Bordone born; dies 1326.

1300 Factions of the Bianchi and Nevi.

1304 Francesco Petrarch born; dies 1374.

1348 Great plague of the Black Death.

1349 "Decamerone" composed by Boccaccio (born in Paris. 1313).

1387 Fra Giovanni Angelico born; dies 1455.

1420 The influence of the Medici begins.

1452 Leonardo da Vinci born; dies 1519. [1517.

1469 Baccio della Porta (Fra Bartolomeo) b.; dies Niccolo Machiavelli born; dies 1527.

1493 Republic proclaimed.

1498 Niccolo Machiavelli chief secretary. Savonarola burned, May 23; born 1452.

1860 Florence annexed to Sardinia.

1864 Florence becomes the capital of Italy.

GENOA.

[Genoa is first mentioned in history during the second Punic war. It was destroyed by Mago, a Carthaginian general, 205 B.C., and rebuilt by the Romans 203 B.C. On the dismemberment of the Latin empire, it fell under the sway of the Lombards, Franks, and Germans successively.]

1000 Genoa becomes a free commercial state.

1284 The Genoese destroy the naval power of Pisa.

1293 Wars between Venice and Genoa.

1339 Simon Boccanegra, the first doge.

1446 Columbus b. about this time, date uncertain.

1522 Sacked by the Spaniards and Italians.

1528 Andrew Doria restores the independence of Genoa.

1797 Genoa becomes the Ligurian Republic.

1805 Annexed to the French empire.

1814 United to the kingdom of Sardinia.

[See *Italy.*]

LOMBARDY.

[The Longobardi (or Langobardi), a Teutonic tribe of obscure origin, descended into Italy about 568, under their king Alboin, and established a kingdom which lasted until 774, when its last king, Desiderius, was dethroned by Charlemagne.]

774 Becomes part of the Carlovingian empire.

843 Created a separate kingdom.

961 Annexed to the German empire.

1167 First Lombard League.

1176 The Lombards defeat Frederic Barbarossa.

1226 Second Lombard League formed.

1540   Spain obtains possession of Lombardy.
1748   Comes into the hands of Austria.
1797   A part of the Cisalpine Republic.
1815   Restored to Austria.
1859   Joined to the new kingdom of Italy.

[See *Italy*.]

MILAN.

[Milan, Mediolanum, capital of the ancient Liguria, now Lombardy, is reputed to have been built by the Gauls, about 408 B.C.]

B.C.

222   Conquered by the Roman consul Marcellus.

A.D.

286   Seat of government of the Western Empire.
452   Plundered by Attila.
489   Included in the Ostrogothic kingdom ; in the Lombard kingdom, 569.
1101   Becomes an independent republic.
1158   The emperor Frederic I. takes Milan.
1162   It rebels ; is taken by Frederic.
1169   Rebuilt and fortified.
1499   Conquered by Louis XII. of France.
1540   Annexed to the crown of Spain.
1714   Ceded to Austria.
1805   Made the capital of the kingdom of Italy.
1848   Insurrection against the Austrians.
1860   Victor Emmanuel enters Milan as king, Aug. 8.

PISA.

[The origin of Pisa is involved in obscurity. Strabo mentions it as one of the bravest of the Etruscan cities. In 225 B.C. it was the friend of the Romans, became their ally, and was finally subjected to their rule. It was one of the most flourishing Italian cities in the Middle Ages.]

1004 Attacked by the Saracens: again in 1011.

1099 Takes part in the second crusade.

1114 Between this date and 1116 the Pisan fleet attacks the Moslems, and rescues a multitude of Christian captives.

1118 War with Genoa, lasting many years.

1174 Construction of Campanile (famous leaning tower) begun.

1222 War with Florence.

1228 The Pisans defeat Lucca and Florence.

1260 Defeat the Tuscan Guelfs at Montaperto.

1284 Sustain crushing defeat from Genoa, Aug. 6.

[For more than two centuries Pisa was engaged in fierce struggles with other Italian cities, and was finally subdued by Florence in 1509.]

1564 Galilei (Galileo) b. Feb. 15; d. Jan., 1642.

1597 Thermometer invented by Galileo.

1604 Galileo constructs a telescope.

1633 Galileo condemned by the Inquisition.

[See *Italy, Florence*, etc.]

SARDINIA.

[Sardinia, an island in the Mediterranean, successively pos-
sessed by the Phœnicians, Greeks, Carthaginians, Romans,
Vandals, Saracens, Genoese, Pisans, Aragonese, and Spaniards.
Victor Amadeus, duke of Savoy, acquired Sardinia in 1720,
with the title of king.]

1708   Sardinia conquered by English naval forces.
1720   Victor Amadeus becomes king.
1849   Charles Albert, king, abdicates, March 23.
         Victor Emmanuel II. king.
1851   Cavour minister of foreign affairs.
1855   Convents suppressed, March 2.
1857   War with Austria; peace, November, 1859.

[For later history, see *Italy*.]

SICILY AND NAPLES.

B.C.

735   Naxos built by the Greeks from Eubœa.
734   Syracuse founded by Archias from Corinth.
579   Agrigentum founded by the Dorians.
405   Dionysius the elder becomes supreme in Sic.
397   Dionysius declares war against Carthage.
387   Dionysius plants colonies in Italy.
343   Timoleon restores the republic.
317   Agathocles overthrows the republic.
263   War with the Romans.
212   Syracuse taken and Archimedes slain.
210   Sicily becomes a Roman province.
135   Servile wars, much slaughter.

73	Tyrannical gov. of Verres, accused by Cicero.
35	Sicily held by Sextus Pompeius.

A.D.

79	Eruption of Vesuvius, Pompeii destroyed.
440	Invasion of the Vandals.
493	Invasion of the Goths under Theodoric.
536	Taken by Belisarius for Greek emperors.
832	Conquered by the Saracens.
1038	Partly recovered by the Greek emperors with assistance of the Normans.
1061	Roger I. takes title of Count of Sicily.
1131	Roger II. crowned king of the Two Sicilies.
1266	Charles of Anjou becomes king.
1282	*Sicilian Vespers*, massacre of the French. Sicily conquered by the kings of Aragon.
1435	Alphonso of Aragon takes pos. of Naples.
1501	Naples and Sicily united to Spain.
1544	Torquato Tasso born in Naples; died 1595.
1615	Salvator Rosa born; dies 1673.
1711	Discovery of buried Herculaneum.
1713	Victor, duke of Savoy, king of Sicily.
1735	Charles of Spain becomes king.
1755	Excavations begun at Pompeii.
1759	Charles abdicates, and is suc. by Ferdinand.
1767	The Jesuits expelled. [lost.
1783	Great earthquake in Messina, 40,000 lives
1799	The French established a republic, Jan 14. The king restored by aid of the British, June.
1805	Fearful earthquake in Naples, thousands per.
1806	Joseph Bonaparte made king, Feb.

1808 Bonaparte abdi. for throne of Spain, June.
Joachim Murat king, July 15.

1815 Kingdom of Two Sicilies restored.
Murat seized and shot, Oct. 13.
Ferdinand abolishes the constitution.

1821 The Austrians invade the kingdom.
Fall of the constitutional government.

1825 Ferdinand d. Jan. 4, having reigned 66 yrs.

1828 Insurrection of the Carbonari in Naples, Aug.

1848 Revolution, rising of the great cities, Jan.
Messina taken by the Neapolitans, Sept. 7.

1849 Catania, Syracuse, and Palermo taken by
assault, April–May.

1860 Garibaldi lands in Sicily, May 11, and as-
sumes dictatorship, May 14; defeats the
Neapolitans in various engagements, May–
July.
New Sicilian constitution proclaimed, Aug. 3.
The Sicilians vote for annexation to Sar-
dinia, Oct. 21.   [19.

1862 Garibaldi estab. a provisional governm't, Aug.

1865 First Eng. Prot. church consecrated, Mar. 11.

1866 Cholera rages in Naples, autumn.

1867 Great eruption of Vesuvius begins, Nov. 12.

1871 Maritime exhibition op. at Naples, Apr. 17.

1872 Revival of brigandage and murder, Aug.

1877 National exhibition of fine arts opened at
Naples, April 8.

1891 Italian national exhib. at Palermo, Nov. 15.

1893 Increase of socialism.

1894 Frequent bloody conflicts.

Destructive earthquake at Messina, Nov. 16.

1895 Disorders cause the suspension of studies in the universities, Feb.

[See *Italy*.]

VENICE.

452 Venice founded by families from Aquileia and Padua.

697 First doge chosen.

811 Rialto made the seat of government.

997 Becomes independent of the Eastern Empire.

1157 Bank of Venice established.

1177 Ceremony of wedding the Adriatic instituted.

1202 The Venetians aid the Crusaders.

1204 Crete purchased.

1229 The four bronze horses by Lysippus brought from Constantinople and placed in St. Mark's.

1263 War with the Genoese; also in 1350–81, 1377, 1380.

1346 Defeats the Hungarians at Zara, July 1.

1355 The doge Marino Faliero beheaded, Apr. 17.

1404 War with Padua.

1428 War against Milan; also 1430.

1461 War with the Turks; loss of many Eastern possessions.

1466 The Venetians take Athens; Cyprus, 1475.

1474 Michel-Angelo Buonarotti born (at Chiusi); dies 1561.

1477 Giorgione born : dies 1511.
Titian born (at Capro del Cadora) ; d. 1576.
1483 Venice excommunicated.
1494 Aldine Press established.
1497 Injured by the discovery of America.
1508 Nearly ruined by the siege of Cambray.
1571 Takes part in the battle of Lepanto.
1592 The Rialto Bridge and the Piazza di San Marco erected.
1651 Naval victories over the Turks. [39.
1683 Recovers part of the Morea ; loses it, 1715–
1775 Antonio Canova b. (at Passagno) ; d. 1822.
1797 Occupied by Bonaparte.
1805 Annexed to the kingdom of Italy. Dec. 26.
1814 Transferred to the empire of Austria.
1830 Declared a free port, Jan. 24. [Manin.
1848 Insurrection ; the city defended by Daniel
1849 Sur. to Austrians after long siege, Aug. 22.
1866 Venetia sur. to France, and transf. to Italy.
[See *Italy*.]

NORWAY.

630 Olaf Trætelia establ. a colony in Vermeland.
940 Haco the Good reigns ; dies 963.
998 Olaf I. establishes Christianity by force.
1066 Harold Hardrada invades England ; slain at Stamford Bridge.
1096 Magnus III. killed in Ireland, 1103. [war.
1136 Numerous competitors for the crown ; civil

1389 Norway united with Denmark, separated 1448, reunited 1450.
1624 Christiania, the modern capital, built.
1814 Given to Sweden by the treaty of Kiel.
1821 Nobility abolished.
1832 Björnstjerne Björnson born.
1873 King Oscar crowned at Drontheim, July 17.
1884 Crown prince of Sweden appointed Viceroy, March 19. [June 10.
1892 Norway desires autonomy in foreign affairs,
1893 Nansen starts for arctic regions, June 24; reaches 86° 14′ N., April 7, 1895; arrives at Christiania, Sept. 9, 1896.
1897 Herr Andrée starts in a balloon for the discovery of the North Pole, July 11.

[See *Sweden, Denmark*.]

POLAND.

842 Piastus, a peasant, elected duke.
992 Christianity introduced.
1080 Boleslas II. murders St. Stanislaus.
1241 Tatar invasion.
1370 Louis of Hungary elected king.
1444 Battle of Varna; Ladislas VI. slain by Turks.
1410 War against the Teutonic knights.
1498 The Wallachians carry off 100,000 Poles, and sell them to the Turks as slaves.
1548 Splendid reign of Sigismund II.

1569 Lithuania incorporated with Poland.

1654 Poland conquered by Swedes and Russians.

1660 Recovers its independence.

1668 John Casimir abdicates.

1683 John Sobieski defeats the Turks at Vienna.

1770 Stanislaus abolishes torture.
Pestilence destroys 250,000 persons.

1772 First partition of the kingdom by Russia, Aust., and Prussia; second partition, 1793.

1794 Rising under Kosciusko, March.   [Nov. 9.
Warsaw and Praga sacked by Suwarrow,

1806 Napoleon enters Warsaw.

1815 Central provinces made the kingdom of Pol.
Cracow a free republic, Nov. 27.

1830 Revolution at Warsaw.

1831 Battles with the Russians.
The insurrection suppressed, Oct. 5.

1832 Poland becomes integral part of Rus. empire.

1846 Cracow annexed to Austria.

1847 Poland declared a Russian province, May.

1861 Prince Gortschakoff governor of Poland.
Great agitation throughout Poland; reign of
terror in Warsaw.

1862 Rigor of Russian government relaxed, April.
Grand Duke Constantine appointed gover-
nor, May 28.   [murdered, Jan. 22.

1863 Insurrection at Warsaw; many Russians
Fruitless intervention of European powers,
June.   [executions.
Mouravieff rules with great severity; many

1866 Church property appropriated, Jan. 9.
1868 Complete union with Rus. effected, Feb. 29.
The Polish language interdicted in public places, July.
1885 Over 30,000 Poles exp. from Prus. Oct.–Nov.
1886 Movement for denationalizing Poland, Feb.
1889 Conciliatory measures towards Polish landowners.
1890 Congress of Polish historians and archæologists at Leopol, July 17.
1892 Emp. William II. of Ger. favors the Poles.
1894 Political demonstration in Warsaw; many arrests, April 16.

[See *Austria*, *Prussia*, *Russia*.]

PORTUGAL.

B.C.

137 The Lusitanians submit to the Roman arms.

A.D.

472 Settlement of Alains and Visigoths.
713 Conquered by the Moors.
1139 Alfonso I. defeats Moors.
1308 University of Coimbra founded.
1415 John I., the Great, invades Africa.
1419 Era of maritime discoveries begins.
1420 Madeira and the Canaries seized.
1433 Lisbon becomes the capital.
1460 Prince Henry, the navigator, dies.

1497 Passage to East Indies discovered by Vasco da Gama, Nov. 20.

1524 Luiz de Camoens born; dies 1579.

1526 The Inquisition established.

1531 University of Evora founded.   [4.

1578 King Sebastian slain at Alcazar, Africa, Aug.

1580 Philip II. of Spain seizes the kingdom.

1640 Yoke of Spain thrown off; John IV., Duke of Braganza, becomes king. Dec.

1668 Treaty of Lisbon, with Spain.

1755 Lisbon destroyed by earthquake, Nov. 1.

1758 The Jesuits expelled.   [by English.

1762 French and Spanish invade Portugal; saved

1792 Queen Maria becomes insane.

1801 War with Spain, March 3; peace, June 6.

1807 Invaded by France; the court sail for Brazil.

1808 Battle of Vimiera; Wellington defeats Junot, Aug. 21.

1809 Oporto taken by Marshal Soult, March 29.

1810 Almeida taken by Massena, Aug. 27; he is defeated at Busaco, Sept. 27; at Fuentes de Onoro, May 5, 1811.

1815 Union of Portugal and Brazil.   [Oct. 1.

1820 Revolution; Constitutional Junta establ.,

1821 Return of the court, July 4.

1826 Dom Pedro abdicates the throne, May 2.

1828 Dom Miguel assumes the title of king, July 4.

1833 Donna Maria proclaimed queen, July 24.

1846 Civil war; the Great Powers assist the queen.

1853 Maria II. dies; Pedro V. succeeds.

1861 Pedro V. dies; Duke of Oporto succeeds, Nov. 11.

1865 International exhibition at Oporto, Sept. 18.

1872 Great fire at Lisbon, June 13.

1882 National art exhib. at Lisbon, about Apr. 15.

1889 Luis I. dies Oct. 19; Carlos succeeds.

1890 Dispute with England in relation to Africa. Anglo-Portuguese difficulties settled, Aug. 20.

1891 Military revolt at Oporto, Jan. 31.

1892 Violent cyclones and gales, Feb. 27, Mar. 6.

1895 Reconciliation with Brazil. Re-organization of the House of Peers.

PRUSSIA.

997 St. Adalbert preaches Christianity; is slain.

1018 Boleslas of Poland ravages the country.

1061 The Prussians renounce Christianity.

1163 Berlin built by a colony of Netherlanders.

1283 The Teutonic Knights subjugate Prussia.

1286 Königsberg made the capital.

1415 Frederick IV. of Nuremberg becomes Margraviate of Brandenburg.

1473 Copernicus b. Feb.; d. May 24, 1543.

1525 Albert of Brandenburg embra. Lutheranism.

1544 University of Königsberg founded.

1608 John Sigismond elector of Brandenburg.

1648 Sir Godfrey Kneller b. Aug. 8; d. Nov. 7, 1723.

1684 George Frederick Händel born Feb. 24; dies April, 1759.

1701 The Order of the Black Eagle instituted.

1740 Frederick II., the Great, reigns.

1756 Seven Years' War begins; ends, 1763.

1757 Battle of Prague, May 6; of Kolin, June 18; of Rosbach, Nov. 5.

1760 An Austrian army marches to Berlin. [War.

1763 Peace of Hubertsburg ends Seven Years'

1767 Karl Wilhelm von Humboldt b.; d. 1835.

1769 Friederich Alexander Humboldt b.; d. 1859.

1770 Ludwig van Beethoven b.; d. 1827.

1786 Frederick the Great dies, Aug. 17.

1792 Frederick William II. invades France.

1805 Kaulbach born Oct. 15; dies 1874.

1806 Prussia joins the allies against France.
Battles of Jena and Auerstadt, Oct. 14.

1807 Peace of Tilsit, July 9.
Formation of the Tugendbund.   [Germany.

1813 The people rise to expel the French from

1819 Marshal Blücher d. Sept. 12, aged 77.

1848 Insurrection in Berlin, March 18.

1849 The king declines the imper. crown, Apr. 29.
Armistice betw. Prus. and Denmark, July 10.

1850 Hanover withdraws fr. Prus. alliance, Feb. 25.
Hesse-Darmstadt withdraws from the Prussian League, June 30.
Treaty of peace with Denmark.

1852 Industrial exhibition at Berlin, May 28.
Repudiates customs' union with Austria.

1858 Prince Frederick William marries Princess Victoria, Jan. 25.

1861 William I. ascends the throne, Jan. 2.

Attempted assassination of the king, July 14.

1862 Bismarck-Schönhausen, premier, Sept. 23.

1863 King resolves to govern without Parliament.

1864 War with Denmark; treaty of peace, Oct. 30.

1865 International exhibition at Cologne, June 2.

1866 Prussia prepares for war with Austria, Mar.

Alliance with Italy, May. [June 14.

1866 Prussia decl. the Germanic Confed. dissolved,

War declared against Hanover and Saxony,

June 15; against Austria, June 18.

Treaty of peace signed at Prague, Aug. 23.

North German Confederation formed, Aug.

1867 North German constitution accepted, May 8.

1868 Naturalization treaty with U. S., Feb. 22.

Workmen's Congress at Berlin, Sept. 26.

1870 French decl. of war rec'd at Berlin, July 15.

North German Parliament engages to support Prussia, July 19.

1870 Day of general prayer in Prussia, July 27.

Strasburg surrenders, Sept. 28.

1871 The king of Prussia proclaimed emperor of Germany, Jan. 18.

[See *Austria, France, Germany, etc.*]

— -

RUSSIA.

376 The Huns invade Russia.

862 Ruric the Norman becomes grand duke.

907 Oleg successfully invades the Greek empire.

988	Vladimir the Great is baptized.
1223	The "Golden Horde" of Tatars conquer a large part of Russia.
1252	The khan of Kaptschak grand duke.
1300	Moscow made the capital.
1380	Tatar war.
1395	Tamerlane invades Russia.
1462	Ivan the Great founds the present monarchy.
1475	Fire-arms and cannon introduced.
1479	Great invasion of the Tatars.
1481	Gen. Svenigorod annihilates their power.
1554	Siberia discovered.
1598	Feodor I., last of the race of Ruric, murdered.
1613	Michael Fedorovitz, a Romanoff, ascends the throne.
1617	Finland ceded to Sweden.
1654	Russian victories in Poland.
1671	The Cossacks subjugated.
1689	Peter the Great sole ruler.
1700	The Russians begin their new year Jan. 1, but retain the old style.
1703	St. Petersburg founded, May 27.
1711	War with Turkey.
1715	Peter the Great visits France, Holland, etc.
1718	The Jesuits expelled.
1730	Peter II., last of the Romanoffs, deposed.
1762	Peter III. dethroned and murdered; Catherine II. reigns.
1774	Rebellion of the Cossacks; suppressed, 1775.
1796	Unsuccessful war with Persia.

1801   Emperor Paul murdered, March.

1805   Russia joins the coalition against France.

1807   Treaty of Tilsit with France, July 7.

1812   War with France renewed, June.

Battle of Smolensko, Aug. 17; Borodino, Sept. 7.

Moscow burnt by the Russians, Sept. 14.

1815   The Holy Alliance formed.

1826   Nicholas I. crowned at Moscow, Sept. 3.

War against Persia, Sept. 28; peace, 1828.

1828   War declared against Turkey, April 26.

1829   Peace of Adrianople, Sept. 14.

1830   War against Poland. (See *Poland.*)

1849   Assists Austria in subduing Hungary.

1850   Harbor of Sebastopol completed, Feb.

1853   War declared against Turkey.

1854   War with France and England.   [22.

Bombardment of Odessa by allied fleet, Apr.

Battle of the Alma, Sept. 20.

Siege of Sebastopol begins, Oct. 17.

Battle of Balaklava, "Charge of the Light Brigade," Oct. 25.

Russian attack at Inkerman, Nov. 5.

1855   Emperor Nicholas I. dies, March 2.

Alexander II. emperor.

Attack on the Malakhoff and Redan, June 18.

The Russians retire from Sebastopol; the allies enter the city, Sept. 8 *et seq.*

Gen. Mouravieff captures Kars, Nov. 26.

1856   Destruction of Sebastopol docks, Feb. 1.

1856 Treaty of peace concluded at Paris, Mar. 30.
The Crimea evacuated, July 9.

1858 Partial emancipation of the serfs, July 2.

1861 Decree for the total emancipation of the serfs,
Feb. 19. [20.

1862 Nesselrode, chancellor of the empire, d. Mar.

1863 Termination of serfdom, March 3.

1864 Emigration of Caucasian tribes into Turkey,
April. [Dec.
Serfdom abol. in Trans-Caucasian provinces,

1865 The cesarevitch Nicholas d. at Nice, Apr. 24.

1866 Inauguration of trial by jury, Aug. 8.
War with Bokhara.

1867 Russian America sold to the U. S., Mar. 13.

1868 Samarcand taken by Kaufmann, May 26.

1871 Schamyl, Circassian chief, dies, April.
Electric telegraph between Russia and Japan
completed, Nov.

1873 Khiva captured, June 10. [27.
Turcomans defeated at Tschandyr, July 25,

1874 Grand Duchess Marie marries Duke of Edinburgh, Jan. 23. [29.

1876 Baltic provinces incorp. with the empire, Jan.

1877 War declared against Turkey, April 24.
Insurrection in the Caucasus, May 18 *et seq.*

1878 Treaty of peace signed at San Stefano; ratified at St. Petersburg, Mar. 17.
Spread of Nihilism in the empire.

1879 Prince Demetrius Krapotkine assas., Feb. 21.
The poll-tax abolished by ukase, April.

1879   Attempted assassination of the Czar, Apr. 14.

1880   Many Nihilists imprisoned and executed.

1881   Czar Alexander II. assassinated, March 13.

Alexander III. becomes emperor.

Treaty of peace with China, April.

Treaty with Persia signed, Dec. 22.

1882   Gen. Kaufmann dies May 16, aged 64.

General Scobeleff, the hero of Plevna, dies July 7, aged 39.

Exhib. of Russian arts and manufactures, summer.

1883   Prince Gortschakoff dies Mar. 11, aged 85.

Grand funeral of Tourgénieff, at St. Petersburg, Oct. 9.

1884   Gen. Todleben dies July 1 ; born 1818.

1885   Great discontent among workingmen and peasantry, Jan.

Ship canal from St. Petersburg to Cronstadt opened, May 27.

Fighting with the Afghans.

Trouble with the British government ; Denmark arbitrates.

Afghan boundaries fixed, Sept. 10.

1886   Russia interferes in Bulgaria, Sept.–Dec.

1887   Baron Hirsch gives £2,000,000 to establish Jewish primary schools in Russia, Dec.

Universities closed ; students in a state of rebellion, Nov.–Dec.

1888   Central Asian railway opened, May.

Great epidemic of influenza, Nov., Dec.

1890 Persecutions of the Jews; protested against
by Tolstoï and many literary men.

Danilesky, historian and novelist, d. Dec. 24.

1891 Gontcharoff, popular nov., d. Sept. 27, a. 80.

On account of severe famine, czar forbids all
state balls and festivities, Oct.

1892 Count Tolstoï, novelist and reformer, active
in relief of distressed people, March.

Provisions to relieve famine received from
America, etc.

Great outbreak of cholera. 260,000 deaths.

1893 Tariff war bet. Russia and Germany, Aug.

Tschaikowsky, musical composer, honored
with state funeral. Nov. 9.

1894 Alexander III. dies Nov. 1, aged 49.

Nicholas II. becomes czar, Nov. 1.

Anton Rubinstein dies Nov. 20, aged 65.

1895 Nicholas II. proclaims his adherence to principle of autocracy, Jan. 29.

A scientific expedition sent to Abyssinia, Jan.

Diplomatic relations op. with Abyssinia, July.

Extensive Nihilist conspiracy disc., Sept.

Decision to abolish private liquor saloons
throughout the empire.

Increased persecution of the Jews.

1896 First official census of the empire, Feb. 10.

Czar assumes direct control of Russ. policies.

Formal coronation of Nicholas II., May 26.

Great disaster on Khodynski Pl., over 3,000
persons crushed to death or wounded.

1896	First "strike" in Russ., textile workers, June.
1897	Exiles to Siberia to go by railway, April.
	Judicial reform in Siberia, July. [25.
1898	100 naval officers arrested for bribery, Mar.

— ---

SAXONY.

[The Saxons, a Teutonic tribe, are first mentioned by Ptolemy as occupying a part of the Cimbrian peninsula, the district now known as Holstein.]

457	Saxons under Hengist land in Britain.
531	Ger. Saxons join Franks against Thuringians.
785	Witikind, the Saxon leader, baptized.
792	Second Saxon war breaks out.
843	Louis the German governs Saxony.
880	Otto the Illustrious duke of Saxony.
919	Henry the Fowler founds the line of Saxon emperors of Germany.
1073	Saxons hostile to the Franconian emperors.
1087	Make peace with Emperor Henry IV.
1106	Lothair, Count of Supplinburg, duke.
1125	Lothair placed on the imperial throne.
1127	Henry the Proud duke of Saxony.
1423	Frederic, margrave of Meissen, first elector.
1429	Country ravaged by the Hussites.
1485	The electorate divided, resulting in the formation of two Saxon lines, Ernestine and Albertine. [supporter of Luther, d. 1525.
1486	Frederic the Wise elector, an illus. prince,
1502	University of Wittenberg founded.

1517 Luther's theses published, Oct. 31; Saxony the cradle of the Reformation.·

1518 Melanchthon prof. in Univ. of Wittenberg.

1525 John elector, a leader of Schmalkald League.

1542 First coal-mine opened.

1547 Maurice, of the Albertine line, elector.

1552 Maurice secures religious freedom through-out Germany.

1553 Augustus I., elector, develops the country.

1629 The elector George joins Gustavus Adolphus.

1632 Wallenstein enters Saxony.   [Nov. 16. Battle of Lützen, Gustavus Adolphus killed,

1648 War ends; population had decreas'd one-half.

1691 John George, the last Protestant elector.

1697 Frederic Augustus I. becomes king of Po-land; the connection disastrous to Saxony.

1706 Augustus gives up the throne of Poland.

1710 Manufacture of porcelain begun at Meissen.

1722 Moravian Brethren settle at Hernhut.

1755 Samuel Hahnemann born April; dies 1843.

1756 Saxony suffers in the "Seven Years' War."

1763 Fred. Augustus III. elector; bec. king, 1806.

1770 Torture abolished.

1796 Treaty of neutrality with France.

1806 Shares the defeat of the Prussians at Jena. Enters the Confederation of the Rhine.

1810 Hahnemann's "Organum of Medicine" (Ho-mœopathy) published.

1813 The Saxon troops desert Napoleon at the battle of Leipsic, and join the allies.

1815 The northern portion annexed to Prussia.

[From the partition of 1815 to the war of 1866 the history of Saxony is mainly a narrative of the slow growth of constitutionalism and popular liberty.]

1849 Uprising in Dresden, barricades erected, May.

1852 Von Beust prime minister; hostile to Prus.

1854 John becomes king: a translator of Dante.

1866 Joins the Austrians against Prussia; occupied by Prussia.   [eration.

Compelled to enter the North Ger. Confed-

1877 Leipsic chosen the seat of the Supreme Court of Law for the German Empire.

[See *Germany*.]

SERVIA.

1159 Stephen Nemanya founds the Racian dynasty.

1336 Stephen Dushan subdues Bulgaria.

1371 The Servians defeated by the Turks.

1459 Subdued by Sultan Mahomet II.

1718 Ceded to Austria; regained by Turkey, 1739.

1806 Rebels, and captures Belgrade.   [1816.

1807 Kara George estab. a governm't; executed,

1829 Alexander Milosch I. recognized as hereditary prince by the sultan, Aug. 15.

1861 Movement to render Servia independent of Turkey.

1862 Turkey grants liberal concessions.

1868 Prince Michael assass. in Belgrade, June 10. Milan IV. succeeds.

1876   Servia declares war against Turkey, July 1.

1877   Peace with Turkey ratified, March 4.

      Servians again declare war against Turkey, Dec. 14.

1878   Proclamation of peace and national independence at Belgrade, Aug. 22.   [6.

1882   Milan proclaimed king by the Assembly, Mar.

1885   Panslavist agitation, Sept.

      War declared against Bulgaria, Nov. 13.

1886   Peace signed, March 3; ratified by the sultan, March 13.

1888   The king divorced from Queen Natalie on political grounds, Oct.   [Mar. 6.

1889   King Milan abdicates; Alex. proclaimed,

1893   Reconciliation of king and queen, Jan. 19.

1894   King Milan's divorce annulled, March 18.

1895   Queen Natalie returns to Belgrade, May 10.

SPAIN.

B.C.

360   Carthaginians settle in Spain.

212   War between the Romans and Carthaginians.

207   The Carthaginians driven out of Spain.

 60   Pompey governs Spain.

A.D.

409   Conquered by the Vandals, Alani, and Suevi.

414   Adolphus founds the kingdom of the Visigoths.

452   Theodoric I. vanquishes the Suevi.

711 Rodrigo, last of the Gothic kings, killed in battle.

Establishment of the Saracens at Cordova.

873 Sancho Iñigo, count of Navarre.

1035 The kingdom of Aragon begins.

1091 The Saracens call in the Moors from Africa.

1094 Dynasty of the Almoravides at Cordova; ends, 1144.

1099 Death of the Cid Rodrigo. [Moors.

1238 The kingdom of Granada begun by the

1253 The Alhambra founded by Mohammed I.

1274 The crown of Navarre passes to France.

1327 Arrival of 200,000 Moors to assist Granada.

1340 Battle of Tarifa; defeat of the Moors.

1474 Las Casas born; dies 1566.

1479 Aragon and Castile united.

1480 Establishment of the Inquisition.

1492 Persecution and expulsion of the Jews.

Columbus sent to explore western world, Aug. 3.

1499 Mohammedans persecuted and expelled.

1503 Garcilasso de la Vega born; dies 1536.

1516 House of Austria acquires the crown of Spain.

1517 Cardinal Ximenes dies; born 1431.

1519 Charles I. elected emp. of Ger. as Charles V.

1534 Society of Jesus founded by Loyola.

1547 Cervantes born; dies 1616.

1554 Philip II. marries Mary of England, July 25.

1561 Great persecution of Protestants.

1562 Carpio Felix Lope da Vega born; dies 1635.

1571 Victory over the Turks at Lepanto.

1598 Philip III. banishes the Moors.

1599 Velasquez born, June; dies Aug. 6, 1660.

1601 Calderon born; dies 1687.

1617 Murillo born; dies April 3, 1682.

1700 Accession of Philip V., House of Bourbon; gives rise to " War of the Succession."

1702 War of the Succession begins; ends, 1713.

1713 Siege of Barcelona.

1762 War with England.

1797 Battle off Cape St. Vincent.

1808 The French take Madrid, March.
Joseph Bonaparte king.   [Jan. 16.

1809 Battle of Corunna, death of Sir John Moore,

1811 Wellington defeats Massena, May 5.

1813 The French totally def. at Vittoria, June 21.
Wellington defeats Soult, Oct. 8.

1817 Slave-trade abolished for a compensation.

1830 Salique law abolished, March 29.
Carlist and Christina parties formed.

1834 Isabella II. suc. to the throne, Apr. 22; deposed, Sept. 29, 1868; abdi.. June 25, 1870.

1837 The monasteries dissolved.

1842 Insurrection at Barcelona.

1843 Success of the revolutionists.

1846 Marriage of the queen to the Duke of Cadiz.

1851 Death of Godoy. "Prince of Peace." Oct. 4.

1854 Military insur. under O'Donnell, June 28.

1859 War with Morocco; peace. March 26, 1860.

1861 Annexation of St. Domingo ratified. May 19.

1861   Intervention in Mexico, Dec. 8.

1862   Much church property in course of sale, Apr.

1864   Rupture with Peru, Apr.; peace, Jan. 27, 1865.

1865   Dispute with Chile.

      Spanish ship *Covadonga* captured by the Chileans, Nov. 26.

1866   Military insur. headed by Gen. Prim, Jan. 3.

      Military revolt in favor of Prim, June; quelled with much bloodshed by Marshals O'Donnell and Narvaez.

      Freedom of the press abolished, Aug.–Sept.

      Re-estab. of tranquillity declared, Oct. 3.

      Public instruc. placed under the clergy, Oct.

1867   Death of Marshal O'Donnell, Nov. 5.

1868   Death of Marshal Narvaez, April 23.

      Marshal Serrano and others exiled about July 10.

      Insurrection begins in the fleet, Sept. 18.

      Prim announces a provisional gov't, Sept. 19.

      Deposition of the queen declared, Sept. 29.

      Freedom of religious worship declared, Oct. 12, 13.

      Insurrections against the provisional gov.

1869   The Cortes votes for a monarchy, May 21.

1870   Isabella II. abdicates, June 25.

      Leopold of Hohenzollern nominated king, July 6; resigns, July 12.   [Nov. 17.

      Amadeus, Duke of Aosta, proclaimed king,

      General Prim shot by assassins, Dec. 27; dies Dec. 30, aged 56.

1871 Sagasta prime minister, Dec. 21.

1872 Insurrection of Carlists, April *et seq.*
Attempted assas. of king and queen, July 18.
Red Republican rising at Ferrol, Oct. 11.

1873 King Amadeus resigns. Feb. 11.
Risings of the Carlists throughout Spain.
The Federal Republic proclaimed, June 8.
Castelar virtually dictator, Sept. 15.

1874 Marshal Serrano president of ministry.
Constant battles with the Carlists.
Alfonso XII. proclaimed king, Dec. 29.

1875 Civil war continues throughout the year.

1876 Don Carlos surrenders, Feb. 27.
The pope opposes religious toleration, April.
Jews (expelled in 1492) petition for re-admission, April.   [Sept.
Repression of Protestant public worship,

1878 The king marries his cousin Mercedes, Jan.
23; Queen Mercedes dies June 26.
End of insur. in Cuba announced, Feb. 21.

1879 Espartero, duke of Vittoria. dies Jan. 8.
King m. Maria Christina of Austria, Nov. 29.
Attempted assassination of king and queen,
Dec. 30.

1881 Russian Jews permitted to come to Spain.
New railway between Madrid and Lisbon
opened, Oct. 8.

1883 Sagasta at head of ministry.

1884 Fall of the Alcudia railway bridge; great
loss of life, April 26.

1884 Severe earthquakes, Dec. 25-31.

1885 Cholera breaks out at Valencia, May.
Alfonso XII. dies Nov. 25.
Marshal Serrano dies Nov. 26.

1886 Bishop of Madrid assassinated, April 19.
Alfonso XIII. born May 17.
Destructive cyclone at Madrid, May 12.

1887 Philippine exhibition at Madrid, Oct. 17.

1888 Republican outbreaks at various places.

1889 Trial by jury first put in force, May 29.
Dispute with Morocco settled, Sept. 29.

1890 Strike of 40,000 workmen in Barcelona, etc.,
March 30.

1891 Great floods and inundations, Sept. 11 *et seq.*

1892 Anarchist riots at Xeres, etc., Feb. 10.

1893 Destructive floods, great loss of life, Sept. 15.
War with Morocco, Oct.; ends Feb. 23, 1894.

1894 Señor Cabrera, first bishop of Spanish Reformed Church, consecrated, Sept. 23.

1895 *Reina Regente*, cruiser, sunk, 400 lives lost,
about March 10.

1896 Personal fracas in the Senate, May 21.
Bomb expl. in crowd in Barcelona, June 7.

1897 Barcelona anarchists executed, June 7.
Assassination of Premier Canovas del Cas-
tillo, Aug. 8.
Señor Sagasta prime minister, Oct. 2. [23.
Scheme of Cuban autonomy approved, Nov.

1898 The cabinet votes an extraordinary war
credit, April 13.

1898 U. S. minister Woodford leaves Madrid, Apr. Declares that war exists with U. S., Apr. 24. Serious food riots, May 5. [Nov. 28. Accepts terms of peace proposed by U. S., American and Spanish commissioners sign treaty of peace at Paris, Dec. 10.

[See *Spanish America*.]

SWEDEN.

1000 Olaf introduces Christianity.
1168 Waldemar I. of Den. destroys pagan temples.
1260 Stockholm founded.
1319 The crown of Sweden made elective.
1363 Albert of Mecklenburg reigns.
1397 Sweden united to Denmark and Norway.
1476 University of Upsal founded.
1520 Nobility murdered by Christian II. of Den.
1521 Gustavus Vasa throws off the Danish yoke.
1523 Gustavus Vasa ascends the throne.
1527 Lutheranism introduced.
1544 The crown made hereditary.
1611 Gustavus Adolphus becomes king.
1628 Gustavus heads the Protestants in Germany; killed at battle of Lützen, Nov. 16. 1632.
1633 Christina queen ; abdicates. June 16, 1654.
1660 Arts and sciences begin to flourish.
1666 University of Lund founded.
1688 Emanuel Swedenborg born Jan. 29; dies March 29, 1772.

1699   Charles XII. begins to reign.

1700   Battle of Narva; defeat of Rus., Nov. 30.

1709   Swedes defeated at Pultowa.

1713   Charles a prisoner to the Turks.   [Dec. 11.

1718   Siege of Frederickshald, Charles XII. killed,

1719   Queen Ulrica abolishes despotism.

1741   Royal Academy founded by Linnæus.

1772   Despotism re-established by Gustavus III.

1792   Gustavus III. assassinated, March 16.

1809   Gustavus IV. dethroned; Charles XIII. succeeds, March 13.
Representative constitution estab., June 7.

1813   Sweden joins alliance against Napo., Mar. 13

1814   Norway ceded to Sweden, Jan. 14.

1818   Bernadotte, French marshal, king, as Charles John XIV.

1844   Oscar I. king, March 8.

1860   Increased religious toleration.

1864   Inauguration of free trade, Jan. 1.
National Scandinavian Society founded, Dec.

1870   Neutrality in the Franco-Prussian war proclaimed, Aug. 4.   [Nordenskjöld.

1879   Northeast passage discovered by Professor

1888   Prince Oscar marries Miss Munck, Mar. 15.

1893   Celebration of 300th anniversary of Reformation, Sept. 5–7.

1894   Birth of Adolphus celebrated throughout Sweden, Dec. 9.   [19.

1897   Jubilee celebration of King Oscar, Sept. 18.
Scandinavian exhibition at Stockholm, Oct.

SWITZERLAND (HELVETIA).

909   Helvetia ravaged by the Huns.

1032   Becomes subject to Germany.

1191   Berne built.

1306   Period ascribed to William Tell; doubtful.

1307   Confederation against Austria.

1315   Battle of Morgarten, defeat of Aust., Nov. 15.

1332   Lucerne joins the Confederacy.

1350   Zurich becomes head of the League.

1351   Berne, Glaris, and Zug join the Confederacy.

1386   Battle of Sempach, defeat of the Austrians.

1388   The Austrians defeated at Näfels, April 9.

1400   League of the Grisons : second League, 1424 ;
       third League, 1436.

1444   Battle of St. Jacob's, 1,600 Swiss and 10.000
       French killed, Aug. 26.

1476   The Swiss defeat Charles the Bold, March 5,
       June 22.

1480   Swiss soldiers first enter service of France.

1481   Fribourg and Soleure join the Confederacy.

1484   Ulrich Zwingli b. Jan. 1 ; killed Oct. 12, 1531.

1499   Maximilian I. acknowledges Swiss ind.

1501   Schaffhausen and Basle join Confederacy.

1519   The Reformation begins at Basle.

1531   Battle of Cappel, Oct. 12.

1544   The Grisons Leagues join Swiss Confederacy.

1597   Appenzell joins the Confederacy.

1602   Geneva attacked by Charles Emanuel of
       Savoy, who is defeated.

1648 Independence of Switzerland recognized by treaty of Westphalia.

1712 Peace of Aargau, end of religious war.

1777 Alliance with France, May 25.   [parties.

1781 Strife in Geneva bet. aristocratic and dem.

1782 Fugitive Genevese seek asylum in Ireland.

1792 Swiss Guards ordered to quit France.

1798 Helvetic Confederation subjugated by Fr.
Helvetian Republic formed.

1799 Switzerland the seat of European war.
The number of cantons increased to 19.
Uri, Schweitz, and Underwald separate from the Republic.

1815 The number of cantons increased to 22.
Independence and neutrality of Switzerland secured by treaty of Vienna.

1846 The Roman Catholic cantons form a separate league (Sonderbund).   [Oct. 7:
Insur. at Geneva against Jesuit teaching,

1847 Civil war, end of the Sonderbund.

1848 New Federal constitution, Sept. 12.

1860 Swiss forbidden to enter foreign service without permission.

1861 Territorial disputes with France.   [28.

1865 Intern. Social Science Cong. at Berne, Aug.

1867 Workmen's International Congress at Lausanne, Sept. 2–7.
International Peace and Liberty Congress meets at Geneva, Sept. 9–12 ; at Berne, Sept. 22–26, 1868.

1872 M. Favre engaged to construct tunnel through St. Gothard in 8 years for £2,000,000, Aug. 8.   [June.

1874 Swiss National Catholic Church constituted, Intern. Postal Congress at Berne, Sept. 15.

1878 James Fazy, eminent statesman, dies Nov. 6.

1882 Opening of St. Gothard railway from Milan to Lucerne, May 20, 21.

1884 National exhib. at Zurich, May. 1–Dec. 27.

1890 Destructive storms and much distress, Aug. 18–23.   [Aug. 18.

1892 Great fire at Grindelwald. near Interlachen,

1895 Carl Schenk, six times president of the Confederation, dies from accident, July 18.

Declares against centralization of the military power, Nov. 3.   [20.

1898 Votes to take gov. control of railways, Feb.

TURKEY.

1299 The Ottoman empire founded by Osman, or Othman.

1330 Turks conquer Nicæa.

1346 The Morea conquered.

1361 Adrianople taken by Amurath I. (?).

1362 Amurath I. remodels the Janissaries.

1389 Bajazet I. overruns the Eastern Empire.

1396 He defeats the Hungarians at Nicopolis, Sept. 28.

1402	Bajazet I. defeated and made prisoner by Tamerlane the Tatar.
1430	Macedonia annexed.
1444	Battle of Varna. (See *Hungary*.) [29.
1453	Constantinople taken by Mehemet II., May
1458	Greece subjected to the Turks.
1480	Otranto taken.
1515	Selim I. overruns Syria. [Egypt.
1516	Selim defeats the Mamelukes, and gains
1521	Solyman takes Belgrade; Rhodes, 1522.
1571	Battle of Lepanto, maritime power of Turkey destroyed.
1637	War with the Cossacks.
1669	Candia (Crete) taken, after 25 years' siege.
1683	Mahomet IV. besieges Vienna.
1703	Mustapha II. deposed by Janissaries.
1717	The Turks lose Belgrade; retaken, 1739.
1745	Defeat of the Turks at Kars.
1770	Great sea-fight in channel of Scio; Russian victory.
1784	The Crimea ceded to Russia, January.
1787	Disastrous war with Austria and Russia; ends 1791.
1798	War with the French in Egypt.
1803	Insurrection of Mamelukes at Cairo.
1807	War against Russia and England.
1809	The Russians defeated at Silistria.
1821	Greek patriarch put to death in Constantinople, April 23.
1826	Massacre of the Janissaries, June 14–16.

1827 Battle of Navarino, the Turkish fleet destroyed, Oct. 20.

1828 War with Russia.

1829 Treaty of peace at Adrianople, Sept. 14.

1830 Turkey acknowledges the independence of Greece, April 25.

Treaty with America, May 7.   [21.

1832 Defeated at Konieh by Ibrahim Pacha, Dec.

1833 The Russians enter Constantinople, April 3.

Treaty with Russia, offensive and defensive, July 8.

1838 Office of Grand Vizier abolished, March 30.

1849 Christians admitted to office, June.

1853 War declared against Russia, Oct. 5.

1854 Rupture with Greece ; conflicts ensue.

1856 Free exercise of religion authorized, Feb. 18.

Great Britain, France, and Austria guarantee integrity of Turkish empire, April 15.

1857 Austrians quit the principalities, March.

1858 Massacre of Christians at Jedda, June 15.

Indecisive conflicts with the Montenegrins, July.

Turkish financial reforms begun, August.

First railway op. from Aidan to Smyrna, Sept. 19.   [Nov. 8.

The Montenegrin boundaries determined,

1859 Electric telegraph completed between Aden and Suez, May.   [destroyed, Sept. 10–14.

Great fire at Constantinople, 1,000 houses

Ill treatment of Christians, May, June.

1861 Christians revolt in Herzegovina, March.

1862 Peace with Montenegro, Sept. 23. [26.

1863 Exhibition of the produce of the empire, July

1864 Great immigration of Caucasian tribes, Apr.

1865 Cholera at Constantinople, nearly 50,000 deaths, August. [Jan. 1867.

Revolt of the Maronites, Dec. 30 ; suppressed,

1866 Revolution in Bucharest.

1867 Omar Pacha, commander of the Turkish army, dies April, 1871.

1868 Dispute with Greece in relation to Crete.

1869 System of compulsory education promulgated, Oct.

Inauguration of the Suez Canal, Nov. 17.

1870 Great fire at Pera, over 7,000 houses burned, June 5. [Oct. 23.

1871 Tunis made an integral part of the empire,

1875 Insurrection in Herzegovina, July–August.

1876 Insurrection in Bulgaria suppressed, May.

Riots in Constantinople, May 10.

Declaration of war by Servia and Montenegro, July 1, 2 ; continued fighting.

Atrocities in Bulgaria, August.

1877 First Turkish Parliament opened, March 19.

War with Russia, April. [28,

Holy war against Russia propounded, May

1878 Treaty of peace with Russia, March 3.

1880 Diplomatic negotiations with European powers throughout the year.

1881 Thessaly ceded to Greece, July 2.

1883 Difficulties with Greek Church, Dec.–Jan. 1884.

1884 Midhat Pacha, statesman, dies May, a. 62.

1885 Turkey asks assistance of Great Powers to settle Roumelian question. [a. 64.

1886 Hobart Pacha, Turkish admiral, d. June 19,

1888 Direct railway communication opened between Calais and Constantinople, August.

1889 Troubles in Servia and Armenia. [June 22.

1890 British yarn-spinning factory op. at Constan.,

1891 Musurus Pacha, diplomatist, 33 years ambassador at London, d. Feb. 12, a. 84.

1894 Diplomatic relations suspended with the Powers in relation to Armenia, Dec. 9.

1895 Commission appointed for reforms in Armenia, June 29. [4; treaty ratified, Dec. 16.

1898 Final treaty of peace with Greece signed, Dec.

WÜRTEMBERG.

1241 Ulrich the first authentic count.

1495 Raised to the dignity of an imperial duchy.

1520 Conquered by Bavaria and sold to Austria.

1534 Recovers its rank as a duchy.
The Reformation introduced.

1571 Johann Kepler born; dies 1630. [etc.

1688 Devastated by French armies, also in 1692,

1699 Offers a home to the exiled Waldensians.

1805 Takes arms on the side of France.

1806 Frederic I. assumes the title of king.

1813 Deserts France, and joins the allies.

1848 A new liberal constitution granted.

1851 The constitution of 1819 reinstituted.

1864 Enters the German Customs Union.

1866 Takes up arms on behalf of Austria.
Defeated by the Prussians.   [France.

1870 Shares in the German enthusiasm against
Becomes part of the German empire.

[See *Germany*.]

ASIA.

[The reputed cradle of the human race, about 4004 before Christ; Noah's deluge is assigned by the old authorities to the year 2348 B.C. Modern science has rejected this chronology, and the subject of the early history of the world is a matter of doubt and mystery.]

AFGHANISTAN.

[A large district in Central Asia, the early history of which is very obscure. Native chroniclers claim descent from the lost tribes of Israel. It formed successively parts of the Persian and Greek empires.]

1200 Early Afghan conquests in India begin.

1221 Conquests of Genghis Khan; of Tamerlane, 1398.

1525 Sultan Baber conquers Cabul.

1720 The Afghans invade Persia.

1738 Nadir Shah of Persia subdues the country.

1826 Dost Mohammed Khan becomes ameer.

1838 Dethroned by the Brit.; Suja Shah restored.

1841 British occupy Cabul; revolt of Afghans.

1842 British army destroyed in the Khyber pass, Jan. 6–13. [Sept. Sir George Pollock forces the Khyber pass, Dost Mohammed, ameer, friendly to the Brit.

1863 Shere Ali becomes ameer.

1878 Shere Ali signs a treaty with Russia, Aug. Gen. Roberts gains vic. at Peiwar pass, Dec. 2.

1879 Yakoob Khan recognized as ameer; continuous fighting.

1880 Constant fighting bet. British and Afghans.
1881 Civil war bet. the ameer and Ayoob Khan.
Abdur-Rahman virtual ruler of all Afghanistan, Oct. [cand, July.
1888 Central Asian railroad finished to Samar-
1891 Great Britain and Russia dispute respecting
the Pamir frontier, Sept.–Oct.

— — — —

ARABIA.

B.C.
24 Invaded by Gallus, Roman gov. of Egypt.
A.D.
529 Abyssinians invade Yemen.
570 Mohammed born at Mecca.
610 The Koran begun; finished, 632.
611 Mohammed announces himself as a prophet.
622 He flees to Medina (the " Hegira "), July 15.
The Mohammedan Arabs, termed Saracens,
begin their career of conquest.
630 Mohammed acknowledged as a sovereign;
dies June 8, 632.
634 Omar chosen ruler; assas. 644; Othman suc.
656 Othman mur. by Ali, who usurps the throne.
660 Ali assassinated; succeeded by Muawwyah.
Damascus made capital of the empire.
750 Merwan, last of Ommiade caliphs, killed.
The good days of Arabia ended.
929 Mecca stormed by Suleyman Abu-Jahir.
1171 Last Fatimite caliph dethroned by Saladin.

1517   Sultan Selim I. receives investiture of Mohammedan caliphate.

1630   Yemenite chief Khasim expels the Turks.

1787   Abd-el-Wahhab, founder of the Wahhabees, d.

1803   Mecca taken by the Wahhabees.

1811   Mehemet Ali begins contest with Wahhabees.

[The later history of Arabia has been a succession of revolts and massacres.]

ASSYRIA.   •

[Originally Assur, between Mesopotamia and Media, was the seat of the earliest recorded monarchy. The chronologists differ greatly in the dates, many of which are now considered mythical.]

B.C.

2245   Nimrod, or Belus, reigns.

2059   Ninus, king of Assyria, takes Babylon.

2007   Semiramis usurps the government.

1446   Belochus, last king of the race of Ninus.

1140   Tiglath-pileser, the real founder of the Assyrian empire.

858   Shalmaneser II. makes large conquests.

823   The empire enlarged by Samas-Rimmon II.

763   A solar eclipse recorded.   [empire.

745   Pul usurps the throne, and consolidates the

705   Sennacherib ascends the throne.   [pire.

680   Esar-haddon reigns, and reorganizes the em-

606   Assyria becomes a Median province.

332   Subdued by Alexander the Great.

A.D.

1637 Conquered by the Turks.

1835 Explored by Col. Chesney.

1848 Layard's " Discoveries " published.

1875 " Assyrian Discoveries," by Geo. Smith, pub.

BABYLONIA.

B.C.

2234 Earliest astronomical observations.

747 Nabonassar governor.

729 Conquered by Pul, king of Assyria.   [king.

722 Becomes independent, Merodach-baladan II.

720 Lunar eclipses observed and recorded by Ptolemy.

705 Sargon king, expelled by Sennacherib.

640 Nabopolassar seizes the gov.; king, 625.

604 Nebuchadnezzar king; his acts recorded in the Bible.

551 Nabonadius king.   [sians, 538.

539 Belshazzar king, slain by Medes and Per-

518 Babylon revolts, and is taken by Darius.

331 Conquered by Alexander, who dies there, 323.

312 Seleucus Nicator transfers the seat of government to Seleuca; Babylon is deserted.

140 Conquered by the Parthians, and becomes part of the Persian empire.

A.D.

650 Conquered by the Mohammedans, and becomes seat of the caliphs till 1258, since 1638 subject to Turkey.

CHINA.

B.C.

2356 Yaou extends the empire.

1123 The Chow dynasty begins with Woo-Wang.

1115 Mariner's compass said to have been invented.

551 Confucius born ; dies 478.

255 Tsin dynasty enthroned.   [finished, 204.

246 Che Hwang-te rules ; builds the " great wall,"

202 Literature and the art of printing encouraged.

15 The religion of Laot-se begun.

A.D.

68 The religion of Fô introduced.

420 Nankin becomes the capital.

635 Nestorian Christians permitted to preach.

845 Christians proscribed and extirpated.

1260 Seat of government transferred to Peking.

1275 Marco Polo introduces missionaries.

Kublai Khan establishes the Mongol dynasty.

1368 Ming dynasty.

1517 Europeans first arrive in Canton.

1616 Manchu Tatars begin conquest of the country ; their rule established, 1643.

1600 Tea first brought to England.

1662 Earthquake buries 300,000 people at Peking ; 100,000 in 1731.   [32.

1692 Jesuit missionaries preach : expelled, 1724-

1812 Edict against Christianity.

1834 Opium dispute begins with Great Britain.

1839 Hong-Kong taken by the British, Aug. 23.

1840 Edict prohib. trade with Great Britain, Jan. 5.

1841 *Hong-Kong Gazette* first published, May 1.

1842 Continued war with the British; peace, Aug. 29.

1850 Rebellion of the Tae-pings breaks out, Aug.

1857 Chinese fleet destroyed by Com. Elliot, May 25–27.

1859 Commercial treaty with America.

1860 War with the British and French. [Oct. 24. Peking surrenders to the allies, Oct. 15; peace,

1863 The English Col. Gordon defeats the Tae-pings.

1868 Burlingame treaty with U. S. signed, July 4.

1870 Massacre of French consul, priests, Sisters of Mercy, and native converts, June 21; French indemnified.

1876 First railway in China.

1877 Equal rights granted Chinese Christians, Feb. 1. Dreadful famine in Northern provinces.

1880 Li-Hung-Chang gov. of metropolitan prov.

1883 *Coup d'état* at Peking; Li-Hung-Chang deposed; subsequently becomes viceroy.

1884 War with France; treaty of peace ratified, Nov. 28, 1885.

1885 Introduction of railways authorized.

1887 Inundation of the Hoang-Ho; millions of people perish.

1891 Formally objects to Henry W. Blair as minister from the United States, April 28.

1891 Continued persecution of foreigners.
1894 War with Japan, July.
      Treaty between China and the U. S., Aug.
1895 Treaty of peace with Japan, April 17.
1896 Li-Hung-Chang visits Europe and America.
1897 German mariners take Kaio Chau, Dec. 3.
1898 Balance of war indem. paid to Japan, Apr. 17.
      Forced abdication of the emperor, Sept. 22.

INDIA.

B.C.
1500 Northern India said to have been invaded and conquered by the Aryans between this date and 1000.
624 Gautama, founder of Buddhism, b.; d.543 (?).
327 Invasion of Alexander the Great.

A.D.
1001 Irruption of Mohammedans under Mahmud Ghuzni.
1186 Extinction of the house of Ghuzni.
1219 Invasion of Moguls under Genghis Khan.
1397 Timour, the Tatar, captures Delhi.
1502 Vasco da Gama estab. a Port. col. at Cochin.
1519 Sultan Baber completes conquest of India before 1527.   [reigns.
1556 Akbar, the greatest sovereign of Hindustan,
1600 The Portuguese introduce tobacco.
1601 The British East India Co. chartered.
      The Dutch first visit India.

1627 Reign of Shah Jehan; golden age of Moguls.

1640 Madras founded; made a presidency, 1652.

1658 Aurungzebe reigns.

1659 Rise of the Mahratta power.

1662 Bombay ceded to England.

1664 French East India Company established.

1698 Calcutta purchased by the East India Co.

1739 Kouli Khan (Persian) captures Delhi, and massacres 150,000 persons.

1746 War between the British and French.

1756 Calcutta taken by Surajah Dowla; suffocation of British in " Black Hole," June 20.

1757 Calcutta retaken by Clive, Jan. 2.

1772 Warren Hastings governor in Bengal.

1780 Hyder Ali defeats the British, Sept. 10.

1782 Death of Hyder; Tippoo Sahib succeeds, killed, 1799.   [dies Feb. 13.

1798 Christian F. Schwartz, " the Apostle of I.,"

1803 Mahratta war; victories of Wellesley (Duke of Wellington).

1824 Burmese war; British take Rangoon, May 5; peace, Feb. 21, 1826.   [Dec. 7.

1829 Abolition of suttees (burning of widows),

1838 Slavery abolished. Afghan war. (See Afghanistan.)

1843 Scinde war; Scinde annexed to Brit. India.

1845 Danish possessions purchased by G. Britain. Sikh war; Sikhs unconditionally surrender, March, 1849.

1851 Burmese war; ends, June, 1853.

1853   First Indian Railway opened, April 16.

1854   Ganges canal opened.

1857   Great mutiny of the native troops; Delhi seized, Cawnpore surrenders to Nana Sahib, Lucknow besieged, etc.

1858   Government of E. India Co. ceases Sept. 1. War in Oude; continues through 1859.

1861   Great famine in the northwest provinces.

1862   Large increase in cultivation of cotton.

1863   War with hill-tribes. Hindu religion deprived of gov. support, Dec.

1864   Gold currency to be introduced Dec. 25.

1866   Awful famine in Bengal; 1,500,000 persons perish.

1869   Rise of Brahmo Somaj, religious reformers.

1871   War with the Looshias; they are subjected, 1872.

1875   Naga tribes chastised. The Prince of Wales visits India, Nov.

1876   Queen Victoria proclaimed Empress of India, May 1.

1878   War with Afghanistan, which see.   [24.

1882   The Sirhind canal (502 miles) opened, Nov.

1886   Upper Burmah annexed to Brit. India, Jan.1.

1887   13,390 miles of railway in India reported.

1891   Factory bill for protection of women and children passed, March 19.

1893   Free coinage of silver suspended, June 26.

1894   First medical Cong. at Calcutta, Dec. 24–29.

1895   First railway constructed by native capital.

1898 The bubonic plague epidemic rages in Bombay, and continues in 1899.

JUDEA.

B.C.

1921 Call of Abraham to enter Canaan.

1896 Isaac born to Abraham.

1837 Birth of Esau and Jacob.

1822 Death of Abraham.

1729 Joseph sold into Egypt.

1571 Moses born; dies 1451.

1491 The Israelites cross the Red Sea.
The law promulgated from Sinai.

1451 Joshua conquers Canaan.

1095 Saul made king; dies 1055.

1055 David king; dies 1015.

1015 Solomon king; dedicates the Temple, 1004.

 975 Death of Solomon, the kingdom divided.

KINGDOM OF ISRAEL.

 975 Jeroboam establishes idolatry.

 901 The Syrians besiege Samaria.

 896 Elijah translated to heaven.

 771 The Assyrian invasion under Pul.

 721 Samaria taken by the Assyrians; the ten tribes carried into captivity.

KINGDOM OF JUDAH.

 971 Shishak, king of Egypt, takes Jerusalem.

 912 Jehoshaphat orders the law to be taught.

884	Usurpation and death of Athaliah.
741	Pekah, king of Israel, besieges Jerusalem.
726	Hezekiah abolishes idolatry. [stroyed.
710	Sennacherib invades Judea; his army de-
588	Nebuchadnezzar takes Jerusalem.
587	Babylonish captivity begins.
536	The Jews return to Jerusalem.
515	The second Temple finished.
445	The walls of Jerusalem built by Nehemiah.
415	Malachi, last of the prophets. [Temple.
332	Alexander the Great offers sacrifice in the
320	Jerusalem taken by Ptolemy Soter.
285	The translation of the Hebrew Bible (the Septuagint) begins about this time.
250	Sect of the Sadducees formed.
170	Antiochus takes Jerusalem.
166	Government of the Maccabees begins. [pey.
63	Jerusalem taken by the Romans under Pom-
54	The Temple plundered by Crassus. [29–18.
40	Herod becomes king; rebuilds the Temple,
4	JESUS CHRIST born.

A.D.

26	Pontius Pilate procurator of Judea.
33	Christ's ministry, miracles, crucifixion, and resurrection, 27–33.
41	Jews receive the right of Roman citizenship.
70	Jerusalem taken and destroyed by Titus.

[See *Syria*.]

JAPAN.

285	Korean civilization introduced.
552	Buddhism introduced from Korea; its hierarchy established, 624.
1192	Shogun (tycoon) usurps supreme power.
1543	Portuguese establish trading settlements; expelled, 1637–42. [strictions.
1600	Dutch settlements tolerated under severe re-
1853	Commodore Perry visits Jeddo.
1854	Treaty of commercial alliance with the U. S.
1856	Nagasaki and Hakodadi opened to European commerce.
1860	Japanese embassy visits Wash., etc., May 14.
1863	Treaty ports closed, June 24. [19.
	Forts bombarded by foreign ships, July 15–
1864	Japan refuses to abide by treaties, ports bombarded by English, French, and American vessels, Sept. 5, 6.
1867	Jeddo and other ports op. to trade, Apr. 25.
1868	Insurrection of the daimios, Jan. 27 - Feb.; rebellion ends, and mikado re-estab., July.
1870	Feudal system suppressed.
1872	First railway opened by mikado, Oct.
	Eng. proposed as the national language, Dec.
1875	Mikado decrees a new constitution, April 14.
1879	Ex-pres. Grant arrives at Nagasaki, June 21.
1883	Japan to be opened to foreign trade, Nov.
1884	Death of the last tycoon, April.
	National religion disestablished, Aug. 11.

1885 Jap. dict. in Roman characters completed.

1887 Western dress and habits intro. by Count Ito.

1888 Complete trans. of the Bible into Jap., Feb. 3.

1889 New constitution promulgated by the mikado, Feb. 11.

1890 First Japanese parliament opened, Nov. 29.

1891 Destructive earthquake on the Niphon Islands, Oct. 28.

1894 Fighting with the Chinese in Korea.

War formally declared against China, Aug. 3.

Victorious campaign of the Japanese army, Sept., etc.

Japanese fleet destroy Chinese fleet, Sept. 17.

Japanese army invades China, Oct. 25.

1895 China makes overtures for peace, Jan.; a truce declared in Mar., and treaty of peace signed, April 17.

Formosa formally transf. to Japan, June 2.

Russia recognizes Japan as a modern power, June 11.

1896 A tidal wave sweeps the northeast coast of Japan, destroying many thousand people.

1897 Japan adopts a gold standard, March 1.

1898 The principle of party gov. adopted, June.

PERSIA.

B.C.

559 Cyrus becomes king of Persia.

521 Darius Hystaspes king; conquers Babylon.

490 Persians defeated by the Greeks at Marathon.
485 Xerxes king, recovers Egypt, 484; defeated
     by the Greeks, 479; murdered, 465.
465 Artaxerxes I. king, marries Esther, 458.
399 War with Greece; Persia invaded, 396.
334 Alexander the Great defeats the Persians at
     river Granicus.
323 Alexander dies; Persia allotted to Seleucus
     Nicator, whose successors rule till con-
     quered by Arsaces I., the Parthian; his suc-
     cessors rule till the Persian revolt, A.D. 226.

A.D.

226 The Sassanides dynasty founded.
227 Religion of Zoroaster restored; Christianity
     persecuted.
309 Sapor II. king, proscribes Christianity.
363 The Roman emperor Julian invades Persia.
428 Armenia again united to Persia.
430 Wars with Huns, Turks, etc.
642 Persia invaded by the Arabs; becomes the
     seat of the Fatimite Mohammedans.
1038 Subdued by the Seljukian Turks.
1123 Omar Khayyám, poet, dies about this time.
1223 Conquered by Genghis Khan and the Mon-
     gols.
1345 Bagdad made the capital.
1388 The poet Hafiz dies about this time.
1399 Timour ravages the land.
1414 The poet Jami born.
1468 Persia conquered by the Turcomans.

1638　The Turks take Bagdad ; great massacre.
1796　Teheran the capital.
1826　War with Russia.
1856　War with England ; peace, April 14.
1858　The shah reorganizes the government.
1865　Railways in process of formation; electric
　　　　telegraphs, 1867.
1873　The shah visits Europe ; again in 1889.
1889　Imperial bank of Persia established, Oct. 23.
1892　Tobacco monopoly abolished, Jan. 7.
1893　Earthquake at Kuchan ; 12,000 deaths re-
　　　　ported.
1894　Coinage and importation of silver suspended.
1895　Russo-Persian frontier settled.
1896　Nasr-ed-Din, shah, assassinated, May 1.

SYRIA.

B.C.

1049　Alliance of David, king of Israel, with king
　　　　Hiram.
1040　Syria conquered by king David.
　898　Benhadad makes war on the Jews.　[syria.
　740　Syria subjugated by Tiglath-pileser of As-
　537　Conquered by Cyrus ; by Alexander, 333.
　301　Great battle of Ipsus, death of Antigonus.
　299　The city of Antioch founded.
　223　Antiochus III. conquers Palestine ; defeated
　　　　at Raphia, 217.
　　83　Tigranes of Armenia acquires Syria.

63 Syria made a Roman province.

A.D. [256.

162 Invaded by the Parthians; by the Persians,

638 Conquered by the Saracens.

970 Conquest of Syria by the Fatimite caliphs.

1095 Crusades begin; continue for nearly two centuries; Christians expelled by the sultan of Egypt, 1291.

1400 Syria overrun by Tamerlane.

1516 Conquered by the Turks, and held till 1799.

1799 Bonaparte overruns the country.

1801 The French evacuate Syria.

1831 Mehemet Ali conquers Syria.

1841 The sultan grants hereditary rights to Mehemet, who gives up Syria.

1860 The Mohammedans massacre Christians at Damascus, July 9 *et seq.;* the English and French intervene.

Pacification of the country effected, Nov.

[No important event in recent years.]

———— —

PALMYRA.

[Supposed to have been the Tadmor of the Bible.]

105 Splendid period of Palmyra.

130 Hadrian gives it the name of Adrianople.

258 Odaenathus wars with Persia.

264 Odaenathus supreme commander.

272 Zenobia defeated by Aurelian.

PHILIPPINE ISLANDS.

1521 Discovered by Magellan, who here lost his life.

1565 Taken possession of by a fleet from Mexico.

1570 A settlement effected at the mouth of the Manila river.   [nish.

1762 Captured by the Eng. under Draper and Cor-

1764 Restored to Spain.

1896 Outbreak of rebellion against Spanish rule, Aug. 31.

Aguinaldo becomes leader.   [1.

1898 Com. Dewey destroys the Spanish fleet, May

Gen. Merritt lands at Cavité, Manila harbor, July 26.

Manila sur. to the American forces, Aug. 13.

AFRICA.

ABYSSINIA.

[Ancient history uncertain.]

330 Christianity introduced.

1490 Visited by the Portuguese.

Court becomes Catholic.

1640 Catholicism suppressed before this date.

1855 Theodore takes the title of king, Feb. 11.

Protestant missionaries received, replacing Roman Catholics. [insults, Jan.

1864 British subjects imprisoned for pretended

1867 England sends war expedition under Sir Robert Napier, Sept. 14.

1868 Theodore's troops defeated by the British, April 10; kills himself, April 13. [12.

1872 Kassa crowned at Axum as Johanni II., Jan.

1875 War with Egypt; Ismail Pacha defeated; desperate fight at Gonda Gouddi, Oct. 16.

1877 Johanni defeats Menelek, king of Shoa, June.

1885 War with Italy. [Johanni, Dec.

1888 Menelek, king of Shoa, rebels against King

1889 Protectorate of Italy over Abyssinia accepted, Oct. 14.

Menelek crowned negus of Abyssinia, Nov. 3.

1896 King Menelek defeats the Italians, March 1.

Italy renounces her claim over Abyssinia, Oct. 26.

BARBARY STATES.

ALGIERS.

935   Algiers founded by the Arabs.

1509   Algiers, the seat of the Barbary pirates, captured by Ferdinand of Spain.

1516   Nominally subject to Turkey.

1816   Bombarded by a British fleet.   [French.

1830   Barbarian government overthrown by the

1833   Abd-el-Kader, an Arab chief, revolts against France; after a long struggle surrenders, Dec. 23, 1847, is reconciled with the French, and dies May, 1883, aged 76.

[The later history of Algiers has been a series of conflicts with the French government.]

MOROCCO.

1051   Morocco subdued by Fatimite Caliphs.

1471   Tangiers conquered by Alfonso V. of Portugal.

1516   The Scherifs, pretended descendants of Mohammed, reign in Morocco.

1662   Tangiers given as a dower to Catherine of Portugal on her marriage with Charles II. of England.

1844   War with France; peace, Sept 10.

1860   A Moorish ambassador in London, the first since the time of Charles II.

1889   Dispute with Spain; settled about Sept. 29.

1892   Rebellion of Angherites, who are defeated,
      July–Sept.   [sharp fighting.
1893   Moors of the Riff tribe attack the Spaniards,

TRIPOLI.

1551   Conquered by the Turks.   [dent.
1741   Hamlet Bey, pacha, makes himself indepen-
1835   Restored to nominal control of Turkey.
1895   Ismail Bey, governor.

TUNIS.

[Tunis stands nearly on the site of Ancient Carthage. It remained under African kings until taken by Barbarossa for Solyman the Magnificent.]

1871   Becomes an integral part of the Turkish
      empire.   [volts.
1881   Controlled by France ; insurrections and re-
1884   French courts of law established.   [canal.
1893   Tunis made a seaport by construction of

CARTHAGE.

B.C.

878   According to legend, founded by Dido ; date
      doubtful.
509   First alliance with the Romans.
379   The Carthaginians land in Italy.
264   The first Punic war begins ; lasts 23 years.
247   Hamilcar Barca commands in Sicily.
      Hannibal the Great born.

242 Hasdrubal founds New Carthage (Cartha-gena).

241 Sicily lost by Carthage.

229 Hamilcar kill'd; Hasdrubal assassinated, 221.

219 Hannibal conquers Spain.

218 The second Punic war begins; lasts 17 years. Hannibal crosses the Alps, and enters Italy. Defeats the Romans at the Ticinus and Trebia; at Lake Trasimenus, 217; at Cannæ, 216.

210 The Carthaginians expelled from Sicily.

206 Expelled from Spain by Scipio.

202 Hannibal totally defeated at Zama by Scipio.

183 Hannibal, in exile in Bithynia, takes poison.

149 Third Punic war.   [Roman senate, July.

146 Carthage taken, and burned by order of the

19 Rebuilt by the Romans.

A.D.

200 Becomes a Christian bishopric.

439 Taken by Genseric the Vandal, Oct. 9.

533 Retaken by Belisarius.

647 Ravaged by the Arabs.   [Egypt.

698 Destroyed by Hassan, Saracenic gov. of

1861 Antiquities excavated, and brought to British Museum.

CENTRAL, EAST, AND WEST AFRICA.

1768 Bruce begins his travels.

1787 Sierra Leone settled by the English.

1795 Mungo Park makes his first voyage to Africa.

1820 Liberia founded; independence proclaimed, 1847, J. J. Roberts president.

1849 Lake Ngami discovered by David Livingstone, Aug. 1.

1856 Du Chaillu travels in Central Africa.

1857 Territories of Liberia incr. by annexations.

1858 Second expedition of Livingstone.

1863 Speke and Grant find a source of the Nile in Lake Victoria Nyanza, Feb. 23.

Du Chaillu starts on a fresh exped., Aug. 6.

1864 Sir Samuel Baker discovers Lake Albert Nyanza.

1870 Expedition of Baker to put down slave-trade.

1871 Henry M. Stanley disc. Livingstone, Nov. 10.

1873 Livingstone dies in Ilala, Cent. Afr., May 1.

1879 Stanley explores the Congo.

1886 The German East African Co. founded.

[Many expeditions from various European countries explored Africa during the succeeding ten years, resulting in the establishment of the Congo State under the protection of Belgium.]

1895 Congo State annexed to Belgium.

EGYPT.

[The chronology of Egypt is very conflicting, the difference in dates being that of centuries. Brugsch and Mariette are the authorities most commonly referred to.]

B.C.

5004 Menes, first known lawgiver (M.), 4455 (B.).

4235 Cheops builds the great pyramid (M.), 3733 (B.).

4100   The worship of Apis established (B.).

2300   Osirtasen III. excavates Lake Moeris, and constructs the Labyrinth and the Nilometer (B.).

2214   The Hyksos, or Shepherd kings, rule (M.).

1750   Arrival of Joseph (B.).   [(B.).

1703   Achmes I. conquers the Hyksos (M.), 1700

1600   Thothmes III. rules; his exploits recorded in his temple at Karnak (B.).

1333   Reign of Seti; makes first canal from the Red Sea to the Nile (B.).

1322   Rameses II. (Sesostris) conquers Ethiopia.

1300   Maneptah, prob. the Pharaoh of the Exodus.

1288   Rameses III. cultivates navigation and commerce (M.).

  980   Shishak (1 *Kings* xiv.), ruler (M.), 966 (B.).

  693   Egypt frequently invaded by Assyrians.

  665   Psammetichus I. (Gr.) restores the monarchy.

  612   Necho II. defeats Josiah, king of Judah, at Megiddo; defeated by Nebuchadnezzar.

  527   Cambyses the Persian conquers Egypt.

  424   Egypt regains its independence by Armyrtæus.   [Persia.

  340   Nectanebes II. conquered by the king of

  332   Alexander conq. Egypt; founds Alexandria.

  323   Ptolemy I., Soter, king of Egypt.

  283   The museum of Alexandria founded; the Pharos completed.

  269   Ambassadors first sent to Rome.

   82   Revolt in Upper Egypt; Thebes destroyed.

47 Alexandria besieged by Cæsar.

43 Cleopatra poisons her brother, and reigns alone.

41 Cleopatra fascinates Marc Antony.

31 Battle of Actium; defeat of Antony and Cleopatra.

30 The kingdom becomes a Roman province.

A.D.

122 Alex. restored by Adrian ; by Severus, 200.

305 Monachism begins in Egypt. [Alex.

365 Great earthquake ; 50,000 persons perish in

389 Destruction of temple and worship of Serapis.

415 Hypatia, neo-Platonic philosopher, murdered by a mob of fanatics in Alexandria.

616 Egypt conquered by Chosroes of Persia.

640 Conquest of Alexandria by the Saracens.

969 Cairo founded by the Saracens. [1691.

1163 Conquest by the Turks begins ; completed,

1250 Government of the Mamelukes established.

1567 Conquered by Selim I., emp. of the Turks.

1798 Bonaparte seizes greater part of the country.

1801 Turkish government restored. [1.

1811 Mehemet Ali massacres the Mamelukes, Mar.

1816 Belzoni removes statue of Memnon.

1820 Construction of the Mahmoud canal, connecting Alexandria with the Nile.

1831 Mehemet revolts, and invades Syria.

1832 Ibrahim takes Acre, May 27 ; defeats the Turks at Konieh, Dec. 21.

1841 Mehemet made hereditary viceroy of Egypt.

1848 Ibrahim Pacha dies, Nov. 10.

1858 Suez canal begun by M. de Lesseps.   [1.

1861 Malta and Alexandria telegraph opened, Nov.

1863 Increased cultivation of cotton; result of American civil war.

1865 Opening of part of Suez Canal, Aug. 15.

1869 Suez canal successfully opened, Nov. 17.

1870 Sir Sam. Baker explores the White Nile, Aug.

1872 Slave-trade apparently subdued.

1875 War with Abyssinia; peace, 1877.

1879 The khedive deposed by the sultan; Prince Tewfik proclaimed successor.

1882 Insurrection at Alexandria, June 11.
Forts bombarded by the British, July 11.
Battle of Tel-el-Kebir, defeat of Arabi Pacha, Sept. 13.

1887 Anglo-Turkish convention respecting Egypt, signed July.

1892 The Khedive Tewfik d. much lamented, Jan. 7; his eldest son, Abbas, succeeds, Jan. 8.
New railway bridge over the Nile, May 5.

1894 Prof. Brugsch Pacha, Egyptologist, d. Sept. 9.

1895 Ismail Pacha, ex-khedive, dies March 2.

SOUDAN.

1881 Mahdi declares himself a prophet, July.
Defeats the Egyptians.

1883 Campaigns of British and Egyptians begin, lasting many years with fierce fighting.

1883 Osman Digna commander for the Mahdi.
1885 Gen. Gordon killed at Khartoum, Jan. 26.
1893 Defeat of the dervishes by the Italians.
1894 Archibald Hunter gov. of frontier prov.
1898 Slavery gradually becoming extinct.

SOUTH AFRICA.

1650 Cape Town founded by the Dutch.
1814 Finally ceded to England.
1820 British emigrants arrive.   [nal colony.
1849 Successful resistance to establishment of pe-
1851 Orange River territory annexed.
1854 First parlia't meets at Cape Town, July 1.
1860 First railway from Cape Town (58 miles) opened, Dec.
1867 Rich diamond fields discovered.
1871 Colony of Griqualand constituted, Oct. 27.
1877 War with the Kaffirs.   [pleted, Dec. 25.
1879 Telegraphic communication with G. B. com-
1885 Railway to Kimberley opened, Nov. 28.
1892 Great fire at Cape Town, Feb. 21.   [2.
1895 Mr. Cecil Rhodes made privy councillor, Feb.
1898 Cecil Rhodes elected as a representative by a large majority.

TRANSVAAL REPUBLIC.

1848 Transvaal Republic founded by Dutch Boers.
1852 Independence declared, Jan. 17.

1876 War with the Kaffirs under Cetywayo.
1877 Annexed to the British dominions.
1879 The Transvaal declared a crown colony, Dec.
1880 The Boers claim independence.
1881 War with the English.
1883 Paul Krüger, president; again in 1888.
1885 Johannesburg founded.
1889 Defensive treaty with the Orange Free State about March 13.
1893 Paul Krüger re-elected president. [June 28.
1894 Brit. subjects exempt from military service, Revolt of the Kaffirs.
1895 The Delagoa railway opened, July 8.
1896 Dr. Jamieson and his raiders defeated, Jan. 1; tried and convicted in London, July 28.
1898 Fresh discovery of diamonds near Pretoria.

AUSTRALIA.

1606 The Dutch discover Australia.
1686 William Dampier lands in Australia.
1787 First transportation of felons to Botany Bay, May.
1788 Sydney founded. [established.
1803 Colony of Van Diemen's Land (Tasmania)
1829 West Australia formed into a province.
1834 South Australia erected into a province.
1835 Port Phillip (Victoria) colonized.
1837 Melbourne founded.

1839	Transportation of felons suspended.
1842	City of Sydney incorporated.
1850	Victoria (Port Phillip) made a province.
1851	Gold discovered by Mr. Hargreaves.
1853	Mints established; transportation ceases.
1859	Queensland made a province, Dec.
1866	Royal Soc. of New So. Wales founded, May.
1883	Completion of railway between Melbourne and Sydney, June.
1885	Federation of Australasian colonies, except New South Wales and New Zealand, completed, Dec. [gration.
1888	Australasia favors restricting Chinese immi-
1891	Uniform colonial postage adopted, Jan. 1. Title "Commonwealth of Australia" adopted, April 1; Victoria requires "Commonwealth" to be changed to "Federation," July 21.
1895	The Australasian Federation League meets at Melbourne; federation of the states approved, Jan. 23.
1898	"Old Age Pension" bill passes the House of Rep. of New Zealand, Oct. 20.

HAWAII.

1778	Discovered by Captain Cook, who is killed there, Feb. 14, 1779.
1789	King Kaméhaméha rules till 1819.

1824 King Kaméhaméha II. and queen visit Lon-
     don, and die there, July.
1840 Kaméhaméha III. promulgates constitution.
1856 Kaméhaméha IV. mar. Miss Emma Rooker.
1875 Reciprocity treaty with the United States.
1876 David Kalakaua elected king, Feb. 12.
1887 Queen Kapiolani present at Queen Victoria's
     Jubilee.   [ceeds, Jan. 29.
1891 King Kalakaua d. Jan. 20 ; Liliuokalani suc-
1893 Liliuokalani deposed ; provis. gov. formed.
1894 Republic proclaimed, S. B. Dole, pres., July 4.
1898 Annexed to the United States, July 7.

SAMOA.

1830 Christianized by Rev. John Williams.
1880 Malietoa king.   [by Tamatese.
1887 Malietoa deposed by the Germans ; replaced
1888 Mataafa gains victory over Tamatese.
1889 Conflicting interests between German, Brit-
     ish, and United States governments.
     Three United States war vessels, *Nipsic*, *Van-
     dalia*, and *Trenton*, and three German,
     wrecked at Apia, March 15–16.
1893 Mataafa exiled to Kakaofo, Sept. 1.   [44.
1894 Robert Louis Stevenson d. at Apia, Dec. 4, a.
1899 Civil war among natives ; British and Amer-
     ican naval officers killed, April.

INDEX.

www.ingramcontent.com/pod-product-compliance
Lightning Source LLC
Chambersburg PA
CBHW021126270326
41929CB00009B/1071